"Who can deny that *Fear and Trembling* looms large in the Kierkegaardian imagination? Many readers assume that this is Søren's last and best word on faith. But it is not his last word, or his best word. It is not even his word. Cudney dwells with this text, wrestling above all with the challenges posed by the pseudonymous authorship. He knows that the pseudonymous nature is not peripheral to the book. It is the key to its successes and its failures. Cudney combines intellectual rigor with personal engagement, pointed critique with generosity of spirit. He is existentially invested in the world of *Fear and Trembling* and its authorship. Surely, the Master would be proud."

—STEPHEN BACKHOUSE
Author of *Kierkegaard's Critique of Christian Nationalism*
and *Kierkegaard: A Single Life*

Where the Truth Lies

Where the Truth Lies

Pseudonymity, Complicity, and Critique
in *Fear and Trembling*

SHANE R. CUDNEY

PICKWICK *Publications* · Eugene, Oregon

WHERE THE TRUTH LIES
Pseudonymity, Complicity, and Critique in *Fear and Trembling*

Pickwick Publications
An Imprint of Wipf and Stock Publishers
199 W. 8th Ave., Suite 3
Eugene, OR 97401

www.wipfandstock.com

PAPERBACK ISBN: 978-1-60608-655-1
HARDCOVER ISBN: 978-1-4982-8575-9
EBOOK ISBN: 978-1-4982-4114-4

Cataloguing-in-Publication data:

Names: Cudney, Shane R., author.

Title: Where the truth lies : pseudonymity, complicity, and critique in Fear and Trembling / Shane R. Cudney.

Description: Eugene, OR: Pickwick Publications, 2021. | Includes bibliographical references and index.

Identifiers: ISBN 978-1-60608-655-1 (paperback). | ISBN 978-1-4982-8575-9 (hardcover). | ISBN 978-1-4982-4114-4 (ebook).

Subjects: LCSH: Kierkegaard, Søren, 1813–1855. Frygt og baeven. | Christianity—Philosophy. | Ethics.

Classification: B4373.F793 C 2021 (print). | B4373 (ebook).

11/22/21

For Jim,
teacher, mentor, therapist, and friend

———————————

In Memory of my Mother and Father

Charlotte Anne Melton
(1938–2020)

Ronald Lee Cudney
(1935–2020)

Contents

Acknowledgments

To say that this project has taken longer than anticipated would be a gross understatement. Indeed, the process has felt Homeric-like, almost epic in scope. For this reason, and many more, not the least of which is my focus here, a work like this exceeds the words that contain it. In other words, it is much more than the sum total of its constituent parts. Put differently, while this is first and foremost an academic and therefore intellectual undertaking, it is inseparable from my personal journey, that is, from existential meaning and significance. Thus, the very words herein, every jot and tittle, if you will, have been woven into the fabric of my life over the past two decades. I am a part of this work even as it is a part of me. If I have learned anything from Kierkegaard, it is this: truth cannot be abstracted or otherwise disconnected from existence without devastating consequences.

In the beginning, projects like this are met with enthusiastic encouragement and thoughtful questions by family, friends, and acquaintances alike. After what seems like a reasonable amount of time the persistent question becomes: "when are you going to be finished?" Still further into the process the inquiries and questions become fewer and fewer; and at some point along the way they stop altogether, and you are left on what feels like a long, dark stretch of road, putting one foot in front of the other. But, of course, "no man is an island," as John Donne once said, and this project could not and would not have even started, let alone been completed, without the unconditional and indefatigable support of those closest to me, all of whom I owe a debt of gratitude I can never repay.[1] I want to thank you all individually, and reverse protocol by starting with my family, confidantes, and close friends. No doubt there will be those I fail to mention, so allow me to both apologize and thank you here at the outset.

I want to begin at the beginning by thanking my parents, Charlotte and Ron Cudney, who have been there quite literally from the start. Thank

---

1. Donne, "Meditation XVII," in *Devotions*, 67.

you for loving me, for pointing the way, and carrying me in your prayers through the best and worst of times. Without your influence this undertaking would not have been possible. Even though you sometimes scratch your heads in curiosity, wonder, and even concern, be assured that I rest in the hands of the one who holds us.

I would also like to thank my brother Ron Jr., his wife Judy, and their daughter Alesha for their quiet support and steadfast love through the years.

How could I not thank my four amazing children, all of whom have been with me and supported me on this odyssey? Thank you for indulging my relentless questions, for accepting me as I am, faults, foibles and all things idiosyncratic. Words on a page cannot begin to describe how much you mean to me or how much I love you. The spirit of this work is dedicated to the four of you.

Thank you, Jenison, for the gift of being my firstborn son. Thank you for your quiet and deliberate manner that harbors unheard cries of the heart; for your profound complexity that is rich with potential beyond what you believe, and for a level of compassion that too few see. It has been a joy watching you find your way in the world. The journey has barely begun, my son. Let go, let live, and let love.

Thank you to my daughter Jessica (Saffron). It has been both a privilege and a challenge watching you become the woman you are. As you follow the Spirit's lead, your kind heart, commanding intellect, and questioning mind will be true to you in your quest for self-discovery. On the road less traveled, I pray for a heightened sense of awareness as you look for the markers that lead to the water of life.

Thanks to my son Spencer who became a combat veteran at twenty-one years old, and who experienced more in one year than most people do in a lifetime. Thank you for your service overseas and for coming home with your body *and* spirit intact. Thank you for your disarming sense of humor and your fierce sense of loyalty. In spite of your war-torn experiences, or perhaps because of them, you will live large and long enough to tell your children and their children of your exploits.

Last, but certainly not least, I want to thank my youngest son Mason. When I think of you I see your wry smile. I celebrate your restless, inquiring mind and your capacity to relentlessly question the status quo. Thank you for your infectious passion to look deeper, reach further, and learn more, qualities that will serve you well on the road to scientific and self discovery. Be true to yourself, listen to your heart, follow your dreams, and remember (Aronofsky's) *Pi*.

For all of you, remember Augustine, remembering the words of Christ: *Dilige et quod vis fac.*

In the context of my children, I would be remiss not to thank Liz who gave me the best years of her life and who accompanied me on the first leg of this journey. Thank you for the life and love we shared, once upon a time.

A heartfelt thank you to Dawn. What can I say about that smile juxtaposed with those cauldron-like eyes that hold a thousand tears? Your love and grace have left an indelible imprint on my soul.

Thank you to Karen for taking my breath away! How could I ever thank you enough for taking my hand, taking the risk, and taking me into a land I hardly knew existed. With you everything is new, and everything is possible.

Thanks to my good friend Eric Flett who has been there since the earliest days of this odyssey. Thank you for your friendship, wisdom, and ongoing support. Grace, strength, and courage as you enter unchartered territory in your own existential quest for self-discovery.

Thanks also to my friends, Grant Ingram and Pete MacDonald. Knowing both of you has made me doubly rich. Thank you for helping to make a death-dealing context a life-giving one.

I would like to acknowledge and thank the unsung workers, students, and faculty—past and present—that make up the Institute for Christian Studies in Toronto. This "graduate school with a difference" made all the difference at a particularly difficult and pivotal time in my life and set my feet on a journey that changed my life. I will thank only a few by name. An affectionate thank you to those who impacted my life directly and helped shape my development, intellectual and otherwise. For those who remain: Bob Sweetman, Henk Hart, and Ron Kuipers; and to those who are now with other institutions: Richard Middleton (Roberts Wesleyan College); Jeff Dudiak (Kings University/College); Brian Walsh (Wycliffe College); and Jamie Smith (Calvin College). Blessings to all of you for your unique and untiring work in the service of angels.

It is important that I thank Jack Caputo whose work has inspired my thinking and helped shape my intellectual development. Your ability to communicate complex ideas with wit and no small amount of literary flare is worth aspiring to. Both the profundity and sheer accessibility of *Radical Hermeneutics* helped convince me that I just might be able to understand philosophy and perhaps even make a contribution of my own. Thank you for your influence, and for helping escort Kierkegaard into the twenty-first century.

It seems only appropriate to thank Geoffrey Hale whose influence is evident throughout this project. His monograph, *Kierkegaard and the Ends of Language* is one of the most daring, groundbreaking, and lofty bits of scholarly business I've had the (pain and) pleasure of wrestling with, one that helped me reimagine Kierkegaard and his work.

Words are inadequate to express how grateful I am to Prof. Dr. Wouter Goris, my former co-promotor at the Vrije Universteit, Amsterdam, now at Rheinische Friedrich-Wilhelms-Universität, Bonn. Thank you for taking an interest in my project at the outset, and for your infinite patience along the way. Your carefully chosen, always encouraging words alongside critical comments made the process far less arduous, and this dissertation infinitely better.

I would also like to thank Prof. Dr. Gerrit Glas for his willingness to join the process at a late stage and for bringing his expertise to bear on this project. His welcomed comments helped shape this project into its finished form.

I would like to take this opportunity to thank the reading committee at the Vrije Universiteit for their time and patient consideration of my work: Rob Compaijen, Reinier Munk, Renée van Riessen, Edward van 't Slot and Pieter Vos. Their collective comments, criticisms, and suggestions pushed for greater clarity which helped put the finishing touches on the dissertation.

An affectionate thank you to Jim Olthuis, my teacher, mentor, guide, therapist, friend, and surrogate father, without whom this work would not have been possible. Jim, you are unique among men and women alike. Simply put, you are love clothed with "Jimness." I have never met anyone quite like you, and I count it a blessing and a high privilege to have learned at your feet. *No one* has allowed me the space to be myself like you. Thank you for encouraging me to become who I am, think for myself, and develop at my own pace. You are an inspiration like no other. Rich blessings to you and yours.

Finally, I would like to thank a man who will never hear my thanks; someone I have never met, whose language is not my own, and whose time is not mine. His living *corpus*, however, has indelibly marked the path of my existential, intellectual, and spiritual development, and whose profound influence will continue to be felt, with or without my help, in the generations to come. Søren Aabye Kierkegaard.

Abbreviations

CUP	Søren Kierkegaard, *Concluding Unscientific Postscript* (1992)
E.FT	Søren Kierkegaard, *Fear and Trembling*. Edited by C. Stephen Evans (2006)
E.KEL	C. Stephen Evans, *Kierkegaard's Ethic of Love* (2004)
FT	Søren Kierkegaard, *Fear and Trembling/Repetition* (1983)
GD	Jacques Derrida, *The Gift of Death*, 2nd ed. (2008)
H.KEL	Geoffrey A. Hale, *Kierkegaard and the Ends of Language* (2002)

Preface

GENERALLY SPEAKING, BOOKS—EVEN THE digital variety—create an immediate, largely implicit, impression. In their immediacy they hold out the illusion that between beautifully designed covers lie perfectly chosen words that will lead the reader down the yellow-brick-road of knowledge and understanding toward the Emerald City of Truth. Like a flower reaching for the sun above and water below, it is our desire to *know*, twisted as it by silence and concealment (to use the words of Johannes de Silentio), that perverts this desire with inflated illusions that we love to employ in order to assuage our deepest fears, illusions we live, die, and sadly kill for. In keeping with *Fear and Trembling* itself, my efforts here do not purport to tell the truth so much as they explore the conditions of that possibility in the context of Kierkegaard's most widely read text. This exploration is my primary focus, one that *testifies* to the truth rather than *delivers* the truth.

My reading of *Fear and Trembling*, therefore, is a faith inspired attempt to "read with" the text in a way that highlights the text's differences, ambiguities, and cross-currents.[1] In the face of this rich and paradoxical prodigality, the goal I have set for myself is to offer a viable alternative to both modern, received, interpretations of the text, and late modern, more transgressive renderings. *Reading with* the text, then, pivots on a treatment of the pseudonym that sees Johannes de Silentio as the sole author of *Fear and Trembling*. While this assumption appears self-evident, on my reading,

---

1. In his "programmatic essay," James Olthuis works toward "a general theory of hermeneutics," one rooted in "a postmodern 'feminist' perspective." See Olthuis, "Otherwise than Violence," 114. What he calls "a hermeneutics of connection" altogether resists traditional, "'mastery' modes of interpretation. Instead of beginning with a Cartesian–Husserlian autonomous subject intent on the creation and control of meaning, or a Hegelian intersubjectivity of oppositional difference," Olthuis begins "with an economy of love (*eros*)" (ibid.). In sum, he "envision[s] a hermeneutics that is 'other-wise than violence,' a reading-*with* as opposed to reading-*against*" (ibid., 115). My *reading with* the text of *Fear and Trembling* is indebted to Olthuis's pioneering work in hermeneutics.

the now common practice of employing the name "Kierkegaard" to interpret the pseudonymous writings assumes that, at the end of the day, he is
the author of those texts.[2] But to the large extent that this occurs, I contend
that it effectively reduces the pseudonymous voice and in turn inflates Kierkegaard's own voice into a universal principle of authority meant to secure
proper interpretation of the text. Ascribing authorship to de Silentio alone,
however, enables the reader to honor the particularity of the pseudonym
and thereby resist any principle of authority designed to corral the text's
disparate elements into an all-inclusive meaning. In so doing, we are able to
see that *what* the text means is inextricably linked with *how* the text functions and *why*. My reading therefore suggests that *Fear and Trembling* is
both *complicit* with and *critical* of metaphysics in a way that resists rational
mediation. As such, the conflicting currents in the text destabilize any and
all attempts (including its own) to establish an all-encompassing textual
truth backed by a universal principle of authority in a way that does not
deny textual meaning.[3]

～

Perhaps more than most, Kierkegaard's texts draw the reader in, teasing,
tempting, and more often than not, trapping us by our own desires and expectations, ultimately throwing us back on ourselves and our own responsibility. As it turned out, this was precisely my experience as I attempted to
"get a handle" on the *truth* of his texts early in my study. What I discovered
was that while many people who speak in the name of Kierkegaard himself claim to know what the truth is, few of them agree with each other.
Armed with all manner of preconceived, conventional notions about how
to approach the text, what was being said, and why, not to mention who
was speaking, I was well into my research and writing when everything was
brought to an abrupt halt by what can only be described as a close encounter
of the hermeneutical, even deconstructive, ultimately transformative kind.
Being thrown back on myself and on my own responsibility exposed my
own desires, expectations, and assumptions about the text in general and
my approach to it in particular. As a result, I had no choice but to start
completely over in an entirely different way, the results of which I offer here.

---

2. See chapter 1.

3. I maintain that long before hermeneutics was organized and subdivided, and
long before Kierkegaard's work was hermeneutically, conceptually and thematically
manhandled, he drew on his (struggle with) faith to help (in)form his approach to writing, and the incarnational logic intrinsic to it. See Smith, *Speech and Theology*, 161–63,
where he pays homage to Kierkegaard as an incarnational thinker.

If it is true that my reading draws on the resources of both modern and late modern influences, it also reaches back to pre-modern, Christian, and pre-Christian, Jewish sources. But of equal importance is the profound influence that Kierkegaard's texts themselves have had on me, even as they are invariably filtered through my current, idiosyncratic sensibilities.

My journey with Kierkegaard, my connection with his texts, and ultimately my reasons for undertaking this project began many years ago, when, as a young student with a newly minted theology degree, I realized that I had more questions than answers. This was disturbing since the whole point of education, or so I thought at the time, was to close the gap of knowledge and finally arrive at the truth; and as a person of faith, it seemed everything was at stake. Thus, finding the *right* answers was imperative. On the surface of things, my questions were simple but they were also complex, and most certainly pivotal. For example, what do the Gospels mean when Christians are called to be *in* the world, but not *of* the world? The New Testament also suggests, paradoxically, that the kingdom of God is both *now* and *not yet*. What does this mean exactly? For that matter, how does one *think* of Christ as *both* human *and* divine? The scriptures also indicate that in order to *find* oneself, one must *lose* oneself; in order to *live*, one must *die*. What role does faith play in all of this? Indeed, what is the relationship between faith and reason?

At that juncture my journey began to take a decidedly philosophical turn, with forays into psychology and phenomenology. Little did I know that these explicitly theological questions and quandaries, not to mention the answers provided for them, were inextricably linked to age-old philosophical dilemmas and paradoxes that have everything to do with rationally driven dualities that find their roots deep in the western intellectual tradition. And chief among these dualisms, that go by many names, is the dichotomy that still exists between (philosophical) truth and (existential) meaning. The radical disconnect at work in this and all similar structures is what, in the end, pointed me toward Kierkegaard and his own parallel preoccupation with the relationship between truth and meaning, particularly as it relates to faith and reason. So, long before Nietzsche, Heidegger, Derrida, and all things postmodern, Kierkegaard had already taken a bite out of Hegel's metaphysical hide (to borrow a playful phrase from Jack Caputo) by emphasizing that truth cannot be abstracted from existence without violent consequences. Moreover, what has been sorely overlooked in the push and pull of modern and late modern, still rational debates—with Kierkegaard caught in the crossfire—is the Dane's emphasis on the Incarnation as the condition for both awakening to and receiving the gift of love's responsibility.

In short, this means that love, received by grace through faith, is the mediating link between truth and meaning.

Significantly, Kierkegaard was among the first modern thinkers, in the tradition of Augustine, Pascal, and Luther, to reclaim the notion that life is *wholly* sacred, the impulse of which is thoroughly and fundamentally religious. Contra Descartes, Kierkegaard might easily have said, 'I was first loved, therefore I exist.' Or perhaps better, "I was loved, therefore I am," and "I love, therefore I am."[4] Kierkegaard's texts everywhere indicate that faith, as fragile trust, is the condition of possibility for life and being as we experience it. Pervasive throughout his *corpus* is the idea that faith, as a foundational mode of human experience, always already expresses itself religiously, devotionally, and purposefully in the shape of commitments, and ethically in the shape of behavior as an outgrowth of those commitments and the beliefs intrinsic to them. And it was precisely because of his commitments that Kierkegaard was able to call into question the very things he was committed to. This challenges, indeed, changes everything, especially if faith, as the blood in the body of existence, is therefore present in every stage on life's way.[5]

As the twenty-first century unfolds at digital speed, I would passionately argue that Kierkegaard's work is more relevant than ever precisely because of the foundational concerns that occupied his attention. Such concerns, however, are becoming increasingly obscured by the sheer rapidity of change, not to mention the spirit numbing effects of digital culture, and the resultant "social saturation," as Kenneth Gergen calls it.[6] If Kierkegaard was a man of faith, coming back again and again as he did to the *relationship* between truth and meaning, as it relates specifically to faith and reason, then the issue of *mediation* and how he approached it becomes a significant pivot point in his texts. If he was concerned that the (particular) individual was at risk of being lost in the (universal) crowd; that faith was being sacrificed on the altar of reason; and that belief and trust were mere stepping stones on the way toward absolute certainty provided by reason, then his texts are arguably even more timely in this current, frenzied, climate of escalating fear, paranoia, and terror.

---

4. See Olthuis, *The Beautiful Risk*, 69.

5. What I want to suggest is that faith is not, in Kierkegaard's texts, limited strictly to the religious sphere of existence. As a foundational mode of human existence, faith is present in the aesthetic as well as the ethical sphere of existence. If it is true that the lower spheres are robustly and functionally religious, it therefore becomes necessary to broaden the notion of both faith and religion (particularly as they relate to reason) to the extent that the former is thought of as the condition of possibility for the latter.

6. See Gergen, *The Saturated Self*, 48–80.

But while we live in perilous and prurient times, lest we unduly disparage them, they are also primed with promise. In fact, these are the very conditions of possibility for reading Kierkegaard in the manner that I suggest here. As a prophetic voice of this present age, it behooves us, therefore, to return again and again to Kierkegaard's texts, specifically, and to the past in general. For each generation does not learn "the essentially human" from the previous one; every generation therefore, must begin anew (*Fear and Trembling*, 121).

January 2020

Beginnings

Will the Real Kierkegaard Please Stand Up!

But we are curious about the result, just as we are curious about the way a book turns out. We do not want to know anything about the anxiety, the distress, the paradox.

—Johannes de Silentio

But this is my limitation—I am a pseudonym.

—Søren Kierkegaard

One of my fond memories as a young boy include watching a television game show called, To Tell the Truth. The premise was quite simple: three people claimed to be the same person, and it was the job of four celebrity panelists to question them and then vote for the one they thought was telling the truth. When the ballots were cast at the end of the hour, the audience waited with anticipation as the host asked for the real person to stand up, at which point, with some hesitation and shuffling of feet to heighten the drama, he or she would rise to their feet. With the secret identity of the mystery guest finally revealed, we, the viewers, could rest easy knowing that the truth had been told; and with the tension gone, my little world was stable and secure once again.

It is not much of an exaggeration to suggest that scholarship in general has conducted itself in the manner of a modern game show; and Kierkegaard scholarship in particular is no exception. At the end of the day, when all the questions are asked and the scholarly work is done, are we not supposed to relax knowing the truth has been told, and, in this case, Kierkegaard's true identity and intentions revealed? Even if scholars concede that the whole story has not yet been told, there is a permeating, all too modern sense that the truth is just around the corner waiting to be uncovered. But even though the Master of Irony is dead and his canon closed, the game is still being played and the drama is still unfolding. Thus, we must conclude that the real Kierkegaard has not stood up.

If it is true that Kierkegaard's real identity and the truth of his intentions remain veiled, in the face of our limited sight we must continue to ask questions, and hard scholarly work must still be done. But the truth is, too much time has already been spent searching for the Holy Grail, looking for something that is simply not available to us, at least not in the objective, fully present manner we would like and often demand it to be. If there is such a thing as clarity when talking about Kierkegaard and his intentions, a few things do seem clear enough, not the least of which was his penchant to restore the mystery to life and faith (or perhaps better, the mystery of faith *to* life); and he achieved precisely this with an emphasis on the fragility of existence, the finitude of language, and the faith necessary to navigate their waters.[1] Indeed, Johannes Climacus argues, with sharp wit, and no small amount of irony, that any truth worth knowing is inextricably linked with existence.[2] And Constantin Constantius, too, suggests that if existence is always on the move, and if truth is inseparable from it, then it is impossible to pin the latter down.[3] But isn't that precisely what scholars have all along attempted, and still attempt to do? To the extent that modern scholarship has demanded that the real Kierkegaard "stand up," is it not guilty of a certain essentialism and therefore fallen prey to the very thing he called into question and sought to destabilize?

If such things are true, what would happen if we pulled back from our Promethean-like propensity to reveal the real Kierkegaard and the so-called truth of his intentions? Would our greatest fears come true? Would his texts be given over to the four winds of dissemination and therefore become anything to anyone? Would we suddenly find ourselves on the road

1. A full-bodied and multifaceted notion of faith will figure prominently throughout this study, one consistent with the body and spirit of Kierkegaard's texts.

2. Kierkegaard, *Concluding Unscientific Postscript* (1992 ed.), 1:23–24.

3. Kierkegaard, *Practice in Christianity* (1991 ed.), 205; Kierkegaard, *Fear and Trembling/Repetition*, (1983 ed.) 131. Hereafter this volume will appear in the text as *FT*. Henceforth, authorial responsibility for Kierkegaard's pseudonymous texts will be solely and assiduously ascribed to their authors alone. Although it may be customary to interchange the pseudonym with Kierkegaard's own name, in my view this less cautious approach all too easily conflates the voice and views of the former with the latter. I hope to show that this easy slide hermeneutically compromises his texts.

to hermeneutical hell, condemned to descend toward the ever-increasing darkness of uncertainty?[4] In the face of Kierkegaard's starkly structured, though richly layered texts, is it still prudent to call upon "Kierkegaard" to mediate the textual differences in order to secure proper meaning? While it may be true that there is not a singular truth to be discovered in his works, neither is it true that they can mean anything at all. For like the earthen vessels that they are, texts have very specific shapes that can hold only so many meanings, meanings that are themselves finite and therefore must be judged accordingly. In other words, even if there is not one true meaning to be revealed, meaning *is* available to us, but only in the shape of particularity. It must be emphasized that this does *not* necessarily put us on a slippery slope that leads to hermeneutical anarchy. But it does give reason for sober pause, especially since finitude and all that it entails actually heightens individual responsibility; and it is precisely this that Kierkegaard's texts achieve. But make no mistake, this does not mean the responsibility to make the right choice between two competing alternatives. Rather, it requires risk and radical faith in the face of otherness and mystery.[5] This is something that I think Kierkegaard understood quite well and made it his life's work to communicate in the unique way that he did.

How then can we appropriately talk about the truth of Kierkegaard's texts in general, and *Fear and Trembling* in particular, if there is no truth, per se, limited as we are to particular languages of truth which cannot help but undo the universal promises they make?[6] How are we to read his texts? Indeed, what are we reading when we read them? I suggest that the general shape of his work provides important clues regarding the central concerns that Kierkegaard (and his pseudonyms) sets out to explore in his corpus. These concerns indicate the need for a certain kind of (writing and) reading that allows the reader and the text to be addressed in a full-bodied way.[7] This is achieved by moving with the full range of textual queries and quandaries.

---

4. The vertigo involved in the disintegration of a worldview that was once thought to be fixed and permanent—as is the case with modernity and the accompanying paradigm of objectivism—is what Richard Bernstein aptly calls, "Cartesian Anxiety." See his *Beyond Objectivism and Relativism*, 16–19. In the "twin pillar" metaphysical scheme of things, existence is *either* grounded, *or* groundless.

5. I am cautious here *not* to suggest that faith is non-knowledge, or an unknowing, to be contrasted with a rational knowledge that knows better. This two-sided metaphysical coin is precisely the currency that Kierkegaard's texts call into question. In fact, his texts everywhere suggest, á la Pascal, that faith knows what reason does not know. See Olthuis, "Introduction," in *Knowing Otherwise*, 1–18.

6. See Hale, *Kierkegaard and the Ends of Language*, 5, where he speaks of the "linguistic promise." Hereafter this volume will appear in the text as *H.KEL*.

7. Hale argues that the difficulty confronting the reader of Kierkegaard "begins

Broadly speaking, the challenges that Kierkegaard's texts address are similar to the concerns of this text, which are not far from the problem of truth. But as we have already probed, what is truth, if it cannot, without detriment, be rationally abstracted from existence? How are we to *think* of that which *both* exceeds the boundaries of human finitude *and* remains within those boundaries? Is it even possible to speak of such a thing, if, indeed, truth is a problem to be solved or a thing to be discovered with the right intellectual tools and the right methodological approach? Both enabled and disabled by existence and it excess, Kierkegaard's texts wrestle with this tension, all the while reaching for a language that honors the tension. Because the "human being is a synthesis of the infinite and the finite," as Anti-Climacus construes it;[8] because we are caught between two worlds, as Pascal might say, the dilemma Kierkegaard's texts keep coming back to again and again in different ways through different voices,[9] seems clear enough: how are we to think of the *relationship* between the infinite and the finite; between the divine and human; Providence and free will; faith and reason; otherness and self, indeed, between truth and meaning? Put differently, how does one responsibly write or otherwise speak of the unspeakable? What can be said about no-thing? Is it possible to talk about a secret without giving it away?

While it may be relatively clear what the central problem is that Kierkegaard's texts explore, what is not so clear are the answers they don't seem to provide for their readers. One of the most interesting, crucial, and certainly controversial issues surrounding his texts concern the very question of final answers and the apparent truth attached to them. In a general way, this project explores this very question, one that bears heavily on the *relationship* between what Kierkegaard says (and does not say), how he is read, who is addressed, and why. Part of my task is to invite the reader to approach Kierkegaard's texts in a faith-inspired, one might even

with the author" and "the inescapable disjunction between 'authorship' and 'authority'" (*H.KEL*, 1). Although he insists that texts are not meaningless, per se, his reluctance, for example, to say anything about the contours of a text and the necessary risk of interpretation, move him in direction of Derrida who maintains that because every interpretation in its specificity, *necessarily* excludes all others, one cannot have or otherwise hold particular, determinate commitments (in this case to a specific interpretation) without the inevitable risk of violence. In the face of that possibility, this project risks a more or less specific interpretation all the while remaining sensitive to issues of authorship and authority, not to mention the easy slide to a "white-knuckle" interpretive posture.

8. Kierkegaard. *The Sickness unto Death* (1980 ed.), 13.

9. Vanessa Rumble persuasively argues that similar to the pseudonymous texts, Kierkegaard's signed works, such as *Works of Love*, also traffic in uncompromising distinctions, to the same disruptive, destabilizing effect, namely, the "displacement of the conscious subject." See Rumble, "Love and Difference," 162.

say, *confessional* way, and thereby more deeply appreciate his unique, and robustly religious contribution to a late modern understanding of the relationship between truth and meaning.

With apparent disregard for his explicit instructions to the contrary,[10] the more orthodox or received interpretations of Kierkegaard's texts, insist on reading them in a more or less straightforward way that ascribes authority to Kierkegaard alone. More recently, the move toward dividing and interpreting his texts along the lines of authorship, evidence this.[11] In a way opposite, yet similar to early interpretations of Kierkegaard's texts, this has resulted in attributing the voice and proper name of Kierkegaard to the pseudonymous authors. This "blunt reading," as Roger Poole calls it, which purports to reveal the real Kierkegaard, along with his true intentions, sees him only "as a 'serious' writer who is didactic, soluble and at bottom, 'edifying.' His puzzles are only seemingly so. His meaning is, by assiduous effort, capable of final solution."[12] According to Geoffrey Hale, from its very inception "Kierkegaard scholarship has tended to follow what have now

---

10. In his "A First and Last Declaration," which appears at the end of the *Postscript*, Kierkegaard is quite clear when he says: "My wish, my prayer, is that, if it might occur to anyone to quote a particular saying from the books, he would do me the favor to cite the name of the respective pseudonymous author." See Kierkegaard, *Concluding Unscientific Postscript* (1941 ed.), 552. In terms of the text of *Fear and Trembling* in particular, if the reader is tempted to align Kierkegaard with the Knight of Faith and his ability to scale the abyss of unknowing with a 'leap of faith', which is impossible on the text's terms, once again we must respect the words of Kierkegaard, who says: "I am just as far from being Johannes de Silentio in *Fear and Trembling* as I am from being the Knight of Faith whom he depicts." Kierkegaard, *Concluding Unscientific Postscript* (1941 ed.), 551. Unless otherwise noted, my choice of translation and referencing is based largely on personal preference and sheer readability.

11. According to Hale, the list of those "[c]ommentaries that interpret Kierkegaard's texts on the basis of their systematic orientation through the proper name of the signatory" are legion. The ones "generally taken as most 'authoritative' include Mark C. Taylor, *Kierkegaard's Pseudonymous Authorship* (1975), and *Journeys to Selfhood: Hegel and Kierkegaard;* Alastair Hannay, *Kierkegaard* (1980); Louis Mackey, *Kierkegaard: A Kind of Poet* (1971), and *Points of View: Readings of Kierkegaard* (1986); Stephen N. Dunning, *Kierkegaard's Dialectic of Inwardness: A Structural Analysis of the Theory of Stages* (1985); George Connell, *To Be One Thing: Personal Unity in Kierkegaard's Thought* (1985); Hermen Deuser, *Kierkegaard: Die Philosophie des religiösen Schriftstellers* (1985); Roger Poole, *Kierkegaard: The Indirect Communication* (1993); and Sylvia Walsh, *Living Poetically: Kierkegaard's Existential Asethetics* (1994)" (*H.KEL*, 185). I would also add, C. Stephen Evans, *Kierkegaard's Ethic of Love: Divine Commands and Moral Obligations* (2004).

12. Poole, "The Unknown Kierkegaard," 61. Even if Poole is sensitive to the hermeneutical issues at stake, it seems clear that he too succumbs to "a kind of idiosyncratic personalism" that functions as a principle of coherence meant to corral meaning by way of Kierkegaard's own name. See *H.KEL*, 11.

become thoroughly predictable patterns. Virtually all commentaries on Kierkegaard," he argues, "fall into at least one of four categories: biography, literature, religion, or philosophy" (*H.KEL*, 5).[13] As such, contends Hale, they inevitably succumb to some principle of coherence, which means one can only conclude that every approach thus far "has attempted, as it were, to force Kierkegaard finally to sign his own name" (Ibid).

AUTHORSHIP, AUTHORITY, AND KIERKEGAARDIAN COMMENTARY

Johannes de Silentio's divided world and the head scratching knots and tangles that it gives rise to, are not only issues for Johannes himself, but for the majority of commentators who have taken up the pseudonyms' cause as Kierkegaard's own. Thus, there have been many and varied attempts in the last century to explain, contain, or otherwise unravel the text's puzzling incongruities by appealing to Kierkegaard's name as a principle of authority called upon to confer a more or less definitive meaning upon his works.

But if what Geoffrey Hale argues is true, even the majority of contemporary approaches to Kierkegaard's text's fall short of the mark to the extent that they share a similar impulse to resolve, once and for all, the complex hermeneutical issues surrounding his body of work. If what I am claiming is faithful to the contours and spirit of *Fear and Trembling*, then the lack of interpretive consensus is itself a testimony to the text's function. In this case, any attempt to finally resolve or mediate its inherent differences, and thereby achieve hermeneutical salvation, is destined to end in frustration and ultimately failure. In fact, a major focus of my efforts overall is to show precisely how the text itself short circuits any and all such attempts. But first things first.

In what follows, I will show, largely with the help of Geoffrey Hale, that if, as we will see in chapters 1 and 2, Evans and Derrida themselves conflate Kierkegaard's voice with the pseudonym's, then they join, what for Hale is a long and illustrious list of commentators who have succumbed to the same

---

13. Hale maintains that, "Kierkegaard's work continually demonstrates that its categorical determination as philosophy, theology, literature, and so on presupposes a system of coherent signification that can always ultimately be shown to be purely imaginary" (ibid., 2–3). In different ways at different points throughout his text, he argues that "any understanding of Kierkegaard's work in its specificity requires first the suspension of any preconceived coherence designated in any principle of authority" (ibid., 3). Hale seems to think, however, that since understanding and interpretation are always and already rational and, as such, coercive, an imperative must exist to suspend any and all "rules of intelligibility" (ibid., 2).

sort of conflation.[14] In fact, says Hale, since its very inception "Kierkegaard scholarship has tended to follow what have now become thoroughly predictable patterns" (*HKEL*, 5). With boldness he contends that the bulk of scholars, from the nineteenth century until now, are guilty of the same thing. "Virtually all commentators on Kierkegaard," Hale argues,

> fall into at least one of four categories: biography, literature, religion, or philosophy. Each has sought, in one way or another, to organize Kierkegaard's papers posthumously in terms of one or another principle of coherence. They have all attempted to explain in terms of a principle of coherence what would otherwise appear to make the whole of Kierkegaard's authorship thoroughly inexplicable. In one way or another, each of these conventional assessments has attempted, as it were, to force Kierkegaard finally to sign his own name. (Ibid.)

Given Kierkegaard's employment of multiple pseudonymous voices, and his creative use of literary styles and devices (paradox, juxtaposition, hyperbole, irony, and satire), not to mention his multi-disciplinary approach, it seems only natural to try and make sense of and therefore understand his writings by way of categorization. Not only is this natural, but necessary, even unavoidable in some sense. The problem, however, is one of posture, which is to say, how one views such categories or otherwise holds them, and to what end.

Hale notes that the first attempts at some "conceptual organization" appeared toward the end of the nineteenth century in the form of two biographies: the first one by Peter Heiberg, and the second one by Peter Rosenberg (ibid., 6). Whereas the former "proposed a psychological profile of Kierkegaard," the latter "attempted to correlate Kierkegaard's life with his literary production" (ibid.). Early in the twentieth century interest in Kierkegaard began to grow, and although scholarship began to take "a more serious turn" the tendency to organize his writings along biographical lines continued, evidenced by Christoph Schrempf's major two-volume contribution, *Søren Kierkegaard: Eine Biographie I / II* (ibid.). If these biographical approaches to, and appropriations of, Kierkegaard's writings focused on his "psychological profile" and "his literary production," still others brought

---

14. In this section, I will shamelessly rehearse Hale's excellent summary of *who* the major commentators were in this regard, *what* they wrote, and *how* their works set the hermeneutical tone for twentieth-century scholarship and beyond. Also, it is important to note at the outset that although it is true Derrida conflates Kierkegaard's name with de Silentio's, his reduction is not ontological but rather hermeneutical. In other words, it is not, as Hale would say, a reduction in the name of a universal principle of authority meant to ascertain and secure proper interpretation.

his philosophy to the fore, that is, to the extent that his "life was taken as philosophically significant in itself" (Ibid). For example, in Georg Lukács's early essay, "The Foundering of Form Against Life: Søren Kierkegaard and Regine Olsen," Hale points out that the author "condensed Kierkegaard's philosophy into the 'gesture,' represented in his famous refusal to marry Regine Olsen . . ." (ibid.). Hale contends, however, that

> in principle, such psychologies or biographies inevitably miss
> the very texts they claim to explicate, ultimately conjuring up a
> life nowhere present as such within the texts, or, as the author A
> of Kierkegaard's *Either/Or* objected, 'poetizing the personality'
> along with them. (Ibid.)

Of course, it was also Kierkegaard's ardently theological writings that scholars paid close attention to; and in particular it was his polemical debates against the Danish State Church that attracted the initial attention. It was these more controversial writings that not only lead to a much "more serious reception" of Kierkegaard's writings but "prompted the translation of his work into German," which in turn promoted a greater interest in his work in general (ibid.). And although responses to "Kierkegaard's critique of the church" varied widely, "his opposition to the church and his deeper rejection of systematic theology ultimately formed the basis for conceptions of dialectical theology or neorthodoxy in the work of such twentieth-century theologians as Karl Barth, Paul Tillich and Friedrich Gogarthen" (ibid., 6–7).

Hale notes that concurrent with these "psychobiographical explications" of Kierkegaard's writings, other writers highlighted his "prolific literary talent" (ibid., 7). Among the first, and arguably one of the most significant studies of this ilk was Georg Brandes's major work of 1877, titled: *Søren Kierkegaard: En Kritisk Fremstilling i Grundrids*. Drawing on aspects of Kierkegaard's life including his own psychological interpretation, "Brandes ultimately concluded that Kierkegaard's primary significance lies in his 'artistry,' thus dismissing any question as to whether the texts address issues of more substantive concern" (ibid.). Significantly, although this treatment helped to broaden the appeal of Kierkegaard, it "had the notable effect of 'de-Christianizing'" his writings which, at the same time, served to play down both their philosophical and theological import (ibid.).[15] It is

---

15. It should be noted that at this time Nietzsche was shouldering his way to the front of the philosophical line in Germany; and with his critique of religion in general, and Christianity in particular, the gap between religion (faith) and philosophy (reason) became even more pronounced. Merold Westphal argues that one of the primary reasons that Kierkegaard is not drawn upon as readily as Nietzsche as a philosophical

also true, notes Hale, that there were commentators during this time who began to take Kierkegaard's philosophy seriously, that is, "as opposed to 'literature'" (ibid.). Hale cites Theodor Haecker's, *Søren Kierkegaard und die Philosophie der Innerlichkeit* (1913), as the first comprehensive treatment of Kierkegaard's philosophy, the hermeneutical reverberations of which are still felt today (ibid.). Hale explains that this text, which "amounts to a more or less uncritical appropriation of Kierkegaard's 'spheres' or 'stages' of existence," paved the way or "set the stage for what would become the thoroughly conventional understanding of Kierkegaardian 'existence' and the religious 'truth' about 'subjectivity'" (ibid., 7–8).

However, to the extent that philosophical renderings of Kierkegaard maintain that 'the truth' of his writings is best understood in terms of the "'religious' sphere," they remain linked with theological discourse "that use Kierkegaard to argue for the 'subjective truth' of 'Christianity'" (ibid., 8). And for Hale, this is yet another example of an all-pervasive reductionism. He emphasizes that the widespread acceptance of Kierkegaard as "the one who prized the 'self' at the same time that he prioritized the religious 'stage' of existence toward which this self was oriented—likely has more to do with Haecker than it does with Kierkegaard" (ibid.). But, for Hale, this conception, "one concerned with establishing an easily transmitted 'truth' about Kierkegaard . . . can only avoid those aspects of Kierkegaard's work that resist such a normative assessment" (ibid.). And even if Karl Jaspers's substantial work on the "[p]hilosophy of existence" is indebted to the likes of Haecker, Hale notes that Jaspers was philosophically sober enough to suggest that "although philosophies of existence may rely extensively on Kierkegaard's work, it remains by no means certain wherein precisely Kierkegaard's significance lies. His importance for various modes of 'existentialism' does not make him an existentialist" (ibid.).

As these "structural and systematic accounts of Kierkegaard" began to give way to more language centered concerns in the latter part of the twentieth-century (Derrida, Foucault, etc.), Hale observes that contemporary "scholarship appears to have come full circle and praises Kierkegaard for his decisively literary technique" (ibid.). He credits Louis Mackey with categorizing Kierkegaard as "A Kind of Poet," a label that invariably

---

resource is because of the still "lingering suspicion that while Kierkegaard is a major religious thinker, he is not really a philosopher." See Matustik, and Westphal, eds. *Kierkegaard in Post/Modernity*, vii. Westphal goes on to insightfully suggest the following: "Insofar as this view stems from the assumption that to be taken seriously, a philosopher must either be secular or abstract from his or her religious identity, it can be dismissed as a prejudice rooted in very dubious Enlightenment conceptions of the autonomy of human thought" (ibid.).

appropriates him and his work in the service of yet another category, that is, "postmodernism" (ibid., 9). Thus, "in the absence of any discovered or revealed principle of coherence, Kierkegaard's notion of 'indirect communication' is called upon to explain the true relationship among the texts, such that the 'aesthetic' or 'philosophical' texts illustrate 'indirectly' the truth 'directly' related in the theological texts" (ibid., 8). Even the attempts by other postmodern figures, such as Mark Taylor, Roger Poole, and Habib Malik, to track the development of Kierkegaard's "influence" in the twentieth century fall under Hale's critical purview. These attempts in particular, he argues, invariably "lapse into a kind of idiosyncratic personalism" (ibid., 11). But, he argues, "to respond 'personally' or 'existentially' is no longer to respond to what Kierkegaard wrote. It is no longer to respond to the work at all, because it absolves one of the responsibility to read" (ibid., 12).

Whether it is the general categories of biography, literature, religion, or philosophy, or the more specific conceptions drawn from Kierkegaard's texts themselves, not to mention those notions that cluster around the term "postmodern," Hale maintains that "what characterizes virtually all studies of Kierkegaard," with few exceptions, "is a rather profound incomprehension, an incomprehension demonstrated rather than resolved by the affirmation of one or another truth in one or another categorical determination" (ibid., 13). With the odds stacked heavily against it, Hale insists, however, that all commentary on Kierkegaard is not guilty of truth telling, and therefore "condemned to failure; rather the condemned are those that take as their presumptive point of departure the explication and hence the affirmation of given modes of subjectivity and the self, on the one hand, or given conceptions of 'God' and 'Christianity,' on the other" (ibid., 12).

In the face of Hale's penetrating critique of Kierkegaardian commentary, I will attempt to show that *Fear and Trembling* is fundamentally about *relationships*, generally speaking, the relationship between the author and Abraham, but more specifically between reason and faith, not to mention meaning and truth.[16] As such, the text concerns itself primarily, if implicitly, with the question of *mediation* which de Silentio explores in the context of the binding of Isaac in Genesis 22. In the end, however, the text is less about Abraham's near sacrifice of Isaac and more about the author's attempt to

---

16. While I do not necessarily disagree with C. Stephen Evans, who argues that *Fear and Trembling* is about faith (and *not* about ethics), the ever-present tension between faith and reason—and by extension, the juxtaposition between Abraham and de Silentio—indicates that the text is more concerned with the *relationship* between these terms and how precisely they are connected. That de Silentio's text is decidedly not about ethics highlights Evans' commitment to the proper name of Kierkegaard that functions as a key to proper interpretation.

relate himself as poet/philosopher to the patriarch, understood as a paradigm of faith. But precisely *how* the author accomplishes this, *why*, and to
what end, are questions that bear heavily on the more probing questions of
authorship, authority and finally how one reads the text.

~

By way of summary, the general aim of my project is to show that the tension-
filled text of *Fear and Trembling* is both *complicit* with the dualisms perpetu-
ated by the Greco-Cartesian-Hegelian metaphysical tradition, and *critical*
of that tradition. While the ostensible purpose of the author's strategy is to
negotiate the assumed chasm between faith and reason—via the teleological
suspension of the ethical in Problema I—and thereby *eschew* rational mediation, *honor* Abraham and *save* faith, I will argue that this gesture remains
resolutely bound by the rules of rationality. But, in the face of the text's stark
structure and its dualistic strategy, I argue that of equal significance is its
creative use of language (ie., irony, satire, hyperbole, paradox, and juxtaposition, etc.), particularly the use of the pseudonym. Coupled then with the
author's detailed exploration of sin in Problema III, the text ultimately puts
a critical finger on its own complicity with metaphysics.

In *Fear and Trembling* we find Johannes de Silentio struggling with
a paradox, an unspeakable truth that lies at the heart of Abraham's near
sacrifice of Isaac in Genesis chapter 22. The focal point of this struggle is
the patriarch's inability to defend himself rationally (ethically) in the face
of God's command to kill his son. If reason demands that Abraham speak
and therefore reveal his murderous plans, faith, de Silentio argues, necessitates silence and concealment. Thus, in order to understand this paradox,
the author writes a "dialectical lyric," the first half of which sees him in the
guise of a poet (the lyrical) attempting to imaginatively depict Abraham
in a way that makes poetic sense of his actions so that he can duly praise
and admire him. In the second half of the text, de Silentio dons the robes
of a philosopher (the dialectical) in order to critically distill and ultimately
justify the patriarch's actions. In the end, based on this divided structure
and the assumptions that undergird it, de Silentio employs a strategy that
suspends the ethical/rational, justifies Abraham, and saves his faith. This
solution is therefore designed to honor both faith and reason.

What are we to think of de Silentio's construction of this problematic
and how he addresses it? Are we to take it simply at face value? If so, why, or
why not? Of course the answers to these questions depend on *how* one reads
the text; and traditionally readers and commentators alike have tended to

collapse the author's views with Kierkegaard's own. While these approaches have yielded an array of interpretations, to the extent that these, or any of the contemporary hermeneutical variations, attempt to reconcile, fuse, or mediate the text's differences once and for all, I maintain that they are confined to a modern orbit where the gravity of metaphysics rules the day. And while contemporary readers of Kierkegaard valiantly attempt to honor the difference in his texts, I will show that even Derrida is guilty of conflating Kierkegaard's voice with de Silentio's, the implications of which cannot be ignored.

But what if we were to take Kierkegaard's injunction against doing so, "seriously," that is, *not* to reduce the pseudonym's voice in this manner? To a large extent my project explores the implications of doing just that. The two-fold question that will help guide this exploration is as follows: what does *reading with* the text of *Fear and Trembling* reveal about the structure of the text, in particular its treatment of the faith/reason problematic; and how do these bear on and ultimately connect with the central issue of mediation? In other words, if the strategy that de Silentio employs to negotiate the tension-filled relationship between faith and reason is "Kierkegaard's" answer to the dilemma facing Abraham, then the obvious question is what or how are we to think of the pseudonym and its use throughout the text? How are we to account for the pervasive use of irony, paradox, satire, hyperbole, and contradiction? And why does an exploration of sin suddenly appear as if out of nowhere in the context of Agnes and the merman in Problema III? What is the significance of this? Where does it all lead? What are we to conclude?

I maintain that taking the pseudonym at his authorial word opens a space that enables the reader to move with the conflicting textual currents. This, in turn, reveals a textual function that is better tuned to the otherness of the text. This means that, on the one hand, while the author's proposed strategy in Problema I and II for addressing the problem of the incommensurability between faith and reason is *complicit* with the logic of metaphysics, on the other hand, by virtue of its creative use of language, and the exploration of sin in Problema III, the text is also *critical* of that logic. I suggest then that resisting the rationalistic notion that "Kierkegaard" is *either* an irrationalist *or* a confused rationalist in need of harmonizing help, puts us in a better position to recognize that something else, something excessive, is happening in the text. On my reading, the conflicted text of *Fear and Trembling* indeed indicates that something larger is at work, something that ultimately frustrates rational mediation and fosters textual connection in a way that takes the faith/reason debate out of a strictly rationalistic orbit.

If, as I contend, that de Silentio's dominant logic draws its strength from the metaphysical tradition, then his attempt to *suspend* ethics, *justify*

Abraham, and *save* faith, reveals his desire to rationally mediate the paradox of faith, even as it simultaneously conceals this desire. This complicity with the logic of metaphysics, however, is only one part of a two-part story, the second half of which involves the author's exploration of sin in Problema III, one that reveals itself as a critique of the text's prevailing logic. When considered in tandem, these contrasting movements *subvert* the dominant logic in the text, *point* beyond de Silentio's explicit intentions, and ultimately *underscore* the mystery of faith and sin that exceed the reach of even the most complex theoretical constructs. If the presenting logic of the text is *complicit* with the gesture of metaphysics, the movement of *critique* reveals the author's hiddenness.[17] Ironically, for de Silentio himself, hiddenness becomes demonic (sin) when the human self crosses the boundary between self and other where the latter is sacrificed on the altar of the former.

On this reading, not only is de Silentio ironically revealed as a counterpart to the merman in Problema III, but the presenting logic of *Fear and Trembling* itself is exposed as an exercise in deceitful silence, on the way toward demonic hiddenness. And to the extent the "System" of philosophy conceals a universal pretense, it too is implicated, perhaps especially so. Thus, rather than reading against the text, *reading with* its conflicting movements draws our attention to it's function, the effect of which *destabilizes* speculative logic, as an end in itself, and thereby *honors* the particularity of the text in a more thoroughgoing way.

~

Chapters 1 and 2 form a critique of both conventional and contraventional readings of *Fear and Trembling*, respectively, with a particular focus on the use of the pseudonym. In my view, the former is best represented by C. Stephen Evans, and the latter by Jacques Derrida. Generally speaking, I want to show that by questioning orthodox and unorthodox assumptions about *what* the text of *Fear and Trembling* communicates, *how* it communicates, and *why*, not to mention on *whose* authority, a space is created that allows it to be read differently. *Reading with* the text, thus enables it to speak differently, that is, in ways that exceed both modern, received readings, and late modern, more transgressive renderings. As for the former, by exploring the relationship between authorship and authority as it pertains to Evans's reading of the text primarily in his monograph, *Kierkegaard's Ethic of Love*,

17. On my reading the dominant or presenting logic in de Silentio's text is thoroughly rational, a (negative) logic that reflects a veiled or hidden attempt to reconcile differences into a higher unity. Traditionally understood, a paradox achieves precisely this, bound as it is by its own internal logic and penchant for totality.

I will emphasize the importance of keeping the tension alive in order to prevent the easy collapse of important hermeneutical distinctions and the concomitant closing of *Fear and Trembling*. As for the latter, by paying close attention to Derrida's reading of the pseudonym in *The Gift of Death*, I will show that his treatment of the author hampers his ability to see the critique at work in the cross-currents of the text.[18]

If, as a representative of the received hermeneutical tradition, C. Stephen Evans maintains that "Kierkegaard" holds to a "meta-ethical position" that metaphysically links (finite/human) moral obligations to (infinite/divine) God, it is crucial to recognize that this first assumes a particular reading of Kierkegaard's texts.[19] In order to highlight that reading I will consider Evans's treatment of the relationship between authorship and authority and its significance for a fair reading of the text. I will then explore Evans's reading of *Fear and Trembling,* with special attention being paid to his interpretation of the pseudonymous author, along with his reading of Johannes de Silentio's reading of faith, understood in the context of a discussion of "infinite resignation" and "faith." In the end, I find my way back to the beginning of Evans's text in order to display, evaluate, and question the philosophical assumptions that condition his hermeneutic methodology. I conclude that while Evans subscribes to a more faith friendly rationality, his allegiance to objective truth and the twin metaphysical pillars that support it, unduly narrows the text. It does so by inflating the name "Kierkegaard" to a universal principle of authority which proves to be deflating, even deadly, for the pseudonym. In the end, my concern is that Evans's philosophical allegiances blind him to the deeply critical aspects of the text.

Having shown that Evans's interpretation of *Fear and Trembling* is tethered to a metaphysical principle of authority that hamstrings his understanding of the text, chapter 2 will focus on Derrida's reading of *Fear and Trembling* as it appears in *The Gift of Death*. I argue that while his approach to the text achieves a kind of openness that eludes Evans, his own reading unduly narrows the text in a way that is hermeneutically reductionistic.[20] My fundamental task then will be to demonstrate that Derrida's treatment of the pseudonym follows in the footsteps of contemporary, orthodox renderings. The very fact that Derrida fails to make a clear, careful, and consistent

---

18. Originally published as *Donner la mort* in *L'éthique du don, Jacques Derrida et la pensée du don*, by Métailié-Transition, Paris, 1992.

19. See Evans, *Kierkegaard's Ethic of Love*, 6. Hereafter will appear in the text as *E.KEL*.

20. As it relates to the author de Silentio, on my reading, whereas Derrida's reading is hermeneutically reductionistic, Evans's treatment of the pseudonym is both hermeneutically and ontologically reductionistic.

distinction between the pseudonymous author, de Silentio, and the proper name of Kierkegaard, carries with it at least two hermeneutically problematic implications: first, it serves to confuse the relationship between authorship and authority in a way that invariably reduces the pseudonymous voice to Kierkegaard's own; and second, it keeps Derrida from recognizing the significance of what is arguably the faith inspired "proto-deconstructive" function of the text.

Having demonstrated that both Evans and Derrida assume that the world of Johannes de Silentio is, in the end, Kierkegaard's world, in chapters 3 and 4 I will question that assumption more thoroughly and point toward a different hermeneutical approach that opens the text of *Fear and Trembling* in a way that allows it to speak differently. To that end, I will emphasize the cruciality, of taking the author, de Silentio, strictly at his authorial word which means bracketing, or separating, "Kierkegaard" from the authorial equation. In turn, this leaves the reader to wrestle with the text's tears, crosscurrents, and ambiguities *without* recourse to the proper name as an overarching principle of authority. This shift in authorial focus then allows the textual differences to stand in their difference thus creating a space where questions can emerge. With an eye toward how the text functions, *reading with* the text then reaches toward textual meaning without reducing the truth of the text to a meaning based solely on Kierkegaard's intention.

With these things in mind, I will argue that *Fear and Trembling* is, from the outset, structured rationalistically, even as the author attempts to resist that structure and the pretensions inherent in it. My task in chapters 3 and 4, therefore, is to focus on *Fear and Trembling* itself beginning with a general summary of each section meant to highlight the tears, cross-currents and ambiguities at work in the text. The very fact that the text assumes an absolute distinction between the human (reason) and the divine (faith) is reason to pause and consider the assumptions involved as de Silentio works first to "lyrically" understand the paradox of Abraham's actions, and then to "dialectically" "perceive the prodigious paradox of faith" that transforms murder into a holy act of sacrifice (*FT*, 53, 30).

After chapter 3, and before chapter 4, we find an "interlude" or "pause," in the form of a "Preliminary Expectoration," that stands between the "lyrical" and the "dialectical" sections where the author begins preparing the ground for the explicitly philosophical section to come. "Dialectical lyricist" that he is, de Silentio has a few things to get off his chest, as it were, even as he continues wrestling with Abraham's actions in a way that tries to make "poetical philosophical" sense of the paradox of faith. In the end, I will argue that de Silentio's "lyrical dialectical" creation of such figures as the "Knight of Faith" and the "Knight of Infinite Resignation" (also the "tragic hero"), along with (later) pivotal notions such as "Absolute Duty to God" and the "teleological suspension of the ethical," are in fact, *"complicit"* with the principle of Reason that he ironically attempts to overcome in order to make room for faith and thereby save Abraham.

In chapter 5 my concern is to draw out the fact that *Fear and Trembling* takes an important, critical turn in Problema III—constituting as it does the last third of the text. I will contend that embedded in the thicket of this section there is a strong critical current at work, specifically in the story of Agnes and merman. With its focus on the phenomenological structure and function of deceitful and demonic silence (sin), it is nothing short of a philosophical show stopper that, when considered against the larger framework of *Fear and Trembling,* indicates that de Silentio's ostensible masterstroke ("the teleological suspension of the ethical") at the very least constitutes deceitful silence that threatens to give way to demonic silence. Thus, in keeping with the split structure and conflicted sensibility of the text, I will emphasize that the overall textual dynamic, in fact, fundamentally undermines its central argument. In other words, on the one (complicit) hand, *Fear and Trembling* assumes that reason and faith inhabit two absolutely separate economies. According to the presenting logic of the text, this means that the former is rational and the latter is irrational (or "absurd"). On the other (critical) hand, because faith, thusly understood, is judged solely on rationalistic terms, reason itself can be seen as absurd by virtue of its belief in and reach for totality. Ironically enough, it is precisely this kind of grasping gesture that de Silentio calls demonic concealment.

If the focus in Problema I and II is on ethics (reason) and its relation to faith, in Problema III the author shifts that focus to esthetics and allows it to guide his inquiry as it leads inexorably to the religious. His ostensible purpose "is to have esthetic hiddenness and the paradox [of religious hiddenness] appear in their absolute dissimilarity" (*FT,* 85). But even as de Silentio's comparative analysis works, on the one hand, to reinforce the stark categories of the text, on the other hand, his exploration of silence ultimately stands in critical contrast to that starkness as he moves from playful silence to the insidiousness of deceitful silence, and then finally to the danger inherent in demonic silence. So, after tracing the contours of silence in Problema III, my primary task is to look closely at the anatomy of demonic silence and its connection to sin in the context of the story of Agnes and the merman with a view toward showing how it functions as a textual critique, and what the implications are.

In the end, I summarize "The Return to Abraham" and the "Epilogue," and then connect them to the overall significance of *Fear and Trembling.*

By way of conclusion, in chapter 6, I summarize my argument, and then draw out the important differences between my understanding of both Evans' and Derrida's reading of *Fear and Trembling* and precisely what the significance of those differences are as they relate to my reading of the text. I conclude that Evans' interpretive strategy, which enables him to employ a universal principle of authority by which proper interpretation is secured, hamstrings his movements and keeps him from being able to fully appreciate the deeply critical dimensions of the text. But if Evans' orthodox rendering of the text prevents him from appreciating its radicality, Derrida's own reading, which follows a similar trajectory, though for different reasons, also prevents him from being able to fully embrace the text's critical import.

PART I

Pseudonymity

1

Authorship as Authority in C. Stephen Evans's Reading of *Fear and Trembling*

I am just as far from being Johannes de Silentio in *Fear and Trembling* as I am from being the Knight of Faith whom he depicts.

After all, I always have a poetic relationship to my work, and therefore I am pseudonymous.

—Søren Kierkegaard

In this chapter, I want to show that by questioning conventional assumptions about *what* the text of *Fear and Trembling* communicates, *how* it communicates, *why*, and on *whose* authority, a space is created that allows it to be read differently, thus enabling it to speak differently, which is to say, in ways that exceed both modern, received readings, and late modern, more transgressive renderings.

As for the former, by exploring the relationship between authorship and authority in the context of Evans's reading of *Fear and Trembling* (in his monograph *Kierkegaard's Ethic of Love*) I will emphasize the importance of keeping the tension alive in order to prevent the easy collapse of that distinction along with the closing of the text in particular. I contend that taking the author, Johannes de Silentio, strictly at his authorial word, is an important first step toward preventing that collapse and keeping the text open.[1] If the bulk of twentieth-century scholarship tended to dismiss the pseudonymous voices, in effect reducing them to Kierkegaard's own voice, I maintain that the counter move in the latter part of the last century to make a clear distinction between those voices—and the connected, interpretive division of the texts along the lines of authorship—blurs the relationship between authorship and authority, effectively repeating a similar problematic. As for the latter, by paying close attention to Derrida's reading of the pseudonym in *The Gift of Death,* I will show, in chapter 2, that because he too collapses the distinction between Kierkegaard's voice and de Silentio's voice he misses the critique at work in the corners of the text. In so doing he misses its critical import.

If, as a representative of the orthodox hermeneutical tradition, Stephen Evans argues that "Kierkegaard" holds to a "meta-ethical" position that metaphysically links (finite) moral obligations to (infinite) divine commands, it is important, nay crucial, to recognize that this first assumes a particular reading of Kierkegaard's texts.[2] In order to explore and evaluate precisely what kind of reading that is, I need to accomplish at least two things. Firstly (1.1.), I will consider the relationship between authorship and authority and its significance for a fair treatment of the text. Secondly (1.2.), I

---

1. I will refer to this problematic, and the dualistic structure that it perpetuates by often employing the term "dual*ism*," inherent to which is a binary logic that is symptomatic of metaphysics with its claim to be able to conceptually unravel the secrets of existence. See Michael Weston, *Kierkegaard and Modern Continental Philosophy,* 11–32. This binary logic or dual*ism* is not to be confused with the terms "duality" or "twoness," intrinsic to which is an existential "excess" that Kierkegaard attempts to honor with a textual dynamic that shows itself differently in each of his texts. An example of this dynamic as it appears elsewhere is the anacoluthic effect that A speaks of and elaborates on in *Either/Or.* See Kierkegaard, *Either/Or* (1944 ed.), 1:135–62. A significant part of my argument seeks to highlight a dynamic at work in the text of *Fear and Trembling,* the twin currents of which underscore both the *complicity with,* and *critique of,* the text's binary logic. This dynamic and the duality intrinsic to it seek to honor both the (universal) promise of meaning, and its resistance to such meaning by underscoring the (particular) finite occurrence of language itself. In a move that extends the argument from a philosophy of finitude to the religious significance of sin, the author's exploration of demonic silence in Problema III highlights the dangers and delusions of misdirected human desire in its boundary crossing bid to grasp the whole truth with finite fingers.

2. Although there are a few exceptions, twentieth-century commentary on, and orthodox readings of, Kierkegaard still dominate much of twenty-first century scholarship. While I hold Evans' hand to the fire of criticism, it must be emphasized that I have the utmost respect for him as a careful and certainly competent reader of Kierkegaard. To be sure, the focused attention that his work is receiving here is itself a testimony to that respect. Ironically, and yet not surprisingly, engaging Evans' orthodox reading of *Fear and Trembling* has helped inform and shape my own rendering, unconventional though it may be. I would like to think Kierkegaard would approve of the difference.

will explore Evans's reading of *Fear and Trembling* with special attention being paid to (1.2.1.) his interpretation of the pseudonymous author, and then
(1.2.2.) his reading of Johannes de Silentio's reading of faith, understood in
the context of a discussion of "infinite resignation" and "faith." Thirdly, and
lastly (1.2.3), I find my way back to the beginning of Evans's text in order to
display, evaluate, and question the philosophical assumptions that condition his hermeneutic methodology. I conclude that while Evans subscribes
to a more faith friendly rationality, his allegiance to objective logic and the
twin metaphysical pillars that support it, unduly narrows the text by inflating the name "Kierkegaard" to a universal principle of authority. In so doing
he simultaneously deflates the significance of the pseudonym and thereby
erases its specificity.[3]

On my reading then, the very fact that Evans's hermeneutical approach necessitates the division of Kierkegaard's texts along the lines of authorship entails hermeneutically problematic assumptions that carry with it
implications that the text of *Fear and Trembling* puts its critical finger on.[4]

3. Understanding the use of the term "metaphysics" throughout this work is
summarized as follows: As a critic of metaphysics, also conceived of as the "System,"
Kierkegaard and his many voices unanimously conclude that while Hegel's dialectic
begins as a movement toward the negativity of death, in the end, it saves itself from having to face it in actuality. Rather than facing death, a posture that generates more than a
little fear and trembling, Kierkegaard's texts conclude that because Hegelian metaphysics works to achieve a higher unity or synthesis (*Aufhebung*) it is spared such anxiety.
By contrast, the conflicting currents at work in *Fear and Trembling*, for example, expose
Hegelian logic to the sharp point of Abraham's upraised, sacrificial knife, and thereby
to its own death—which is to say, its inability to achieve a comprehensive and consistent explanation of reality by reason alone. While the textual dynamic of *Fear and
Trembling* does not deny the promise of redemption and resurrection, made possible
by faith, and mediated by love and trust, it does deny that such a promise can be mediated by the "System," or any other self-appointed principal/principle of authority. In the
context of Kierkegaard's writings, then, the term "metaphysics" represents a complete
and all-encompassing view of reality which claims, by way of reason alone, to render
that view conceptually present as the Truth. While Hegel's "System" is the focal point
of Kierkegaard's criticism, to the extent that any thought project employs a systematic
means by which contingencies and differences are papered over or otherwise erased,
they are subject to that critique. For example, to the extent that Evans employs the
name "Kierkegaard" as a universal, authoritative, hermeneutical principle called upon
to secure the meaning of his texts individually, and all of them collectively, it pushes
him too far into metaphysical territory for my liking. While the same cannot be said of
Derrida, he is subject to a hermeneutical, rather than an ontological critique.

4. That is, the dividing line between Kierkegaard's early, pseudonymous writings
and his later, signed works provides a now accepted hermeneutical ground zero for
the majority of scholars today. See *H.KEL*, 1, 185 n1. On this assumption we are to
conclude that the early, pseudonymous texts are *indirect* expressions of religious truths
expressed *directly* in the later, signed texts. In this way, the latter works, signed by the
author "Kierkegaard," are taken to be the authoritative texts through which the former,

Importantly, though Evans argues to the contrary, this reading provides him
with a principle of authority, or master key, that unlocks the door to "Kierkegaard's" true intentions, allowing him to establish what "Kierkegaard"
meant by how he signed his works. In this way, the name "Kierkegaard"
becomes the self-evident and final authority over/behind the texts, and
therefore the authoritative guide for those texts.[5] I argue that intrinsic to this
hermeneutic is a metaphysics that links these assumptions to an ontological
anchor without which "everything would be permitted."[6]

Although Evans recognizes the importance of the pseudonymous
voice,[7] my reading questions the extent to which he honors that voice and
ultimately the critical function of the text.[8] While Evans wants to be tolerant
of other readings, the fact that he calls upon the name "Kierkegaard" to

---

less authoritative pseudonymous writings, are to be filtered and interpreted.

5. It is important to emphasize the fact that as a Kierkegaard scholar, Evans's own
voice becomes an authoritative one that speaks with authority about "Kierkegaard" and
how it makes good sense that the Dane should interpret his own work. But the question
remains, whose good sense and authority are we talking about here? In other words,
is the division between the early, pseudonymous writings and the later signed works
a hermeneutical divide that obviously and self-evidently indicates how those texts are
to be interpreted? Was this Kierkegaard's intended strategy? The questions themselves
destabilize any attempt to mediate the difficulty.

6. Significantly, in the opening chapter of his book, "God and Moral Obligation:
Is a Link Possible?," and as a way to begin answering its question, Evans approvingly
quotes the famous line from Dostoevsky's *The Brothers Karamazov,* "that if God did not
exist, then 'everything would be permitted'" (*E.KEL,* 1). This is significant because it
sets the hermeneutical tone for his entire book from which his basic assumptions and
conclusions are drawn.

7. While Evans admits that, "the importance of the pseudonyms has become standard among philosophers and theologians who write about Kierkegaard," I will question
whether or not the move in the twentieth century from dismissing the pseudonyms to
now valorizing the signature, achieves essentially the same thing. Interestingly, Evans
confesses that a chapter in his own dissertation did not do justice to the pseudonyms.
Of course this confession is meant to highlight the fact that he now takes the signature
seriously, which I do not doubt. See *E.KEL,* 38 n.13. I also do not doubt that Evans's
use of the pseudonyms have a positive and robust character all their own. In the larger,
hermeneutical scheme of things, it may be better to say that the pseudonyms have an
intrinsically (indirect) negative character. This highlights the fact that, following the
logic of de Silentio, the pseudonyms are designed to display the (direct) positive truth
of Christianity which reflects the true intentions of Kierkegaard himself.

8. As it relates to Kierkegaard, Mark Dooley adopts Richard Rorty's answer to the
charge of taking John Dewey in a direction he did not intend to go when he says: "every
writer who stands in the shadow of a great philosophical forebear is obliged to make a
distinction between the spirit and the letter of that forebear's work. This is so because
each great thinker is the product of his or her time—that is, no philosopher can take up
a neutral standpoint to assess the quandaries of the age." Dooley, *The Politics of Exodus,*
xv.

secure the intelligibility and meaning of each of his texts specifically, and all of his texts generally, indicates a collapse between authorship and authority. If this collapse in turn signals the closing of the text, rather than its opening, it also highlights the limits of that hermeneutical toleration. Fundamentally I will show that Evans's orthodox posture reveals a commitment to a principle of authority that, in effect, pre-exists the text's finite, temporal occurrence. In other words, that Evans effectively ignores the singularity of each pseudonym invariably turns "Kierkegaard" into a veritable master signifier, enabling him to side step the complexities of the pseudonyms themselves and their disruptive presence in the texts. As such, I will conclude that his reading does not escape the metaphysics that *Fear and Trembling* itself is critical of and ultimately exceeds.

With these weighty things in mind, it is imperative to revisit our basic approach to one of Kierkegaard's most popular and accessible texts, particularly as it relates to, not only our fundamental assumptions about that text, but to the crucial connection between authorship and authority. Indeed, the question of ethics, as responsibility itself,[9] is brought to bear on how language is wielded, and how, by extension, the texts themselves are treated in the name of Kierkegaard and his so-called true intentions.[10]

1.1. WHICH INTERPRETATION, ON WHOSE AUTHORITY, AND WHY?

Before we can explore and evaluate Evans's reading of *Fear and Trembling* in a more thoroughgoing way it is important to first consider the relationship between authorship and authority, especially since assumptions about *what* the text of *Fear and Trembling* communicates, *how* it communicates, and *why,* are inextricably linked with the question of authority, one often taken for granted and therefore seldom addressed.

In the face of the tension between the reader and the text/author, arguably the task of interpretation—if there is such a thing—rests squarely on the shoulders of the former. Not without much risk, it is up to the reader, in

9. Rather than a rule based, rationalistic ethics that dictates human conduct, an ethics of responsibility puts the onus on the individual to negotiate the strait between rules and the right behavior they aim at. This is best summed up by Augustine's dictum: *Dilige, et quod vis fac.* ["Love and do what you will"].

10. It is important to note here that I am neither eschewing the notion of authorial intention in general, nor am I suggesting that Kierkegaard's intentions, in particular, are *wholly* inaccessible and therefore fruitless to talk about. What I am concerned with, however, is the question of access to those intentions, what the mechanism of mediation is, and precisely what it promises to deliver.

relationship with the text/author, to help point the way toward a responsible rendering. If early scholarly efforts tended to collapse the divide between Kierkegaard and his pseudonyms, as Evans points out, assuming as it did that the pseudonymous voices were, in the end, Kierkegaard's own voice, the question of how to negotiate that hermeneutical strait is now answered by making a clear distinction between the two, which is to say, between the early pseudonymous writings and the later signed or veronymous works (*E.KEL*, 48). In this way, as common sense apparently dictates, the later texts, signed by Kierkegaard himself in his own name, are considered to be a reasonable, interpretive "baseline" by which the early, pseudonymous texts are to be interpreted (ibid., 40).[11] Thus, the later works are said to be *direct,* faith focused, religious expressions of the early, *indirect,* poetically inspired writings. In order then to understand Kierkegaard's texts, in order to know *what* he meant by what he said, we need to first know *who* wrote the text. The idea is that dividing the texts along the lines of authorship preserves the integrity of the author as the singular, and therefore authoritative voice behind the cacophonous plurality of the pseudonymous voices and their respective orientations, religious or otherwise.

But to argue, as the received tradition now does, that the later writings provide "the decisive, mature view of Kierkegaard" (ibid., 41), through which the early writings are to be hermeneutically filtered, assumes, it would seem, the promise of direct access to the author's true intentions. By conferring final authority on the name "Kierkegaard" as the sole author, ultimate responsibility is placed on that name to determine the meaning of his texts based on how he ostensibly divided and signed them. In this way, the signature, as a means of accessing the truth of Kierkegaard's texts, therefore, mediates the space between the reader and text/author, thus resolving, for all intents and purposes, the hermeneutical tension. But if this is the case, whose authority are we talking about here, and what principle is at work?

Geoffrey Hale suggests that while this straightforward approach to Kierkegaard's texts has common sense appeal, "it amounts to nothing less than the refusal to recognize the problem of authorship altogether" (*H.KEL*, 1). If, in the name of "Kierkegaard," and on his word, the tension between authorship and authority is mediated, then the hermeneutical moment is papered over and left unaddressed. In other words, one might say that the elephant in the room is ignored and the reader is "saved", as it were, from having to bear the full weight of hermeneutical responsibility. As Hale probes, if we accept this approach, the very "attempt to resolve the plurality

---

11. As a rule, Evans believes it is prudent "to take the non-pseudonymous writings of Kierkegaard as a baseline by which to understand Kierkegaard's *own* views" (*E.KEL*, 40; emphasis added).

of Kierkegaard's names under one name effectively abolishes the difficulty *prior* to any purported resolution" (*H.KEL*, 2; emphasis added).

Seen against the horizon of Kierkegaard's proper name, the plurality of pseudonymous names become mere stepping-stones along the way toward proper textual meaning. Among other things, this reduces the pseudonym to the role of a foil or cipher, and effectively robs each name of their own integrity and authority (Ibid). In this way, argues Hale, the name "'Kierkeg-aard' would no longer be the name of the author; instead it would become the sign for the principle of coherence ultimately called upon to secure the intelligibility of each of his texts, and all of his texts together . . . And if 'Kierkegaard' the name designates nothing more than the principle of his authority, there is, in the end, no Kierkegaard" (ibid.). Inflating the proper name to a universal principle of authority then not only nullifies the sin-gularity of Kierkegaard, it simultaneously results in deflating and thereby minimizing the particularity of the pseudonyms. In other words, subsum-ing the pseudonyms under the authorial intention of Kierkegaard all but forces him into the role of a master signifier meant to unify the textual dif-ferences. But the very attempt to unify such differences, at the very same time, eradicates those differences.

According to Hale, attempting to honor the distinction between au-thorship and authority is much more than a meaningless exercise in "tech-nical clarification" (ibid.). Recognizing that distinction and highlighting the irreducible tension intrinsic to it, necessarily "calls into question the very assumptions about what texts mean and how they mean what they mean" (ibid.). As Hale pointed out above, we must keep in mind that for authority to operate authoritatively, which is to say, as a universal principle, "it must *preexist* the very texts that articulate it . . . In spite of all rules of grammar and all the demands of universality in language," he argues, "we can never know what language means prior to its occurrence" (ibid.; emphasis added). Such a claim, like all similar claims, involves a "leap of faith" as it reaches for a promise that can and never will be delivered. As Hale succinctly expresses it:

> The written word is forever caught in the unresolvable tension between the singular temporal specificity of its occurrence and the possibility of a meaning held infinitely in abeyance. Al-though meaning conveyed in language is necessarily 'universal,' its availability depends on a language that can take place only in a finite form and thus has no immediate or secure relation to the universal . . . This predicament lies at the heart of what we might call the linguistic promise. Language always promises access to a meaning that would be universal and totalizable, although

its very occurrence continues to resist complete foreclosure in universality. (*H.KEL*, 5)

Arguably, the desire for and belief in complete disclosure of the truth is tethered to (Greco-Cartesian-Hegelian) Enlightenment sensibilities and the idea of full presence that it promised. Relevant to our discussion here, is the fact that Hegel's dialectic and his attempt to synthesize or otherwise mediate irreconcilable differences represent a high point of that tradition, one that arguably began with Greek philosophy. In the face of the traditional logic of noncontradiction, we remember that Hegel argued that there is an internal connection or relation between identity and difference, which is to say that there is identity amid difference. In Hegel's words, "identity, therefore, is *in its own self* absolute non-identity."[12] The significance here, observes Mark Dooley, is "that the opposition that seemingly emerges between two mutually exclusive entities can be surmounted and overcome in a positive third that is constituted through the dialectical mediation of both."[13] While it is true that Hegel attempted to honor otherness and difference, the fact that he incorporated it in his system and deemed identity (sameness) logically *prior* to difference, effectively reduces the latter to the former. In other words, the spoken of difference or tension between inherently oppositional terms, is, in the end, mediated into a higher unity of meaning.[14] On my reading, to the extent that Evans employs the name "Kierkegaard" as a principle of authority by which his texts are authoritatively interpreted, the signature functions like a positive third, the point of which is to mediate textual differences in a way that serves "Kierkegaard's" "higher, religious purposes" (*E.KEL*, 36). Even if Evans's intention is not to contain all contingencies, the fact remains that the signature operates in this manner.

Any desire then to "go further," one "teleologically" fixated on the "result," to use de Silentio's words, is precisely what *Fear and Trembling* puts its critical finger on (*FT*, 123, 54ff., 62–63). But as a sign called upon to disclose and secure the true meaning of the text, the name "Kierkegaard" ultimately loses its specificity and disappears in a system of signs and signifiers, only

---

12. Hegel, *Science of Logic*, 413.

13. Dooley, *The Politics of Exodus*, 25–26.

14. If it is true that the Hegelian version of philosophy of religion is more radical than Kant, the question is whether or not Hegel's dialectic is authentically open to the future, to radical difference, to death. In other words, does negativity in Hegel go all the way down? While negativity is certainly a chord in Hegel's larger philosophical symphony, Derrida, and certainly Kierkegaard, would argue that it is a minor one, contra thinkers such as Catherine Malabou, Slavoj Žižek, and Quentin Meillassoux. See, respectively, Malabou, *The Future of Hegel*; Žižek, *The Parallax View*; Meillassoux, *After Finitude*.

to reappear as the universal called upon to reveal the truth. If the signified, however, always already partakes of a finite system of signs and signifiers, and therefore remains squarely within that system, how can we employ it in the service of a universal ideal? Yet it appears that Evans does precisely that; and, in fact, we know why he wants to and needs to. His reason is clear from the outset. He needs to employ an ontological anchor in order to ensure proper textual meaning, and therefore prevent hermeneutical anarchy (*E.KEL*, 1, 3, 5). Appealing then to the name "Kierkegaard" as the final authoritative voice over the texts that he obviously authored, provides Evans with just such an anchor.

Arguably, Evans's position, and others like it, stem not only from a fundamental confusion but also from an even more basic fear. The confusion has to do with the often misunderstood relationship between authority and meaning. Conventional scholarly conviction has it, says Hale, that "if the 'author' is deprived of 'authority,' there cannot be any authority at all; and, if there is no authority, one assumes, there can be no meaning" (*H.KEL*, 3–4). But conferring absolute authority on the name "Kierkegaard" does not and cannot guarantee the "true" meaning of a text, since, simply put, the need for reading and its inherent questions remain. Indeed, how can this kind of appeal guarantee such a thing, since every name, and the language it depends on, is shot through with finitude *and* sin?[15] Nevertheless, rooted in its own assumptions and beliefs about what authority is and how it functions, orthodox hermeneutics promises to corral the wild stallion of meaning using the rope of authorial intention. It therefore focuses all its efforts on that task in order to deliver the truth via the meaning inherent in the author's intention—in this case, found in Kierkegaard's later, "mature," or "direct" works.

The unarticulated fear that underlies this confusion is what Richard Bernstein calls "Cartesian Anxiety."[16] This helpful term at once underscores the uncompromising vision of objectivism in general, and reveals its worst fears. At the center of this vision, says Bernstein, "is the belief that there are or must be some fixed, permanent constraints to which we can appeal and which are secure and stable."[17] The self-evident *fact* that there is something rather than nothing, fuels the effort to find and establish such constraints, which at the same time helps nullify the anxiety that haunts such a vision and the beliefs intrinsic to it. For the objective thinker, there *must* be a fixed,

---

15. This is because every reading produces another Kierkegaard with a different voice. More on the issue of sin in chapter 5.

16. Bernstein, *Beyond Objectivism and Relativism*, 16–20.

17. Ibid., 19.

grounded point of reference, otherwise everything is ungrounded; and if everything is ungrounded, then, "everything would be permitted" (*E.KEL*, 1). As far as Kierkegaardian commentary is concerned, this fear is consistent with Hale's observation "that, if the 'author' is deprived of his 'authority,' there cannot be any authority at all; and, if there is no authority, one assumes, there can be no meaning" (*H.KEL*, 3–4). In turn, no meaning means that the truth cannot be secured.

But as Hale argues, "the crisis in authority that Kierkegaard articulated in his work is not the same as a crisis in meaning" (ibid., 4). Meaning, he contends, is neither up-for-grabs in an absolute sense, nor can it be absolutely determined by a single voice of authority (ibid.). But if there is no privileged, authoritative voice or principle of authority to which we can appeal, and if it is necessary to question and ultimately move beyond "Cartesian Anxiety," it would appear that we must adopt an altogether different hermeneutical posture. Such a posture would encourage the kind of reading that honors textual difference and the tensions intrinsic to it, where questions remain, and the hermeneutical moment is preserved. Moreover, such a reading would destabilize any meaning backed by, in this case, the sure convictions and authoritative explications of what a text ostensibly means based on the name "Kierkegaard."

However, in the face of the destabilization of meaning, it is important to emphasize, as Hale insists, that language still means what it says; the important point is that meaning itself, haunted as it is by the "moment"—that is, the existential, finite moment of unknowing and unknowability that undoes our best efforts to paper over the dread inherent in it—cannot be pinned down by a single, determined and determinate authority. To the extent that a hermeneutical posture honors that moment and allows it to have its way, reading to understand the meaning of a text becomes a responsive, productive act of giving and receiving, one laden with responsibility to point the way toward responsible renderings, readings to be held in an open hand with a certain *fear and trembling*. It must be emphasized that while texts are always on the move, by dint of their finite particularity, they have particular shapes and contours that resist being given over to the four winds of infinite meaning, as well as being hermeneutically straight-jacketed.

Having broached the important relationship between authorship and authority as it connects with Kierkegaard's texts, as well as how scholarly convention has conceived that relationship, I now turn to Evans' treatment of *Fear and Trembling* in his monograph, *Kierkegaard's Ethic of Love: Divine Commands and Moral Obligations*. Importantly, by considering the kind of reading Evans employs, along with the assumptions that it entails, we will see *how* a link is achieved between God and moral obligations, precisely *what* the mechanism of mediation is, and ultimately *why* this is hermeneutically problematic as it connects with the issue of authorship and authority specifically in the text of *Fear and Trembling*. To that end, I will first show what kind of reading Evans entertains, including its rationale, and second, why that reading is necessary for him. This will go a long way toward answering the third and fourth questions: what do these findings reveal; and what are their implications?

1.2. READING EVANS READING
FEAR AND TREMBLING

In this section I will show that Evans's reading of *Fear and Trembling* pivots on the division of his writings along the lines of authorship. As an interpretive gesture this appeals to a universal principle of authority that effectively pre-exists the articulation of that principle; and as such, it raises important critical, hermeneutical and methodological questions. By looking closely at Evans's project, I will consider the assumptions undergirding his work, trace them to a modernist, rationalistic interpretation of Kierkegaard's texts, and in the end call them into question. Rather than trying to find a happy medium or "balance" through mediation proffered by metaphysics, my *reading with* the text of *Fear and Trembling* attempts to honor textual differences by allowing them to stand in their difference. (*E.KEL*, 35–36).

Chapter 1 of *Kierkegaard's Ethic of Love*, "God and Moral Obligations", framed as it is with a question as its subtitle, "Is a Link Possible?", suggests a spirit of exploration and a posture of openness. We quickly learn, however, that not only is such a link possible, but that it is necessary, indeed, essential. Importantly, as we will see, this necessity carries with it the promise of immediate, though conditional, delivery. In the opening paragraphs, Evans lays out clear project markers by which we can both identify and track his working assumptions. But even as we connect those assumptions to the project that he articulates in the beginning sections, it is not until the final section of that chapter that we get a clearer, overall hermeneutical picture and the implications that it entails.

By not beginning at the beginning with questions of hermeneutics and the problem of interpretation as it relates to authorship and the question of authority; and by not discussing, first and foremost, how his interpretation entails assumptions about what Kierkegaard's texts mean by what they say according to who wrote each text and why, Evans conceals a secret with one hand that he reveals with the other. Thus, before exploring those assumptions, I will closely consider his project and the kind of reading those

assumptions give rise to as it relates both to his treatment of the pseudonyms, and to his reading of key figures and themes in *Fear and Trembling*.

1.2.1. Interpreting the Pseudonyms

In chapter 2 of Evans's text—"The Ethical as a 'Stage' of Existence: *Either/
Or* and Radical Choice"—one notes that the title of section 2—"Interpreting
the Pseudonyms"—puts the focus directly on the pseudonym, immediately
suggesting that their proper interpretation is the key to unlocking the meaning of Kierkegaard's texts as a whole. Not only does this focus necessarily
create a disjunction between the pseudonymous and non-pseudonymous
(signed) writings, it also assumes, as suggested, that when the pseudonyms
are rightly viewed, that is, as ciphers or foils meant to serve Kierkegaard's
higher religious purposes (*E.KEL*, 40), his own voice (which reflects his true
intentions) becomes the self-evident truth that bubbles to the surface of the
text, thereby alleviating the hermeneutical tension.

Quoting from the well known "A First and Last Declaration" that appears at the end of *Concluding Unscientific Postscript*, Evans, in an effort to
make his point, highlights the fact that Kierkegaard himself explicitly and
wholly distances himself from the work of the pseudonyms: "'Thus in the
pseudonymous works there is not a single word by me. I have no opinion
about them except as a third party, no knowledge of their meaning except
as a reader . . .'" (ibid., 38). Evans therefore rightly concludes that such a
statement militates against any effort to cobble together various viewpoints
from across the authorship in order to come up with a fully unified philosophy.[18] If it is true that early generations of Kierkegaard scholars tended to
do precisely that, that is, reduce all voices in the authorship to Kierkegaard's
own, Evans believes that things are quite different now. To be sure, he says,
recognizing "the importance of the pseudonym has now become standard
among philosophers and theologians who write about Kierkegaard, most of
whom today understand that the views of the pseudonyms must be understood in relation to those pseudonymous characters' own agendas" (ibid.).

But while this recognition is an important hermeneutical first step, it
does not necessarily mean that the textual voices are taken seriously or ad-
equately honored, especially if this now means that Kierkegaard's own voice
is given interpretive primacy *over* the pseudonymous voices. Evans's major

---

18. But the fact that, in the end, Evans proposes a theory of interpretation that is
backed by the authority of Kierkegaard's own voice implies a singularity of purpose
and intent which itself points toward a unified, philosophical vision entertained by
Kierkegaard himself.

concern, or fear, seems to be the critics who take the literary, pseudonymous character of the authorship *too* seriously. According to Evans, giving too much credence to the pseudonymous voice ultimately "makes it *impossible* to see in it *any* overall purpose or thrust" (ibid., 38–39; emphasis added). In order to counter this kind of interpretive danger, he appeals to Kierkegaard's own voice by underscoring the self-evident fact that the latter "describes his task from beginning to end as an attempt to 'reintroduce Christianity to Christendom'" (ibid., 39). In so doing, contends Evans, Kierkegaard's clear intention was to "awaken his contemporaries to the questions of existence" (ibid.).[19] Thus, the interpretive task for Evans is not unlike cutting a wide swath through dense tropical undergrowth, the goal of which is to unearth the truth found in the treasure box of intentionality located in the later works. "Given the multivocity or polyphony of the authorship, how can we get a sense for Kierkegaard's *own* purposes and aims, since these can by no means be identified with any or all of the pseudonyms? Well," says Evans, "we could *decide* to take Kierkegaard's *own* word for what he was about, as developed primarily in *The Point of View for My Work as an Author*" (ibid.; emphasis added). And who could argue with the apparent reasonableness or self-evidence of such a claim?

What Evans is suggesting is that it is hermeneutically prudent "to take the non-pseudonymous writings of Kierkegaard as an interpretive "baseline" by which to understand Kierkegaard's own views. "After all," he argues, "Kierkegaard's admonition not to confuse the views of the pseudonyms with his own can hardly be taken as warning against attributing to him the views he puts forward under his own name" (ibid., 40).[20] In addition, says Evans, this is not to say that one cannot also *selectively* draw on Kierkegaard's Journal entries, so long as "we are using material that reflects his own voice" (ibid.). When one has confidence and clarity as to what Kierkegaard *himself* says, the reader is in a far better position to judge precisely "how the pseudonyms serve his wider purposes . . . where the pseudonyms provide him with a foil, [and] where they prefigure or seem to be developing views he personally held" (ibid.).

For those "'postmodern' interpreters of Kierkegaard . . . who have announced the 'death of the author' and have claimed that 'S. Kierkegaard' should be seen as simply one more pseudonym, another persona," Evans

19. While I do not contest this, per se, I contend that the text destabilizes the pervasive dialectical logic by showing *performatively* that metaphysics, with its penchant for universal reason, avoids these very questions and the exigencies intrinsic to existence.

20. But it seems clear that attributing absolute authority to "Kierkegaard" collapses the pseudonymous voices with Kierkegaard's own voice, thus confusing them in precisely the same manner he warns against.

insists that "anyone who seriously advances this line of thought cannot possibly argue that the view I propose to develop is not that of the 'real Kierkegaard' since such a reader denies the possibility that there could be such a thing" (ibid.). But since Evans appears to believe that postmodern interpreters are cut from the same cloth, all of whom invariably subscribe to some form of hermeneutical nihilism that undermines both positive and negative accounts of textual meaning, it seems clear that his positive appropriation of Kierkegaard's meaning and intentions is designed precisely to reveal the "real" Kierkegaard via the proper name.[21] But how does one not stagger under the hermeneutical weight given to Kierkegaard's *own* voice to determine the meaning of his own intentions—which of course the reader alone bears? To "simply drop the claim" that his interpretation *is* Kierkegaard's, as Evans suggests, does not change anything substantial. While this appears to be a gesture of open-handed, interpretive tolerance, all indications suggest that he himself cannot and would not drop the claim because his own interpretation stands or falls on an objective, metaphysically backed, and ontologically rooted argument.

If Evans argues that it is "reasonable to take the later works as providing the decisive, mature view of Kierkegaard," he also rightly recognizes the "lack of uniformity" in those works (ibid., 41). In an attempt then to remain true to his founding hermeneutical principle, and therefore pave a straight road through Kierkegaard's literary jungle, Evans makes yet another interpretive decision and subsequent distinction. If the later works are supposed to provide the "baseline" from which we read and therefore understand Kierkegaard's own views, he finds it necessary to take his *"very* late writings" with an interpretive grain of salt (ibid., 40–41; emphasis added). This is due largely to the fact that here, Kierkegaard's "*end* seems only to be the negative

---

21. If Evans wants to agree with Johannes Climacus who insists that "the existing thinker, particularly the religious existing thinker, cannot simply move through the negative and leave it behind in a higher 'positivity,'" by contending that, in his dissertation, "Kierkegaard defends irony as essential to human life, but argues that irony must be 'mastered' or 'controlled', directed to a higher end," he side-steps the hermeneutical difficulty here by appealing to Kierkegaard's own name as the *final* authority over his own work (*E.KEL*, 34–35). Indeed, Evans insists that "there is no reason to think that Kierkegaard *himself* thinks that the presence of irony is incompatible with positive convictions" (ibid., 35; emphasis added). He then harks back to *Concluding Unscientific Postscript* and insists that, "Johannes Climacus sees a precise balance between inappropriate seriousness and inappropriate laughter" (ibid). In the next paragraph he concludes this of "Kierkegaard": "Though his situation in Christendom demanded that he begin with aesthetic writings that constituted a kind of godly deception, the *real* irony in his authorship is that the irony masks a serious purpose which contemporary readers missed" (ibid., 36; emphasis added). This "serious purpose" I take to be the "positive" intent that informs and ultimately *precedes* negativity.

one of inspiring people publicly to confess that the official Christianity was not the Christianity of the New Testament" (ibid., 42; emphasis added). As we have seen, what Evans wants (with Johannes Climacus?) is to make sure that there is "a precise balance" between the negative and the positive, and that cannot be done if the "very late writings" are not distinguished and kept separate from the late writings in general (ibid., 35). Whether or not Kierkegaard himself wanted the same thing, however, remains to be seen.

In general, it seems clear that Evans's interpretive method is focused primarily on bringing order to the chaos that Kierkegaard's texts represent. But are we entirely sure that a straightforward, rationalistic approach does justice to such a multi-layered, multi-textured, and multi-colored corpus? Does Evans's interpretation get us any closer to the truth of those texts? Indeed, if *the truth* is even attainable, that is, using the logic that Evans traffics in, what would it look like exactly, and whose truth would it be? What hermeneutical recourse then do we have if the truth is not available to us in a direct, objective manner? Are we to suggest that a whole-hearted embrace of Kierkegaard's apparent irrationalism is therefore in order? But if a straightforward, rational approach to his texts is in question, is it not logical to assume that its irrational opposite would also be called into question since they represent both sides of the same coin, the deflated value of which Kierkegaard's texts resist?

On my reading, at issue here is the existential fact that not only is reason, and the language which props it up, fraught with finitude, it is freighted with human fallenness. In this fractured light, how are we to talk seriously about meaning and truth in language when, à la Hale, by dint of its finite occurrence, there is no immediate connection to the objective, universal truth it promises to deliver? In the sober face of human fallenness, connected as it is to the rabbit hole of self-deception, should we not altogether resist the penchant to attempt such a thing? Indeed, does not the very attempt constitute a transgression of creaturely boundaries that de Silentio draws out in Problema III?[22] As we will see, far from revealing an objective, metaphysical principle of authority that pre-exists the text's temporal occurrence, one that has Kierkegaard's name written on it, his texts instead highlight both the finitude of language and human fallenness in ways that frustrate any and all attempts to rationally mediate the space between the early and late writings, not to mention the space between faith and reason.[23]

22. See *GD*, 3–6, where Derrida, in the footsteps of Jan Patočka, employs strikingly similar language to de Silentio in the service of his "religion without religion"—albeit without biblical or expressly theological references to sin (*GD*, 50).

23. Evans would likely say that the wholly negative emphasis on finitude and fallenness is all well and good, and certainly important, so long as *in the end* it gives way to

But before I say anything else in this regard, it is only fitting to follow Evans's argument a little further, all the while keeping in mind the challenges he faces, particularly the challenge of language and its limits. What Evans assumes about *Fear and Trembling* and how he negotiates the stark structure of the text is as revealing as it is instructive. Thus, as we explore his reading of its central focus, figures and themes, I will continue teasing out those assumptions and highlight how the interpretive framework that follows, forms and informs the details of his reading. Even if Evans takes the pseudonym with an interpretive grain of salt, the fact that he takes the stark structure and logic of the text as Kierkegaard's own is really not that surprising since it is consistent with Evans's own logic. But that logic, I contend, is ultimately inconsistent with the contours of the text and the questions raised by its conflicting currents, the very currents that Evans wants to manage with an hermeneutical dam.[24]

1.2.2. Interpreting the Text of Fear and Trembling

In his Introduction to the 2006 Cambridge edition of *Fear and Trembling*— co-edited with and translated by Sylvia Walsh—Evans there too emphasizes the importance of taking the literary character of Kierkegaard's early writings seriously.[25] "A proper interpretation of *Fear and Trembling* must therefore try to understand the figure of Johannes de Silentio" (*E.FT*, ix). But, as we have seen, on Evans' reading, understanding de Silentio, specifically, and the pseudonyms generally, involves separating the (false) pseudonymous signatures from Kierkegaard's own (true) signature. In what functions as an authoritative principle, then, Evans argues that the late, non-pseudonymous works constitute a hermeneutical ground zero for interpreting the early

---

a "positive end," understood as "Kierkegaard's" "higher religious" or "serious purpose" (*E.KEL*, 35–36). For Evans, there must be an "overall purpose or thrust" to Kierkegaard's work, otherwise one could say anything, hermeneutically speaking (ibid., 38–39).

24. I am attempting to demonstrate throughout that Evans' approach to the text of *Fear and Trembling* is overly rationalistic. Without subscribing to an anti-rationalist, non-rationalist, or irrationalist position, all of which in some way fall within the purview of metaphysics and are therefore seen as antithetical to the text's logic, my hope is to map out a different path through the territory of reason and language, one that follows in Kierkegaard's footsteps. Even if Evans traffics in a more benevolent, faith friendly reason, because the latter precedes the former and therefore has the teleological last word, I propose a construction that sees the former as the condition of possibility for the latter. In this way, conditioned as it by faith (as trust), reason begins with faith and ends with faith.

25. Kierkegaard, *Fear and Trembling* (2006 ed.); hereafter this volume will appear in the text as *E.FT*.

pseudonymous writings based on the signature. How Kierkegaard signs his work, therefore, ultimately determines what the text means based on who signed it. If then the proper name provides the lens through which Evans views Kierkegaard's texts, that name ultimately has the final, authoritative say.

In chapter 3 of *Kierkegaard's Ethic of Love,* Evans's argument centers on *Fear and Trembling* in particular. He argues, in essence, that while the central focus is both the ethical and religious stages, the text is less about ethics, per se, and much more, indeed, "primarily about faith, and the role faith should play in the formation of the self's identity" (*E.KEL,* 62). In keeping with his interpretive principle that, for all intents and purposes, keeps the pseudonymous and signed writings separate, Evans argues that for a more definitive view of ethics one must look to the later texts signed by his own name. So rather than grapple with the sharp textual disjunction between faith and reason, Evans, proposes a kinder, gentler version of reason, one designed to make more room for faith. On my reading, this proposal remains not only in basic agreement with de Silentio's own construction of the relationship between faith and reason, but with the text's overall presenting logic, one designed to keep the former and the latter philosophically separate from each other.

While I agree with Evans that *Fear and Trembling* is written from within a Hegelian, intellectual worldview that sees ethical obligations 'embedded in the historically relative institutions and practices of societies', I maintain that the textual focus is on the inherent contrast between faith and reason, and how that *relationship* is conceived, wrestled with, and ultimately mediated by a man struggling with faith within a particular philosophically laden milieu.[26] Rather than question the author's relationship to Hegelian logic as it relates to the textual tension, Evans, for the most part, works to preserve de Silentio's overall negative logic as Kierkegaard's own. But assuming that the dominant logic of the text is Kierkegaard's own distracts the reader from the larger issue of the tension itself and the utter failure of that logic to "understand" Abraham.

In the extended preface to the dialectical section of *Fear and Trembling* ("Preliminary Expectoration"), which can also be seen as an interlude

---

26. While it is true that de Silentio confesses that he is not a person of faith, this is largely because, as a product of the Hegelian intellectual milieu, he is honestly, yet with much difficulty, wrestling not only with the notion that one simply inherits faith as a birthright, but with the tension between fideism and rationalism. While Johannes may (rationalistically) *think* of himself as being on the outside looking in, the very fact that the entire text reaches for an understanding of faith, grappling as it does with the assumed disjunction between faith and reason, demonstrates that the faith he does have is firmly rooted in the soil of reason.

between the poetical and philosophical sections of the text, Johannes introduces two characters in order to illustrate the relationship between faith
and reason, and the immense difficulty of negotiating the space between
them. One might safely say that on these personages, and all other similar
couplets, the split sensibility of the entire text pivots. De Silentio calls these
figures, the "knight of infinite resignation," and the "knight of faith," both of
whom connect with the figures he also calls, the "tragic hero," and the "hero
of faith" (*FT*, 38, 57). On Johannes's accounting, both knights have made
the first "movement of infinite resignation," one that precedes the second
movement of faith (ibid., 41ff). Even though these are posited as absolutely
separate movements, the former is seen as a stage that necessarily precedes
the latter, so that "anyone who has not made this movement does not have
faith" (ibid., 46). This preliminary stage, as the last way station before faith,
represents a willingness to sacrifice everything finite (the creaturely world)
for the sake of "the infinite," "the eternal," or "God." This movement, says de
Silentio, is thus, "purely philosophical," one that "I make all by myself, and
what I gain thereby is my eternal consciousness in blessed harmony with my
love for the eternal being" (ibid., 48).

De Silentio illustrates infinite resignation by imaginatively depicting
a young man who falls in love with a princess, a love, however, that cannot
and will never be fulfilled in the here and now of temporality. As de Silentio
frames it, "this love is the entire substance of his life, and yet the relation is
such that it cannot possibly be realized, cannot possibly be translated from
ideality into reality" (ibid., 41). In the face of this impossibility, the young
man renounces all hope, all temporal possibility of love's fulfilment and
thereby sacrifices everything on the altar of "eternal love" (ibid., 43). In this
way, Johannes says that the lad's love for the princess becomes a symbol,
"the expression of an eternal love," one that

> would assume a religious character, would be transfigured into
> a love of the eternal being, which true enough denied the ful-
> filment but nevertheless did reconcile him once more in the
> eternal consciousness of its validity in an eternal form that no
> actuality can take away from him. (Ibid., 43–44)

"Infinite resignation then," as Evans rightly observes, "embodies a kind of
other-worldly religiousness, a life-stance that Johannes himself claims to
understand and even . . . able to realize" (*E.FT*, xiv). The fact that Johannes
boasts that if ordered to do so he too would undertake the journey to Moriah and ultimately fulfil God's command, highlights the suggestion that he
himself is a knight of infinite resignation who dreams of faith (*FT*, 34–35).
Importantly, this underscores the disjunction between faith and reason; and

this *absolute* divide is best illustrated by Johannes' own posture of resignation as he imaginatively attempts to put himself in Abraham's shoes. Unlike the patriarch, however, he cannot follow in his footsteps since there are no footprints in the rarefied terrain beyond the boundary of reason where only God and Abraham dare to tread. Consequently, all that he can do is resign himself to the loss. "The moment I mounted the horse," says de Silentio,

> I would have said to myself: Now all is lost, God demands Isaac, I sacrifice him and along with him all my joy—yet God is love and continues to be that for me, for in the world of time God and I cannot talk to each other, we have no language in common. (Ibid., 35)

Indeed, a paragraph earlier, when contemplating the enormity of faith and the ability of Abraham to make the necessary, second movement of faith, Johannes is paralyzed by the sheer impossibility of it all. Compared to Abraham and his faith, Johannes says that "I do not have faith; this courage I lack. To me God's love, in both the direct and [indirect] converse sense, is incommensurable with the whole of actuality" (ibid., 34). According to de Silentio, then, infinite resignation, by itself (as is the case of the young man's love for the princess) is a mere substitute for faith—simply because it is *not* faith. Nevertheless, as we have seen, it is, paradoxically, an essential ingredient of faith. While Abraham himself has made this initial movement, it is the second movement that baffles Johannes. For having thus resigned the whole of actuality (the finite world), the patriarch receives it all back "by virtue of the absurd" (ibid., 37). By way of a "double-movement," then, Abraham was able to receive Isaac the second time "more joyfully than the first time" (ibid., 36).[27]

After a fairly straightforward exposition of this section ("Preliminary Expectoration"), the focus of which are the two (ideal) personages, Evans sets out to, as it were, salvage "Kierkegaard's" notion of faith and thereby rescue him from an obvious irrationalism. In the face of the absolute disjunction between the religious (faith) and the ethical (reason), not to mention the rational contradiction that it entails, Evans argues that "Abraham" neither holds to a logically contradictory belief, nor is he a shrewd figure who has rationally determined the outcome beforehand (*E.FT*, xvi. ff.). On my reading, the issue here has less to with Evans's argument, per se—ie., whether or

---

27. "I can," "I cannot"—it is precisely these absolutely separate economies that force de Silentio at different times and in different ways to say: 'I can make the movement of infinite resignation', 'I cannot make the movement of faith'. I will argue that the "yes and no" of which I speak is fundamentally different from the "paradoxical" economy that de Silentio assumes overall.

not it is cogent or valid—and more about the rationalistic attempt to recast and thereby reconcile the text's notion of faith with the patriarch's, which is to say, "Abraham himself" (which is also to say, the "genuine," or the "actual Abraham"), why that is, and what it indicates in the light of the text (ibid., xviii, xvii, xi).

In keeping with his operating assumptions that we will consider momentarily, assumptions that entail the privileging of Kierkegaard's name over the pseudonym's name, we are not surprised to find Evans separating de Silentio's sensibilities from those of the *real* Abraham. Of course, the use of the proper name is directed toward determining precisely what is happening in the text and what it all means. But, as I have already indicated, the quest for textual truth, driven by an over-arching principle of authority, distracts us from the uncomfortable idea that the truth is not *in* the text and therefore not objectively available to us as some-thing to be discovered with the right intellectual tools and the right methodological approach. Rather, in the case of *Fear and Trembling*, it points to the performative failure of the text's presenting logic.[28] In other words, in keeping with the emphasis throughout, the text is meant to *do* something, even as it *explains* something.

Nevertheless, Evans's rationalistic sensibilities compel him to save Abraham and his faith from the absurdity of "Kierkegaard's" apparent irrationalism. But the attempt to make reason shake hands with faith in this way fundamentally ignores and does nothing about what I argue is Johannes's own rationalistic distinction between the former and the latter. For example, on several occasions Evans emphasizes, with de Silentio, that anyone "who looks at things from this viewpoint of the absurd has completely rejected human calculative reasoning" (ibid., xvii). Nevertheless, in the face of this absolute distinction "faith requires a clear-headed understanding that from the perspective of human experience the situation appears impossible" (ibid.). But by emphasizing that the "absurd" only looks that way from a (human) rational standpoint, and that by looking at it from a (divine) faith perspective it is no longer absurd, does not address the absolute divide dictated by reason. On my reading it therefore achieves little in the larger hermeneutical scheme of things. This may, at best, smooth off the edges of de Silentio's stark depiction of faith, but the dichotomy itself, and the rationalist assumptions that undergird it, remain firmly in place.

This attempt to round out the edges of Johannes's faith may allow for a more benevolent reason, but on my reading, the former is still confined to

---

28. Geoffrey Hale rightly reminds us that the "truth" of a text is its intrinsic incompleteness, its finitude, its fragmentation. "This 'truth'—the fragment—thus is not the goal of meaning, but its condition. And as its condition, it must also be understood paradoxically to condition the very meaning it cannot secure" (*H.KEL*, 15).

the latter's front yard, in which case the relationship is subject to the text's critique of it's own logic. As we will see, because the text of *Fear and Trembling* is structured in an uncompromising way, it makes any kind of strictly rational reconciliation (mediation) impossible.[29] Nevertheless, we watch as de Silentio, shaped and tempted by reason, reach precisely for that impossibility in Problema I (via the "teleological suspension of the ethical"), a gesture then called into question and ultimately destabilized in Problema III (via the exploration of deceitful and demonic silences). Rather than smooth off the sharp edges of de Silentio's faith so that it will comfortably fit the contours of reason, I contend that it makes better textual sense to allow the inconsistencies and contradictions in the text to hang there until they turn a little blue—to borrow a colorful phrase from Jack Caputo.[30] Allowing for this level of textual difference enables us to view the text itself in another way and thereby read it differently.

But before we can more fully appreciate such a reading, we need to look a little more closely at Evans' philosophical starting points with a view toward understanding where they come from, and why. While this next section will be excursive in some sense, it is important to consider his divine command theory of moral obligations in order to see these starting points, and the assumptions that undergird them, more clearly.

1.2.3. Divine Commands, Moral Obligations, and Philosophical Starting Points

The fact that Evans begins his text by quoting, approvingly, the famous line from Dostoevsky's *The Brothers Karamazov*, "that if God did not exist, then 'everything would be permitted'" (*E.KEL*, 1), arguably sets the hermeneutical tone for the entire book, one that is concerned to establish "overriding," "objective" and "universal" (ibid., 2) moral obligations that depend directly on God, understood as the "ontological" (ibid., 3), and therefore "absolute" (ibid., 16) foundation for such obligations. With these concerns as his focus, the "meta-ethical" theory that Evans ascribes to Kierkegaard himself is in keeping with the theories of moral obligation that ethicists Robert Adams

29. The term "irrational," as the polar opposite of "rational," only makes sense on reason's terms. Importantly, the idea of the "paradox" itself functions similarly and therefore makes sense only against the horizon of reason.

30. See Caputo, *Radical Hermeneutics*, 1–2. One of the best examples of the text's stark, conflicting structure is found embodied in the author's split view of himself, insisting as he does, on the one hand, that he "is by no means a philosopher"; then declaring, on the other hand, that he is "not a poet" but rather a philosopher and therefore approaches "things only dialectically" (*FT*, 7, 90).

and Philip Quinn argue for respectively. Both thinkers, says Evans, defend "plausible versions of the metaphysical linkage claim by defending a 'divine command theory' of moral obligation . . . This kind of meta-ethical theory entails a *direct* link between God's reality and this aspect of morality . . ." (ibid., 5; emphasis added). In particular, Evans applauds the efforts of Adams to develop an ethical framework that connects the Platonic idea of the Good with the theistic idea of God. According to this logic, since both notions are "conceived as infinite and transcendent," one can safely conclude that the former is not only consistent with, but also "identical with a personal God" (Ibid).

In this way, one can see that "this broadly Platonistic framework" provides the general condition of possibility for a *direct* linkage between the infinite "Good"/God and finite, goods/creaturely things. As it is with Platonism, so it is with theism, says Evans, that finite goods are good precisely because of their likeness to the "Good"/God. One might say then that if the goodness that finite goods enjoy derives from the "Good," it is also true that creaturely things derive their goodness from God. It is safe to conclude then, that in and of themselves, that is, apart from the infinite Good, finite goods are not good. How could they be, since without the infinite Good as their source, finite goods would not even exist, let alone be good. On these terms, it follows that because finite goods are directly dependent on the infinite Good, it cannot also be said that the latter is dependent on the former. As we will now see, these assumptions figure prominently in Evans' divine command theory, the fundamental, philosophical lines of which extend to his hermeneutic methodology.

Still in the opening pages (section 3 [ibid., 8–10]), in an attempt to argue his point, Evans contrasts what he calls "religiously based human nature theories" (HNT) with "divine command theories" (DCT) of moral obligations in order to show that the former theories, best developed and taken in a religious direction by Aquinas, fall short of the standard set by Platonic metaphysics (ibid., 8). By maintaining, for example, that moral obligations are best "understood in relation to God's purposes in creation and the potential goods there to be realized," Evans believes that such an argument is simply not strong enough (ibid., 8, 12). Even as a religiously based, explicitly Christian, human nature theory, the link to God here is indirect at best, and as such it lacks the strength of a *direct* linkage. Although Evans recognizes the complementarity between Aristotelian (from which Aquinas' theory derives) and Christian positions, the fact that postmodern versions of the latter are suspicious of any claims to universality is a central issue for him (ibid., 11). Indeed, linked as they ought to be with a more robust account of moral obligations, he insists that "Christian versions of a human nature theory must see our nature as grounded in God's creative intentions" (ibid.). To be sure, argues Evans, as the creator, God has endowed all human beings with "a particular nature, with a distinctive set of potentialities, because he willed them to become particular kinds of creatures" (ibid.). Importantly, in carefully distinguishing human goods from the Good, Evans is also emphasizing that the latter precedes the former, metaphysically speaking.

By looking at the "characteristic strengths and weaknesses" of both HNT and DCT through the lens of a "variation on a question posed in Plato's *Euthyphro*," Evans will argue that the former lacks sufficient grounding (ibid., 8). In other words, if God commands particular actions because they are morally right, then human, moral commands *precede* divine commands and therefore lack grounding (ibid., 17). Conversely expressed, however, the latter achieves the necessary grounding, which is to say, if particular actions are morally right because God commands them, then divine commands *precede* human, moral commands. For Evans, the difference here makes all the difference.

In the form of a question, then, the metaphysical problem Evans sets for himself, based on Plato's text, can be summarized as follows:[31] does God command particular actions because they are morally right, or, are particular actions morally right because God commands them? On Evans's accounting, HNT maintains the former—that God commands particular actions because they are morally right—while DCT holds the latter—that particular actions are morally right because God commands them (ibid.). For the sake of argument, Evans says that while DCT depends on God, it could be argued that it renders moral obligations arbitrary in the sense that acts understood to be immoral, such as murder, theft, etc., could become moral if God so commanded them—case in point being God's command

---

31. While it is true that this section traffics primarily in Platonic metaphysics, there are important connections between Plato's dialogical communication and Hegel's dialectical mediation. "For both Plato and Hegel," says Weston, "man's highest form of activity is philosophical knowing in which the ground . . . is discovered as at one with man himself. For Plato, this ground is the idea of the Good, of the purposiveness which binds together all that can be said to be and which provides us with the notions of a final truth and unchanging being . . . For Hegel, this purposiveness becomes the activity of unifying thought itself . . ." (Weston, *Kierkegaard and Modern Continental Philosophy*, 27). Quoting Kierkegaard referring to Hegel, Weston highlights the fact that "'Philosophy is the purely human view of the world, the human standpoint . . .' It leads, that is, towards an identification of the human with the divine, a process which has its roots in the Platonic conception of a divine element in man's nature. Hegel's thought, for Kierkegaard, is the culmination of this tradition of philosophy, within which the nature of that human project becomes transparent, for there the human being thinking 'the system of the universe' becomes divine" (ibid., 27–28).

to Abraham to sacrifice his son (ibid., 8–9).[32] If moral obligations are not arbitrary, which is to suggest that they are sufficient, in and of themselves, then they do not, therefore, necessarily, depend on God or his existence. As a theist, Evans contends that neither alternative is acceptable because in both instances there lacks a direct linkage to God (ibid., 9). Thus, the only way to solve the problem is to defend a robust version of theism where moral obligations are directly and necessarily linked to God.

Thus, in an attempt to provide an absolute foundation that will mediate the difficulty inherent in the Platonic tension, Evans argues that divine commands are metaphysically "rooted in God's broader teleological vision of the good" in a way that sees moral obligations directly linked to God; and it is precisely this linkage that honors and ultimately fulfils human nature in the truest, most authentic sense. What Evans wants to emphasize is that DCT differs from HNT, fundamentally, by "claiming that moral obligations do not follow directly from human nature alone" (ibid.). In other words, he argues, "one cannot deduce our moral duties simply from a knowledge of human nature" (ibid.). Put differently, if moral obligations are absolute in character, they must necessarily be anchored to the absolute source of those obligations; and a God that is metaphysically conceived (after the manner of Plato's 'Good') is precisely what he has in mind (ibid., 3). According to this logic, as alluded to above, genuine (read, "absolute") moral duties do not and cannot derive from the *finite* goods which certain acts and practices make possible. Rather, they stem from the *infinite* source of those goods. For Evans, then, (divine) essence must precede (human) existence, *necessarily* so.

1.3 CONCLUSIONS

In this chapter I argued that a close consideration of the relationship between authorship and authority in Evans's thought highlights the hermeneutical problematics that follow from the collapse of that distinction. I showed that his interpretation of Kierkegaard's texts along the lines of authorship—one that posits the proper name as a principle of authority—results in precisely such a collapse, one that unduly narrows the hermeneutical scope of *Fear and Trembling*. I concluded that this narrowing is traceable to Evans' metaphysical assumptions, the interpretive methodology that it gives rise to, and the logic that supports them.

32. At this point, Evans surmises that a human nature theorist might say that as long as the actions that God commands "fulfil the good potential present in the natural order," then such actions are moral actions (*E.KEL*, 9).

In the next chapter, I will deal with Jacques Derrida, whose reading of *Fear and Trembling* is almost faithful, one that reflects a certain religious sensibility, albeit with a deconstructive twist. To be sure, the publication of *Donner la mort* in 1992 marks Derrida's more explicit turn to the religious (and the political), and in some sense anticipates his own death; and it is in this text that he engages Kierkegaard in a sustained way for the first time with a close reading of *Fear and Trembling*. It is to Derrida's text that we now turn with a view toward exploring the significance of his treatment of the relationship between the author's voice and Kierkegaard's own voice.

2

Pseudonymity in Jacques Derrida's Reading of *Fear and Trembling*

But it is Kierkegaard to whom I have been most faithful and who interests me the most.

—Jacques Derrida

In the last chapter I attempted to show that Evans's interpretation of *Fear and Trembling* is tethered to a metaphysical principle of authority that hamstrings his understanding of the text. Rather than opening the text, this tethering unduly narrows its hermeneutical scope, thus preventing him from reading it differently.

In this chapter I will argue that while Jacques Derrida's approach to *Fear and Trembling* achieves a kind of openness that eludes Evans, his own reading hampers his ability to honor the text in a way that fully appreciates its more critical dimensions.[1] This means that Derrida also unduly narrows

---

1. I will maintain that, what might be called, the *performative* function of *Fear and Trembling*, together with its faith inspired motivation and its religious character, mediate the textual differences in a relational, non-binary way that is not necessarily coercive or violent. The model for this is the biblical Incarnation woven throughout Kierkegaard's textual fabric. Contrary to the Socratic mode of conceptual mediation, the god's actual, historical presence "is not incidental to his teaching but is essential. The presence of the god in human form . . . is precisely the teaching, and the god himself must provide the condition . . . otherwise the learner is unable to understand anything." See Johannes Climacus', *Philosophical Fragments/Johannes Climacus*, 55–56.

the text for strikingly similar reasons. My task overall then is to demonstrate that this narrowing is due largely to Derrida's treatment of the pseudonym which, at its most basic level, follows in the footsteps of contemporary, orthodox readings. The very fact that Derrida fails to make a clear, careful, and consistent distinction between the pseudonymous author, de Silentio, and the proper name of Kierkegaard, carries with it at least two hermeneutically problematic implications: first, it serves to confuse the relationship between authorship and authority in a way that invariably reduces the pseudonymous voice to Kierkegaard's own; and second, it keeps Derrida from recognizing the significance of what is arguably the faith inspired "proto-deconstructive" function of the text.[2]

On my reading, to take the pseudonym *strictly* at his pseudonymous word, as Kierkegaard implores his reader to do (see his "First and Last Declaration" at the close of *CUP,* where he also insists that "I am just as far from being Johannes de Silentio in *Fear and Trembling* as I am from being the Knight of Faith whom he depicts." [551]), opens the door to think otherwise about the function of the text, in general. Even if Derrida's reading of the pseudonym is informed by orthodox commentary, it is clear that he does achieve a unique "deconstructive" reading. That reading is not the issue, per se. The primary issue here is that his treatment of the pseudonym eclipses and thereby dismisses the more radical aspects of the text. In this way, it parallels the concern I have with Evans's treatment of *Fear and Trembling*, in general, and the pseudonym in particular.

In the following sections I will consider Derrida's treatment of the pseudonym and its hermeneutical implications. Firstly, in section 2.1., I will focus on Derrida's reading of *Fear and Trembling* in the context of his discussion of "Kierkegaard's" understanding of the relationship between faith and reason (ethics), and how he negotiates it. Secondly, in section 2.2., we find Derrida holding "Kierkegaard's" hand to the fire of deconstruction in order to burn the ties that bind him to metaphysics. While I will consider *what* Derrida says by way of his response to "Kierkegaard's" strategy for negotiating the space between faith and reason, I am fundamentally concerned with *how* he reads the pseudonym. In the end, Derrida's reading of

---

2. I use the word "proto-deconstructive" only to emphasize that while Kierkegaard's texts, in general, achieve a deconstructive-like effect, this is not to be confused with Derrida's deconstruction, especially in the face of the obvious fact that Kierkegaard appeared on the philosophical stage a century before Derrida. Moreover, I want to preserve the uniqueness of Kierkegaard's contribution to postmodern thought in a way that is distinct from Derrida. In so doing, I hope to implicitly demonstrate the extent of Derrida's debt to Kierkegaard, one that shows itself in its difference. Note that all references to *The Gift of Death* are taken from the second English edition from 2008 and will appear in the text as *GD.*

Fear and Trembling, in general, and his critique of "Kierkegaard" in particular, fundamentally assumes that the textual strategy is Kierkegaard's own. In so doing, Derrida unwittingly conflates the author de Silentio with Kierkegaard which in turn undermines his otherwise novel approach to the text.

2.1. READING DERRIDA READING FEAR AND TREMBLING

If, in chapters 1 and 2 of *The Gift of Death*, Derrida details not only what ails modern civilization, but how that malaise connects with the relationship between responsibility and religion, not to mention how that relationship is negotiated, we find him in chapter 3 ("Whom to Give to [Knowing Not to Know]") looking to "Kierkegaard's" understanding of faith and its relation to ethics (reason) in the context of *Fear and Trembling*. As it relates to the modern malaise and the collapse of responsibility and religion, Derrida is keenly interested in "Kierkegaard's" approach to writing which is a remedy that the latter employs to negotiate the "paradox" between Abraham as a "Knight of Faith," and as a murderer.

Arguably the uncompromising structure of *Fear and Trembling* is its best known feature, one on which its reputation rests. But since there is little consensus on the significance of that structure, it is also its greatest point of controversy. And while it is true that Derrida effectively sidesteps much of that controversy by finding a unique way through those debates, nevertheless, his reading of the text in general, and his treatment of the pseudonym, in particular, depends on taking the starkness of the author's structure as Kierkegaard's own. In spite of Derrida's novel reading, I maintain that this dependence entails the assumption that, at the end of the day, Kierkegaard is the author and final authority of *Fear and Trembling*. But by highlighting the fact that Kierkegaard is *not* the author, and therefore *not* the final authority of *Fear and Trembling*, I will emphasize the importance of taking Johannes de Silentio at his authorial word, and how that opening impacts our reading and understanding of the text.

2.1.1. Derrida and New Testament Theology

After a short introduction to chapter 3 ("Whom to Give: [Knowing Not to Know]"), which sees Derrida connecting his notion of the secret (or "the *mysterium tremendum*"), as "the gift of death," to the title of de Silentio's dialectical lyric, he provides a brief exegesis of Philippians 2:12–13—the

New Testament passage from which the title of *Fear and Trembling* is drawn (*GD*, 54–58). This section is important because here we glimpse how closely aligned Derrida is with de Silentio's overall split sensibility, which, on my reading, does not reflect Kierkegaard's own, strictly speaking.

But first, by way of a brief but important digression, we need to keep in mind that Derrida's concerns here, which parallel Jan Patočka's, pivot on the tension between *religion* (as demonic, orgiastic mystery) and *responsibility* (as faith, in general), at the center of which is "the secret," a notion inextricably linked with "the gift of death" (ibid., 3–10). In order to prevent the reduction of the latter to the former, the collapse of which, fueled by orgiastic desire and a "fervor for fusion," leads to "demonic rapture," Derrida reaches for a kind of thinking or logic that, as we will see, is at once close to and far from the sensibilities of *Fear and Trembling* (ibid., 3). Importantly, this "thinking," says Derrida, "has no need of *the event of a revelation or the revelation of an event*" (ibid., 50). Such "logic," he continues,

> needs to think the possibility of such an event but not the event itself. This is a major point of difference, permitting such a discourse to be developed without reference to religion as institutional dogma, and proposing a thought-provoking genealogy of the possibility and essence of the religious that doesn't amount to an article of faith. (Ibid.)

To be sure, Derrida has already insisted that just because "Christian themes are identifiable does not mean that this [Patočka's] text is, down to its last word and in its final signature, an essentially Christian one, even if Patočka could himself be said said to be. It matters little in the end" (ibid., 49).[3] Along with the likes of Levinas, Marion, and Ricoeur, Derrida says that Kierkegaard belongs "to this tradition that consists in proposing a nondogmatic doublet of dogma, a philosophical and metaphysical doublet, in any case a *thinking* that 'repeats' the *possibility* of religion without religion" (ibid., 50). And it is precisely this *thinking* that Derrida will use to hold "Kierkegaard's"[4] hand to the fire of deconstruction in order to burn the vestiges of metaphysics from his philosophy. On the one hand, then, Derrida applauds the uncompromising structure of *Fear and Trembling,* along with its excesses, because it is

---

3. I maintain that the faith infused religious character of the text of *Fear and Trembling*, including its primary figures and themes, are integral to the work, specifically, and to Kierkegaard's writings in general.

4. For the most part, throughout this chapter I will refer to the name "Kierkegaard" within quotations. In doing so, my primary aim is to highlight the many times throughout *The Gift of Death* (particularly chapter 3) that Derrida uses the name "Kierkegaard" in the place of the author, de Silentio. But secondarily, it serves as a constant and necessary reminder to give authorial credit precisely where credit is due.

not far from his own philosophy that reaches for the "impossible." In fact, there are many points of intersection between Derrida and de Silentio, particularly the language that the latter employs as he himself approaches the edges of otherness and impossibility. "Everyone shall be remembered," says Johannes, "but everyone became great in proportion to his *expectancy*. One became great by expecting the possible, another by expecting the eternal: but he who expected the impossible became the greatest of all" (*FT*, 16).[5] To be sure, de Silentio's notion of the "impossible" is very close to the heart of Derrida's philosophy, closer than he might even imagine.

With these things in mind, and with the notion of the *mysterium tremendum* as a guide, Derrida argues, in a similar fashion to de Silentio, that an absolute divide or "dissymmetry . . . exists between the divine regard that sees me, and myself, who doesn't see what is looking at me . . . the disproportion between the infinite gift and my finitude, responsibility as culpability, sin, salvation, repentance, and sacrifice" (*GD*, 56–57). This split sensibility and the assumptions that give rise to it are therefore brought to bear on his reading of Philppians in particular, which mirrors his treatment of *Fear and Trembling*, in general. On Derrida's reading, the disciples are told by the apostle Paul to "work out your own salvation with fear and trembling" (Philippians 2:12 KJV). Consistent with the starkness that we have seen, Derrida says that the Philippian believers "have to work for their salvation knowing all along that it is God who decides: the Other has *no* reason to give to us, and *no* explanation to make, *no* reason to share his reasons with us . . . We fear and tremble before the inaccessible secret of a God who decides for us although we remain responsible, that is to say, free to decide, to work, to assume our life and our death" (*GD*, 57; emphasis added). For Derrida, that this injunction is conditioned by the fact that Paul is not present with them, is telling. On his reading, then, the Philippians

> are asked to work toward their salvation not in the presence *(parousia)* but in the absence *(apousia)* of the master. Without knowing from whence the thing comes and what awaits us, we are given over to absolute solitude. No one can speak with us and no one can speak for us, we must take it upon ourselves, each of us must take it upon himself . . . (Ibid., 57–58)

Moreover, Derrida continues:

> If Paul says 'adieu' and absents himself as he asks them to obey,
> in fact ordering them to obey (for one doesn't ask for obedience,

---

5. If, for Derrida, the "impossible" must always remain futural, on de Silentio's reading of the Akeidah, Abraham believed and expected the impossible and, impossibly, received it as concretely possible, that is, in the here and now (the temporal "moment").

one orders it), it is because God is himself absent, hidden and
silent, separate, secret, at the moment he has to be obeyed. God
doesn't give his reasons, he acts as he intends, he doesn't have to
give his reasons or share anything with us: neither his motiva-
tions, if he has any, nor his deliberations, nor even his decisions.
Otherwise he wouldn't be God, we wouldn't be dealing with the
Other as God or with God as *wholly other [tout autre]*. If the
other were to share his reasons with us by explaining them to
us, if he were to speak to us all the time without any secrets, he
wouldn't be the other, we would share a type of homogeneity.
Discourse also partakes of that sameness; we don't speak with
God or to God, we don't speak with God or to God as with others or to our fellows. (Ibid., 58)[6]

Aside from the debatable theology at work, along with the assumptions undergirding it, the structure and logic here could easily be lifted from
the pages of *Fear and Trembling*.[7] That "Kierkegaard" chose this Pauline
phrase as the title for *his* text makes perfect sense to Derrida, drawing as it
does on the "Jewish experience of a secret, hidden, separate, absent, or mys-
terious God, the one who decides, without revealing his reasons, to demand
of Abraham that most cruel, impossible, and untenable gesture: to offer his
son Isaac as a sacrifice" (ibid., 58–59).

---

6. On my reading this oppositional structuration highlights both the similarities
between Derrida and de Silentio, and their significant differences. If they both employ
stark and uncompromising language to articulate the (absolute) difference between the
human (self) and the divine (other), but if de Silentio is not reducible to "Kierkegaard"
then their similarities give way to differences rooted in different assumptions about
and remedies for the breach that exits between the finite and the infinite. If, for Derrida, difference and opposition 'go all the way down', as it were, the remedy for which,
consequently, is a way of thinking that "has no need of *the event of a revelation or the
revelation of an event*," one "that 'repeats' the *possibility* of religion without religion"
(embodied in the "gift of death") (*GD*, 50), interestingly, and not without significance,
Johannes Climacus' "thought project" in *Philosophical Fragments* involves meeting this
challenge via an "incarnational" way of thinking that mediates the ostensible incommensurability between the human and divine via the gift of love. For example, Climacus says that "only in love is the different made equal, and only in equality or in unity is
there understanding" (25). But because the learner cannot ascend to or otherwise reach
the truth on his own, and in order "not to destroy that which is different" in the fullness
of God's arrival (Ibid), he concludes that "for unity to be effected, the god must become
like this one. He will appear, therefore, as the equal of the lowliest persons" (31).

7. See especially *FT*, 32–35.

2.1.2. Derrida and de Silentio

On one level then, Derrida's reading reflects the divided structure and logic of *Fear and Trembling* itself. The fact that a silent and separate God keeps Abraham in the dark, suggests Derrida, is mirrored by the fact that *Fear and Trembling* "is not signed by Kierkegaard, but by Johannes de Silentio . . . This pseudonym keeps silent, it expresses the silence that is kept. Like all pseudonyms, it seems destined to keep secret the real name *as* patronym, namely the name of the father of the work, in fact the name of the father of the father of the work" (ibid., 59). But if de Silentio is the author of *Fear and Trembling*, a text that Derrida clearly understands is "not signed by Kierkegaard," is it appropriate, at any point, to reference "Kierkegaard" on substantial textual matters? If the answer is yes, at what precise point is it appropriate to do so? Who makes that judgment, and why exactly? If the answer is no, then why does Derrida use the names interchangeably, which suggests that such usage is of no real consequence?

Rather than muddy the hermeneutical waters in this way, I contend that taking de Silentio strictly at his pseudonymous word is the most obvious way to honor Kierkegaard's texts in general, and *Fear and Trembling* in particular—especially since he made it explicitly clear to do just that.[8] Thus, to pay loose heed to Kierkegaard's request carries with it hermeneutical implications that conspire against the text in ways that miss its deeply critical dimensions. So while, on the one hand, it is clear that Derrida recognizes the presence and significance of the pseudonym, on the other hand, the fact that he uses the name "Kierkegaard" interchangeably with de Silentio is inconsistent at best, and hermeneutically problematic at worst. Apart from Derrida's novel reading of the text, which certainly has its merits, his handling of the pseudonym signals that his treatment all too easily blurs the lines between author, authorship, and authority.

This interchangeability of names appears harmless enough, at least on the surface of things, after all most readers of Kierkegaard realize, on the one hand, that de Silentio is the author of *Fear and Trembling*, yet, on the other hand, we also know that he is not the *real* author, strictly speaking. The very fact that readers in general move all too easily between the two names indicates, it would seem, that we are simply covering our bases and hedging our bets. But isn't the reader supposed to read the text and play the game; and is it not true that the player can best understand the game by playing it on it's own terms and by its own rules? Thus, this begs an important threefold question: what precisely is being said in the text, who is saying it, and

---

8. See Kierkegaard's "A First and Last Declaration" at the close of *CUP.*

why does it matter? I argue that not paying scrupulous attention to what is being said by who, invariably and unduly ascribes to Kierkegaard a textual structure and logic that is simply *not* Kierkegaard's. The very fact that *he* is the target of Derrida's critique is clear evidence of the pseudonymous voice being confused with Kierkegaard's own voice. To be sure, his critical conclusion is that "Kierkegaard" is still too tangled with metaphysics, and this is precisely why he nudges him toward the deconstructive edge—in order to save him from his latent metaphysics and onto-theology.

If it is true that Derrida unwittingly adheres to an orthodox treatment of the pseudonym, I contend that it keeps him, at least in part, from fully appreciating the text's robustly religious character, and its connected critical function. The question, however, is not whether Derrida recognizes the role of faith, as that which precedes and pervades language and existence (his "arche-originary *yes*"), rather it involves the structural dissymmetry that exists between faith (as the "impossible") and the content (the possible) of that faith.[9] On my reading, at issue here are the character and implications of that divide as Derrida understands it in connection with his reading of "Kierkegaard's" understanding.

With a view toward confirming Derrida's orthodox treatment of *Fear and Trembling* in general, and the pseudonym in particular, in what follows I will outline his critique of "Kierkegaard's" logic, the split stage for which has already been set in the first two chapters of *The Gift of Death*, along with the introductory comments to chapter 3.

2.2. DERRIDA'S CRITIQUE OF "KIERKEGAARD"

In *The Gift of Death* we find Derrida reaching for a way of "thinking" that does justice to otherness in general, one that does not reduce difference to sameness, he finds in *Fear and Trembling* a strategy and logic that is at once close to and far from his own. In the early part of *The Gift of Death* Derrida's concern, alongside Patočka's, clusters around the twofold question of what precisely ails modern civilization and why. This concern, it turns out, has everything to do with the reduction of responsibility to religion, the collapse of which signals "the removal of responsibility" (*GD*, 3).[10] On

---

9. Of course Derrida likes "Kierkegaard's" stark economy because it is quite close to his own, in a manner of speaking.

10. I maintain that the text of *Fear and Trembling*, with its focus on the relationship between faith and reason, and the question of how to negotiate the space of difference inherent in that relationship, shares a similar concern with *The Gift of Death*. But, as I have already alluded, if de Silentio's and Derrida's concerns are similar, the remedy that the former points toward, reaches beyond the logic of the latter.

Derrida's reading, for Patočka, the first step toward remedying the situation involves freeing responsibility from the grip of demonic "irresponsibility, or, if one wishes, nonresponsibility" (ibid., 5). And the way to do that is to subject the latter to the former. In the end, only responsibility can "make orgiastic or demonic mystery subject to itself" (ibid., 4). But even if Patočka is on the right track and recognizes that the demonic secret can "never be destroyed" because history "always keeps within itself the secret of whatever it encrypts, Derrida wants to extend and radicalize his explicitly Christian language in the direction of "a logic that at bottom . . . has no need of *the event of a revelation or the revelation of an event*" (ibid., 23, 50).[11]

As we will now see, in his critique of "Kierkegaard's" logic, Derrida sets out to hold his hand to the fire of deconstruction in order to disabuse him of his allegiance to metaphysics. In so doing, Derrida will help "Kierkegaard" achieve something similar, something minimalist that resembles what the former later refers to as a kind of "desertification" that repeats the possibility of "messianicity without messianism."[12] Such arid thinking, says Derrida, signals "the opening of the future or . . . the coming of the other as the advent of justice, but without a horizon of expectation and without prophetic prefiguration."[13] To reiterate, while I will consider *what* Derrida says by way of his response to "Kierkegaard's" strategy for negotiating the space between the singularity of (Abrahamic) faith and the universality of ethics, I am fundamentally concerned with *how* he reads *Fear and Trembling* in general, and the pseudonym in particular. What this reading reveals, what the implications are, and why all of this matters in the larger hermeneutical scheme of things, then, are my primary foci overall. But first it will be important to get a sense of what precisely de Silentio himself is struggling with and ultimately how it connects with Derrida's logic.

2.2.1. De Silentio's Logic, or, Fear and Trembling in a Nutshell

Steeped as he is in the Hegelian milieu of his time, the author of *Fear and Trembling*, Johannes de Silentio, is a man struggling with faith. While the text seems to indicate that de Silentio is on the outside of faith looking in, suggesting that he is *not* a man of faith, I maintain that he is always already *in* faith. Indeed, Kierkegaard's texts everywhere suggest that faith, as a

---

11. It seems clear enough that Derrida has little need of the concrete "event" because as soon as (in this case) religion is instantiated the risk of violence increases exponentially.

12. Derrida, "Faith and Knowledge," 17.

13. Ibid.

fundamental mode of human existence *[Existents]*, has us, even as we have faith, whether one is a Christian or not. De Silentio, then, is man torn asunder because of his inability to reconcile the faith of Abraham (expressed in his willingness to sacrifice Isaac), and the obvious imperative to uphold ethical duty, love his son, and thereby preserve his life at all cost. Faced then with a paradox and the need to explain his (ethically) unfounded admiration for Abraham, as *both* a man of faith *and* a murderer, the task de Silentio sets for himself in the second half of the text is to tease out the "dialectical aspects implicit in the story of Abraham" (*FT*, 54). At the end of his "Preliminary Expectoration," Johannes says that the point of his undertaking in the Problemata is "to perceive the prodigious paradox of faith, a paradox that makes murder into a holy and God-pleasing act, a paradox that gives Isaac back to Abraham again, which no thought can grasp, because faith begins precisely where thought stops—" (ibid.).

Given his desire to make sense of Abraham's faith and therefore honor him as it relates to the relationship between faith and reason, de Silentio proposes three problems in the latter half of his text. Whereas the first half of *Fear and Trembling* is more poetical or "lyrical" in tone and scope, the second half is philosophical or "dialectical," consisting as it does of three "Problemata," each of which is presented in the form of a question: "Problema I—Is there a Teleological Suspension of the Ethical?" (ibid., 54–67); "Problema II—Is there an Absolute Duty to God?" (ibid., 68–81); and "Problema III—Was It Ethically Defensible for Abraham to Conceal His Undertaking from Sarah, from Eliezer, and from Isaac?" (ibid., 82–120).

On my reading, the short answers to these questions are: yes, yes, and no. (P.I.) If, along with de Silentio, we are to take Abraham's faith seriously, that is, to consider the patriarch worthy of admiration; and if, at the same time, we are not to dismiss ethics, then, on the stark terms assumed by the author, the ethical must be suspended in order to preserve or otherwise make room for faith. (P.II.) In this way, the hermeneutical road is paved and ready for the necessity of absolute duty to God. Otherwise, says de Silentio, the ethical itself "is the universal, and as such the divine" (ibid., 68). "If this is the highest that can be said of man and his existence," contends de Silentio, "then the ethical is of the same nature as a person's salvation . . ." (ibid., 54). If there is nothing beyond ethics, "faith has never existed . . . [and] Abraham is lost . . ." (ibid., 81, 113, 120). (P.III.) On these terms then, what Abraham proposed to do is not *ethically* defensible; nevertheless, it is admirable from the standpoint of faith because Abraham obeyed God and suspended ethics for the sake of absolute duty to the divine.[14] As such, as

14. Throughout de Silentio's text we note that while he admires Abraham, he does

we have seen, faith lies beyond the realm and reach of ethics. This means that the only way to honor Abraham and his faith, and at the same time not dismiss ethics, is to propose what de Silentio calls "a teleological suspension of the ethical" (ibid., 54, 66). In this way, he says, "the ethical relation is reduced to the relative in contradistinction to the absolute relation to God" (ibid., 71).

2.2.2. Derrida and the Logic of Responsibility

As we have seen, Derrida closely identifies with "Kierkegaard's" attempt to tease out the extreme aspects of the Abraham story, inherent to which is a paradox. This kind of logic confronts us with the tension between Abraham as both man of faith and murderer, leaving us with no absolute criteria to decide which one he is. Consequently, this brings us face-to-face with what Derrida calls, "the gift of death" (variously called the "*mysterium tremendum*," or the "secret," the veritable seat of responsibility). But the fact that "Kierkegaard," in the end, has recourse to a religious realm beyond esthetics and ethics, is troublesome for Derrida and smacks too much of onto-theology. A significant part of Derrida's project in *The Gift of Death* then, is a deconstructive mission of mercy to save "Kierkegaard" from the machinations of metaphysics. As Jack Caputo playfully puts it, by dropping a "bit of deconstructive solvent" on "Kierkegaard's" treatment of the Abraham story, Derrida means "to distill by a slow drip the (un)essence, to get to the messianic structure, the messianic-in-general, the general messianic *tout autre*, without biblical baggage."[15]

In essence, what Derrida wants his readers and "the knights of good conscience" to understand "is that 'the sacrifice of Isaac' illustrates . . . the most common and everyday experience of responsibility" (*GD*, 68). In other words, he says, "responsibility binds me to the other, to the other as other, and binds me in my absolute singularity to the other as other. God

---

not understand him. To be sure, what the patriarch proposed to do was not only *not* understandable, it was reprehensible, from the standpoint of ethics and fatherly love. In this way, Abraham embodies the paradox because he is both a man of faith and a murderer.

15. Caputo, *The Prayers and Tears of Jacques Derrida*, 189–90. Interestingly, Caputo also casually uses the author's name, de Silentio, interchangeably with Kierkegaard's proper name. Consider the following quote: "*Donner la Mort* takes us by the hand up to Moriah and shows us how to put the torch to the particular messianisms in order to get to the messianic in general, to learn how to read *Fear and Trembling*, the *Kierkegaardian* rendering of this famous story, as a story for everyman and everywoman, with or without a determinable faith, even if one rightly passes for an atheist" (ibid., 190; emphasis added).

is the name of the absolute other as other and as unique . . . As soon as
I enter into a relation with the absolute other, my singularity enters into
relation with his on the level of obligation and duty" (ibid.). Thus, by virtue
of my absolute relation with the absolute, I am bound to every other, and
every other other. In keeping with the Abraham story, Derrida says that
"what binds me in my singularity to the absolute singularity of the other
immediately propels me into the space or risk of absolute sacrifice" (ibid.).
But in this economy, he contends that one "cannot respond to the call, the
request, the obligation, or even the love of another without sacrificing the
other other, the other others" (ibid., 69).[16]

Aside from the significance of this last sentence it is important to see
that it is here Derrida begins to part ways with "Kierkegaard," and he does
so by eschewing the name of God as a metaphysical placeholder and by
replacing absolute duty (to the Other) with general responsibility (to every
other other). In turn, this levels the distinction between the ethical and the
religious. "If God is the wholly other," argues Derrida, "the figure, or name
of the wholly other, then every other (one) is every (bit) other. *Tout autre est
tout autre*" (ibid., 78). Derrida continues:

> This formula disturbs Kierkegaard's discourse on one level while
> at the same time reinforcing its most extreme ramifications. It
> implies that God, as wholly other, is to be found everywhere
> there is something of the wholly other. And since each of us . . .
> is infinitely other in its absolute singularity, inaccessible, solitary,
> transcendent, nonmanifest, originarily nonpresent to my *ego* . . .
> then what can be said about Abraham's relation to God can be
> said about my relation without relation to *every other (one) as
> every (bit) other [tout autre comme tout autre]*, in particular my
> relation to my neighbor or my loved ones who are inaccessible
> to me, as secret, and as transcendent as Jahweh. (Ibid.)

But if "God" is a mere substitute name for the absolute other as other with
whom I enter on the level of obligation; and if the absolute obligatory character of that relation puts me in a space of absolute risk and sacrifice where
I am infinitely obligated to every other who is infinitely other (and therefore infinitely guilty), we are not far from saying that every other is God
even as God is every other. Even if we are not Jahweh, as Derrida insists,
neither are we not not Jahweh (ibid., 79). As I alluded to above, this levels

16. For Derrida, not completely unlike the thrust of the dominant logic of *Fear and
Trembling*, absolute sacrifice, which entails absolute risk, involves absolute guilt. In his
famous "cat" analogy below, Derrida says, in essence, that because he cannot take care
of every other cat in the world along with his own, he is always already guilty by virtue
of his finite inability to answer the call of an infinite obligation.

the philosophical playing field such that every other is equally distributed across the spectrum of otherness where every other is equal to all others.

This levelled space of absolute difference and infinite obligation is also, as we have seen, the place of the paradox, the *mysterium tremendum,* where there is no mediating link or "middle term," as de Silentio says, "that saves the tragic hero" (*FT,* 57). In this economy, argues Derrida, one "can respond only by sacrificing ethics, that is to say by sacrificing whatever obliges me to also respond, in the same way, in the same instant, to all others" (*GD,* 69). In this way, "I don't need to raise my knife over my son on Mount Moriah for that. Day and night, at every instant, on all the Mount Moriahs of this world, I am doing that, raising my knife over what I love and must love, over the other, to this or that other to whom I owe absolute fidelity, incommensurably" (ibid.). On these terms, Derrida famously asks: "How would you ever justify the fact that you sacrifice all the cats in the world to the cat that you feed at home for years, whereas other cats die of hunger at every instant?" (ibid., 71). The fact that Abraham, as the "knight of faith," did not suspend his decision in the face of his blindness, nonknowledge, and his ethical duty to Isaac, but rather responded to the call/command of the other, is, for Derrida, "the paradoxical condition of every decision," one that "structurally breaches knowledge and is thus destined to nonmanifestation; a decision is, in the end, always secret" (ibid., 78).

2.2.3. Derrida, Levinas, and "Kierkegaard"

In chapter 4 (*"Tout autre est tout autre"*), in the context of his comments on Levinas' critique of "Kierkegaard" and the connections between the two thinkers, Derrida clarifies his own critique. On my reading, the comments here highlight his problematic treatment of the pseudonym in particular, and by extension, his reading of *Fear and Trembling,* in general. Derrida notes the fact that in his "critique of Kierkegaard concerning ethics and generality Levinas' thinking stays within the game—the play of difference and analogy—between the face of God and the face of neighbor . . . If every human is wholly other." argues Derrida, and

> if everyone else, or every other one, is every bit other, then one can no longer distinguish between a claimed generality of ethics that would need to be sacrificed in sacrifice, and the faith that turns toward God alone, as wholly other, turning away from human duties. (Ibid., 83–84)

On Derrida's reading, if Levinas insists on making a distinction "between the infinite alterity of God and the 'same' infinite alterity of every human, or of the other in general, then he cannot simply say something different than Kierkegaard either" (ibid., 84). For Derrida, since neither Levinas nor "Kierkegaard" are able to assure themselves "of a concept of the ethical and of the religious that is of consequence . . . they are especially unable to determine the limit between those two orders" (ibid.). This means that "Kierkegaard" would have to concede,

> as Levinas recalls, that ethics is also the order of and respect for absolute singularity, and not only that of the generality or of the repetition of the same. He can therefore no longer distinguish so conveniently between the ethical and the religious. But for his part . . . Levinas is no longer able to distinguish between the infinite alterity of God and that of every human: his ethics is already a religion. In both cases the border between the ethical and the religious becomes more than problematic, as do all discourses referring to it. (Ibid.)

On the one hand, Derrida is fundamentally right in his critique of the structure and logic of *Fear and Trembling*. As he rightly suggests, precisely because the text posits a religious sphere that lies beyond the horizon of (esthetics and) ethics where the *Wholly Other* resides, the author must suspend ethical duty ("teleological suspension of the ethical"), that is, if absolute duty to God is to be upheld. On these terms, the absolute necessity of absolute duty to God, and the absolute faith required for it, becomes, for all intents and purposes, the same as ethical duty. But because all language takes place within the confines of existence, talk of absolute duty, one must admit, is circumscribed by its finite occurrence, which is to say, à la Hale, by the very finitude that conditions it. In other words, absolute duty here simply becomes inscribed higher in the sphere of the same. So, rather than putting ethics on hold, the author's method is in fact dictated by it; and this connects precisely with Derrida's concern, one that puts its critical finger on the metaphysics that *Fear and Trembling* paradoxically wants to avoid.[17]

On the other hand, however, I am at odds with Derrida's reading of the text, specifically his treatment of the pseudonym and the implicationshat follow. The point I want to make is simple, even delicate, the larger implications of which will become evident in the next two chapters. The point is his: the author of *Fear and Trembling* is Johannes de Silentio, *not* Kierkegaard.

---

17. If Derrida and I agree that the author's method is dictated by the logic of metaphysics, my insistence that de Silentio is the author and *not* Kierkegaard is the critical point of our difference.

I argue that not maintaining that distinction confuses and complicates the issue of authorship and authority, and in turn leads to an unduly confusing and complicated hermeneutical state-of-affairs. Derrida's argument, notwithstanding, I contend that his rendering of the text is hampered by his treatment of the pseudonym and ultimately hinders his ability to recognize its more critical dimensions. I contend, therefore, that assiduously ascribing authorship to de Silentio alone would necessarily and fundamentally alter Derrida's reading of the text. Indeed, treating de Silentio as the author of *Fear and Trembling* is the condition of possibility for seeing the conflicting (complicit/critical) textual currents that are central to my reading.

On my reading, it is crucial to be *clear* about who the author of *Fear and Trembling* is, *careful* of the distinction between de Silentio and Kierkegaard, and *consistent* with how, when and why those personalities are employed. This matters because rather than narrowing the text, taking the pseudonym at his authorial word opens it, inviting us to read it otherwise, thus enabling it to speak differently to a different time. If neither the strategy nor the notion of faith in *Fear and Trembling* can be attributed to Kierkegaard, and if the larger narrative framework is not an attempt by him to, in fact, "perceive" the dialectical truth of faith, then what does the text indicate by what it says? What does it say in its unsaying? As it pertains to the previous two chapters, how does *Fear and Trembling* itself call into question both Evans's reading of the text and Derrida's?

As I will attempt to show, beginning in the next chapter, the textual dynamic at work in *Fear and Trembling* cries out for a different approach and calls the reader to be attentive to the text's difference. Even if it is true that Derrida's deconstructive reading of *Fear and Trembling* in general, and his critique of "Kierkegaard's" methodology in particular, pivot on the reduction of the pseudonymous voice to Kierkegaard's own, my concern is less with his laudable emphasis on responsibility, and more with the implications of that reduction as it relates to the critical dimensions of the text.

2.3 CONCLUSIONS

In this chapter I have taken steps toward showing that Derrida's treatment of *Fear and Trembling* in general, and the pseudonym in particular, hampers his ability to full appreciate its deeply critical character, intrinsic to which are a faith inspired motivation, and a transformative function. This inability, as we have seen, is due largely to Derrida's reading of the text which follows in the footsteps of contemporary orthodox renderings. To the extent that he accepts the text's presenting structure and logic as Kierkegaard's own, I maintain that Derrida unwittingly ascribes authorship and final authority to the proper name. In so doing he involves himself in the reduction of the pseudonymous voice to the voice of Kierkegaard himself. This hermeneutical reduction is evident in his critique of the text and his attempt to save "Kierkegaard" from himself by proposing a deconstructive strategy meant to disabuse him of his religion and its inherent onto-theology. On my reading, however, the focus on and critique of "Kierkegaard's" strategy not only misses the text's motivation and critical function, but its fundamentally religious and faith infused import.

As we will see with greater clarity in the chapters to come, the dynamic at work in *Fear and Trembling* puts it at once close to and far from deconstruction, highlighting as it does both the same concern for the question of language and mediation, and the different approaches that Derrida and de Silentio employ, approaches that carry similar implications for understanding the text. In the context of *Fear and Trembling* those answers and the reasons for them have everything to do with the relationship between philosophy and the language of faith, and between human finitude and the notion of sin. The different "remedies" that Derrida and de Silentio provide for the challenge of language and its connection to the human predicament, serve to underscore the significance of the differences between the philosophical motivation of deconstruction and the religious, faith focused vision of Kierkegaard's texts.

In the next two chapters I will undertake a close reading of *Fear and Trembling* with a view toward demonstrating that when freed from orthodox hermeneutical constraints a textual excess emerges, the significance of which lies in its ability to disrupt our best attempts to mediate the text's difference in order to secure final and definitive textual meaning. If *Fear and Trembling* functions in a way that frustrates any and all attempts to determine what it means by determining who the author (and therefore final authority) is, I maintain that instead of throwing up our arms in hermeneutical despair, this shift in focus opens a space to read the text in a way that does more justice to the intricacies and idiosyncrasies of the textual fabric.

PART II

Complicity

3

The Complicity of Silence
Making Lyrical Sense of Abraham's Faith

The present author is by no means a philosopher. He is a poetice et eleganter [in a poetic and refined way] a supplementary clerk who neither writes the system nor gives promises of the system, who neither exhausts himself on the system nor binds himself to the system.

—Johannes de Silentio

Having demonstrated that both Evans and Derrida assume that the world of Johannes de Silentio is, in the end, Kierkegaard's world, in this chapter I will question that assumption more thoroughly and suggest that a different hermeneutical approach opens the text of *Fear and Trembling* in a unique way, thus allowing it to speak differently. To that end, I will argue that it is important, nay, crucial, to take the author, de Silentio, strictly at his authorial word which means effectively separating, "Kierkegaard" from the authorial equation. In turn, this leaves the reader to wrestle with the text's tears, cross-currents, and ambiguities *without* recourse to the proper name as an organizing, universal principle of authority.[1] On my reading, this shift

1. In this current hermeneutical climate, it is imperative to emphasize the importance of honoring the text of *Fear and Trembling* and its author de Silentio by *not* referring back to Kierkegaard in what is all too often a knee-jerk interpretive reaction that foists final authority onto his name. In other words, authorial intention is one thing, but author intentionality backed by the proper name as a metaphysical principle of

in authorial focus allows the textual differences to stand in their difference. Importantly, not only does this create a space where questions can emerge, but it calls for a respectful *reading with* the text in an effort to reach toward its meaning and significance. *Reading with* the text, and the implications that it entails, represents a large part of my task both in the present chapter and in the larger scope of this project.

With these things in mind, I will argue that *Fear and Trembling* is, from the outset, structured dualistically even as the author clearly attempts to resist that structure and the metaphysical pretensions inherent in it. As such, I will make the claim that the text is *both* "complicit" (chapters 3 and 4) with *and* "critical" (chapter 5) of metaphysics in a way that cannot be reconciled or otherwise mediated.[2] What this *means*, I contend, is connected to the text's function, the dynamic of which shows itself *both* as an attempt to pull itself up by the philosophical bootstraps, *and* as a warning against the utter futility, even sin, of such an attempt. In a more general sense, therefore, one might say that *Fear and Trembling* is a performative exercise that invites the reader to think critically, but also imaginatively about how the text functions and its relationship to textual meaning.

After introducing the conflicted text of *Fear and Trembling*, the following sections (3.1–3.4), then, will attend to the text itself beginning with a general summary of each major section meant to underscore the tears, cross-currents and ambiguities at work in the text. The express purpose here is to highlight the text's complicity with the logic of metaphysics. The very fact that, from the very outset, the text assumes an absolute distinction between the human/finite (reason), and divine/infinite (faith) is reason to pause and consider the assumptions involved as de Silentio works first to "lyrically" understand Abraham's actions (chapter 3), and then to "dialectically" "perceive the prodigious paradox of faith" (chapter 4) that transforms murder into a holy act of sacrifice (*FT*, 53, 30). In the end, I will argue that de Silentio's imaginative creation of such figures as the "Knight of Faith" and the "Knight of Infinite Resignation" (also the "tragic hero"), along with

---

authority designed to mediate the distance between the text and its meaning, is something else entirely. Because an author (in this case, Kierkegaard) crafts a text with intention, clearly he is not without authority as to its meaning. The question, however, is this: to what extent is the reader able to appeal to that authority as a basis for definitively determining textual meaning? How is such a feat even possible? In other words, it is a question of *access*, which all too often entails a mechanism of mediation designed to secure, more or less, a definitive meaning.

2. This is not to say that the first two thirds of the text do not have critical elements, or that the last third does not display complicity. My argument is that the former comes to the fore in Problema III and explicitly so in the account of Agnes and the merman, specifically.

later notions such as "Absolute Duty to God" and the "teleological suspension of the ethical," are in fact, complicit with metaphysics that he ironically attempts to overcome in order to make room for faith and thereby save Abraham.

What then are we to make of *Fear and Trembling*? How are we to treat both its stark simplicity, and its rich complexity? If, in the past, commentators largely dismissed the pseudonyms and their voices as impediments to finding Kierkegaard's real voice behind the pseudonymous subterfuge, I argue that the counter move in the latter part of the last century to clearly distinguish those voices, via the authorship, achieves a similar conflation, one that continues to blur the relationship between authorship and authority. In both cases we find that an unavoidable reduction takes place in the service of a principle of authority designed to determine the *real* or *true* meaning of Kierkegaard's texts. In the former instance the pseudonym is sacrificed on the altar of Kierkegaard's proper name, and in the latter instance the pseudonymous writings are sacrificed on the altar of the later works effectively repeating the same problematic. In either case, when the f/actual name of Kierkegaard is contrasted with the fictional names of the pseudonyms in the service of a higher ideal, it necessarily reduces the latter to the former.

In the face of the ongoing quest for the Holy Grail of hermeneutical "results," I propose that *reading with* the text yields a different understanding. Rather than an interpretive mining expedition fixated on unearthing the gold nuggets of meaning using the pick axe of Kierkegaard's proper name, I suggest that an exploration of the textual terrain focuses less on results (textual meaning) and more on movement (textual function). If the former dismisses the latter as irrelevant to the more important task of determining what the text means, I maintain that the latter entails the former and thereby works to keep the text open in a way does not eschew textual meaning. In other words, à la Hale, what any text means hinges first and foremost on what conditions language. The truth or meaning of a text, he argues, lies in "its fragmentation, its incompleteness within itself, not some ideal and therefore external meaning" (*H.KEL*, 15). He continues:

> This "truth"—the fragment—thus is not the goal of meaning, but its condition. And as its condition, it must also be understood paradoxically to condition the very meaning it cannot secure. There can be no language without meaning, and yet there can be no meaning that is not already fragmented in and by the finite occurrence of language. Any assumed system or method can never secure for what is fragmentary a "truth" that would be any less of a "fragment" itself. (Ibid.)

In the next four sections I will summarize the explicitly "lyrical" first half of *Fear and Trembling* with a view toward highlighting its fundamental structural tension, as well as the tears, conflicting currents, and ambiguities that are intrinsic to it. I will argue that de Silentio's split textual structure and the solution he proposes for the problem of language as it reaches, first to *lyrically* understand Abraham's unethical choice to sacrifice his son (chapter 3), and then to *dialectically* to perceive such a paradox (chapter 4), is hamstrung before his project begins. In other words, as we will see, even as the *Preface* begins, for example, laden as it is with Cartesian language, a "given" divided hermeneutical structure is already assumed and firmly in place. Based then on this pre-given, two-tiered philosophical structure, de Silentio proceeds to work out (lyrically and then dialectically) a solution to the problem of "God-talk" and the assumed chasm that exists between reason and faith; the temporal and eternal; the visible and invisible, etc. As we will see, the solution Johannes proposes is epitomized in his employment of what he calls the "teleological suspension of the ethical." But, as I will contend, because the author's argument emerges between the twin metaphysical pillars of the "known" (human/philosophy) and the "unknown" (divine/faith), his solution is inescapably complicit with the metaphysics that he resists and ultimately attempts to overcome.

The following questions and comments then will help frame my exploration with a view toward highlighting the textual divide, and ultimately the text's complicity with metaphysics. As I have suggested, the issues involved are both simple and complex. On the simple side, the question is this: what is the central problem facing Johannes de Silentio in the text of *Fear and Trembling*? More pointedly, what is the crux of the problem as the author understands it, and how does he go about solving it? On the complex side of things, we need to ask more fundamental, hermeneutically salient questions if we are going to sufficiently honor the voice of the pseudonym and in turn read the text in a judicious way. If the central problem is directly connected to the absolute divide between the human (reason/murder) and the divine (faith/sacrifice) that the author assumes; and if the solution to that problem involves "absolute duty to God," the condition for which is the "teleological suspension of the ethical," it is crucial to recognize the rationalistic character of this solution and precisely whose it is. The all too common assumption here is that since "Kierkegaard" is the *real* author of the text, in the end it is *his* solution. But if this is the case, we are left scratching our heads and confronted with more questions than answers. Ironically, this perplexing hermeneutical state-of-affairs is perhaps why the reader is pressed more than usual to find answers—on behalf of "Kierkegaard's" true intentions.

But this begs the question: other than their use as a mere literary prop, cipher, or foil, why employ the pseudonym in the first place? Moreover, to simply assume that "Kierkegaard" is the author of the text not only flies in the face of the obvious, it all but forces the reader to save "Kierkegaard" from his own convolutions, contradictions, and apparent confusions. If we maintain, however, that de Silentio is the author, it frees the reader to indulge the text's excesses which function as an invitation to move *with* the cross-currents and contradictory movements rather than against them in an attempt to reconcile them. In other words, if we are clear and consistent in maintaining that de Silentio is the author of *Fear and Trembling*, I contend that the text's stark structure, the problem central to it, and the author's solution to that problem, take on a different tone and significance. Instead of fixating on ways to save "Kierkegaard" from his own devices, which are ironically bent toward our own "result" driven solution to "Kierkegaard's" problem, the hermeneutical shift in focus that I am proposing keeps the focus on de Silentio and thereby opens the textual door in a way that allows us to both see and hear the text differently.

With these things in mind, let us begin at the beginning.

3.1. EPIGRAPH: INDICATIONS OF A BEGINNING

Johannes de Silentio, the author of *Fear and Trembling*, is a man torn asunder, caught, as it turns out, between two worlds.[3] This tension is felt throughout the text, one "rich in paradox—paradoxes too tangled to be unraveled by speculative reflection," as Mark Taylor suggests.[4] This inherent tension is immediately apparent in the subtitle (*Dialektisk Lyrik*), which "seems to impute to its pseudonymous author, the self-contradictory status

---

3. The two worlds of de Silentio are expressed in a multitude of ways. Most notable and pertinent to the text of *Fear and Trembling* is the divide between Abraham and the author himself followed closely by the faith/reason divide, not to mention the particular/universal and the silence/utterance distinctions. On these connected dichotomies (and many more) the entire text pivots. Exploring how they function and why is a central concern of this study.

4. Taylor, "Sounds of Silence," 165. Oddly enough, in the end, Taylor attempts to resolve the tensions in *Fear and Trembling* by way of Hegel's dialectic, a movement that ultimately reduces difference to sameness. The fact that Taylor refers to Kierkegaard instead of de Silentio throughout most of his essay is an indication of that reduction. On my reading, Hegel's metaphysics is precisely what the text of *Fear and Trembling* destabilizes. Interestingly, even though Taylor has since moved on with digital speed to bigger and better things, his later work indicates that his Hegelianism (with a twist) has never been far behind. See John Caputo's insightful comments in his review of Taylor's book, *After God*, in *Journal of the American Academy of Religion* 77 (2009) 162–65.

of 'dialectical lyricist,' or, perhaps more colloquially, 'philosophical poet.'"[5] Accordingly, the text is uneasily split into two main sections: the first part "lyrical," the second part "dialectical."[6] Although it appears that attempts are made throughout to unite these literary realms—and all other such dichotomies—paradoxically, and not insignificantly, the text itself works against such efforts. Whether in the guise of a poet (lyricist) or a philosopher (dialectician), at the end of the day, any attempt to reconcile the paradoxes are brought up short where he is rendered silent.

In the face of the enigmas confronting both the author and the reader, even before the text of *Fear and Trembling* formally begins, there are signs that serve as indications of how to proceed and what to expect along the way. It is not insignificant that the text's title is a fragment drawn from the New Testament (Philippians 2:12–13) which is connected explicitly to the theme of individual salvation. It is also not insignificant, as we will see, that the title carries with it the force of a traditional, literal (rationalistic) interpretation of scripture that is itself consistent with the stark structure and the accompanying hermeneutical tension of de Silentio's text.

As an exegetical aside, Gerald Hawthorne suggests that while the command to "work out your (own) salvation" has led many to conclude that the apostle Paul's primary focus here is on "the eternal welfare of the soul *of the individual*," there is reason to think otherwise[7] He argues, for example, that the immediate context, the grammar used (the verb, together with the reflexive pronoun), and the wider context of the epistle itself, "suggests that this command is to be understood in a corporate sense."[8] Moreover, there are strong indications that the word "salvation" is employed in a "non-eschatological" way by the author. "Thus the church at Philippi is urged to work at its spiritual well-being until its well-being is complete, until its health is fully established, until every trace of spiritual disease—selfishness, dissension,

---

5. Joseph Westfall, "Saving Abraham," 276. Westfall notes that the kind of "disciplinary 'boundary crossing'" one witnesses in *Fear and Trembling* "was not unfamiliar to writers and philosophers in Copenhagen during Denmark's Golden Age. When writing of himself, however, Johannes de Silentio seems incapable of unifying the two realms in a manner suited to his subtitle" (ibid.).

6. Textual evidence suggests that the "Preliminary Expectoration" is a kind of preface to the Problemata that follows. Thus, it makes a certain sense to draw the dividing line (between "part 1" and "part 2") immediately after these preliminary remarks (ibid., 285). In this way, it might also be seen as an interlude or pause between the lyrical and dialectical where de Silentio attempts to, as it were, reconcile the gap between the two parts.

7. Hawthorne, *Philippians*, 98.

8. Ibid.

and so on—is gone."[9] In this light, the second modifying phrase ("with fear and trembling") "has no reference to the anxious concern that individual Christians might be expected to have as they face the last judgment."[10] In addition, while the word "fear" might suggest "'alarm,' [or] 'dismay' in the face of danger, it also carries the meaning of 'awe' and 'respect.' Coupled with *tromos*, a word which means 'a trembling,' or 'a quivering,' the phrase could picture a person standing with quivering fear or trembling awe before something or someone."[11] But since this phrase is unique to Paul, and since he never uses it in connection to an attitude one should have toward God, it appears that the phrase "may well have meant something far less forceful than what one might expect from considering separately each word of which it is composed."[12] One might therefore translate the phrase accordingly: "'*Obediently* work at achieving spiritual fitness within your community.'"[13]

To step into the text then is to *fall* down a rabbit hole where paradoxes abound, silence reigns, and, as I will argue, reason is called upon to save the day. Concerned as it is about silence, the very fact that *Fear and Trembling* was even written is perhaps the most perplexing paradox of all.[14] "Consider the author: Johannes *de Silentio*, [or "John of the realm or kingdom of silence"].[15] Consider the central character: Abraham, who not only does not speak, but who cannot speak. Consider the book's preoccupation: silence. A book by Johannes de Silentio, about a person named Abraham who cannot speak, devoted to an exploration of silence."[16]

As a character in his own text, Johannes appears as much taken with silence as silence has taken him. And while this theme is not dealt with explicitly until Problema III ("Was It Ethically Defensible for Abraham to Conceal His Undertaking from Sarah, from Eliezer, and from Isaac?" [*FT*,

9. Ibid., 99.

10. Ibid.

11. Ibid., 99–100.

12. Ibid., 100.

13. Ibid. Significantly, Hawthorne's exegesis would fit de Silentio's assessment of that contemptible, "pious and accommodating exegete," who finds "in one or another exegetical resource book" that the gale force of a literal rendering of, in this case, Luke 14:26 ("If any one comes to me and does not hate his own father and mother and wife and children and brothers and sisters, yes, and even his own life, he cannot be my disciple") is reduced to a warm afternoon breeze (*FT*, 72). Not to mention the "contemplator," who loves to relax and "smoke his pipe while cogitating" (ibid., 28); or the unthinking "preacher," who unwittingly reduces the impact of the Abraham story and then forbids his insomniac parishioner to do the same (ibid., 29).

14. Taylor, "Sounds of Silence," 165.

15. Mackey, "The View from Pisgah," 395.

16. Taylor, "Sounds of Silence," 165.

82–120]), Johannes moves steadily in that direction, "discussing it in the context of other issues, touching it briefly when he peeks through the cracks in the System."[17] Although many commentators ignore the significance of this later, more lengthy and meandering section, dismissing it as personal and therefore anecdotal at best, it is here where we find the text's critical strength bubble to the surface, particularly in the context of de Silentio's discussion of "demonic silence" as it relates to the legend of Agnes and the merman.[18]

If we can liken the text of *Fear and Trembling* to an architectural structure, even a sacred structure, where silence is honored, one might say that the epigraph functions as a beginning point, a kind of entranceway that opens into the Preface or "vestibule." Here the reader already hears the sounds of silence that set the tone (*Stemning*) for what is to come. Passing through the entrance, one is struck dumb by a shroud of secrecy and the accompanying mystery that surrounds the enigmatic epigraph: *Was Tarquinius Superbus in seinem Garten mit den Mohnköpfen sprach, verstand der Sohn, aber nicht der Bote* [What Tarquinius Superbus said in the garden by means of the poppies, the son understood but the messenger did not] (*FT*, 3).[19] Although the communication shell game here stupefies the reader, paradoxically, it calls for a response. Keeping in mind that *reading with* the text is different than penetrating its mystery, it is therefore appropriate, even imperative that the reader risk moving with the unfamiliar cross-currents. Facing a language that is not straightforward or self-evident is a challenge that requires a cautious trust, especially when dealing with a king who speaks without speaking; a messenger who hears without hearing; and a son who understands without understanding.

While this confounds a one-to-one correspondence theory of rational mediation that promises to remove the hermeneutical veil and deliver the truth as it really is, it does not mean that nothing is communicated here.

---

17. Ibid.

18. Taylor concurs, and rightly argues that all "[t]oo often this section [Problema III] of *Fear and Trembling* is read either as a repetition of points stated more precisely in Problems I and II, or as musings on Kierkegaard's personal experience that stray from the primary concerns of the work. But such judgments are usually rash, insensitive to the care with which Kierkegaard composes his works" (ibid.).

19. The gist of the story, which ostensibly draws on several historical figures and their sources, including Johann Georg Hamann, G. E. Lessing, and Aristotle, is as follows: "When the son of Tarquinius Superbus had craftily gotten Gabii in his power, he sent a messenger to his father asking what he should do with the city. Tarquinius, not trusting the messenger, gave no reply but took him into the garden, where with his cane he cut off the flowers of the tallest poppies. The son understood from this that he should eliminate the leading men of the city." (*FT*, 339).

Paradoxically, in the face of secrecy and silence something is said even though it is veiled. In other words, communication does take place though it is by no means self-evident or direct in any straightforward or literal sense.[20] To be sure, the son had to interpret the messenger interpreting what the father did not say. And let us not forget that Kierkegaard's de Silentio is quoting Hamann (from the German) who is recounting an early Roman story that is retold here in English some two-hundred years later. The point is that in the face of hermeneutical ambiguity, the son risked an interpretation that was informed primarily by a trust-based relationship with his father, *mediated* by a messenger.

If a similar dynamic is inherent in *all* forms of communication, including the relationship between the text and reader, then trust itself is fundamental to discourse, in which case mediation is always already necessary, yet never without risk and never complete in an absolute sense. Importantly, mediation and risk are not only necessary but also fundamentally *good* since they are the very components that enable communication, even though the potential for miscommunication and communication breakdown simultaneously exists. But as we will see, caught as he is between two realms, as it were, de Silentio, as both lyricist and dialectician, reaches for a language that does justice to both the human (ethics/reason) and the divine (faith), even as these realms are fundamentally at odds with one another.

If silence and the mystery intrinsic to it are the focus of this fragment, then the question of language, mediation, and the possibility of faith knowing, are all at issue here and explored in the pages of *Fear and Trembling*. What is significant is how de Silentio plays the game, and how he is played by it.

3.2. PREFACE

Since in many respects de Silentio follows Descartes's lead, it is significant to note that *Fear and Trembling* begins with an explicit homage to the Father of Modern Philosophy (*FT*, 5–6). In fact, one might even say that the text's point of departure is thoroughly Cartesian, assuming as it does a philosophical disjunction between faith and reason. It becomes clear that

---

20. Hale argues that "[i]t would appear that there should be two kinds of communication: a subjective communication that ought to be 'doubly reflected' and therefore always indirect, and an objective one that, spared the necessity of the 'double reflection,' is thankfully capable of communicating itself directly. But, Climacus implicitly asks, is direct communication still communication? Can there even be such a thing? The answer, quite simply, is no. 'Double-reflection is already implicit in communication itself' (*Postscript*, 73)" (*H.KEL*, 22).

the tension generated by this and a host of other connected, contrasting terms is essential to the structure of the text without which there would be no drama, at least how de Silentio tells the story. As it turns out, separating faith from reason and maintaining that distinction is the veritable ground from which de Silentio's strategy emerges, one that reaches back to the twin pillars of ancient Greece,[21] and forward to the modernity of Descartes.

Harking back to a time before *de omnibus dubitandum est* became a vehicle for everyone to ride on the way toward the certainties of Hegel's "System," de Silentio is reaching for a time when faith was beyond the pale of reason, and reason itself was held in doubt. "Descartes," argues de Silentio, "a venerable, humble, honest thinker, whose writings no one can read without being profoundly affected," stopped at doubting where he questioned, scrutinized, and wrestled with the natural light of reason (ibid., 5–6). And although for Descartes, faith "'is incomparably more certain than anything else,'" it involves a different kind of struggle since it lies infinitely beyond reason (ibid., 6).

But in the modern age, says de Silentio, everyone begins with doubt "in order to go further" to the assurances of the System (ibid., 7). If, however, people are unwilling to stop with doubt, the same can said of faith as it too becomes a mere stepping stone on the way toward the House of Reason. Thus, in an age that is driving the value of faith (and doubt) into the ground, de Silentio wants to "jack up the price" (ibid., 121). In the spirit of both the Greeks and Descartes, then, Johannes's project will involve recapturing what he sees is the place and prominence of faith. As we will discover, this is a place beyond reach, beyond all pricing, something extremely difficult, nay impossible, to afford or otherwise attain.

While it is true that Descartes took his faith seriously, he assumed that it did not and could not impinge on his work as a philosopher, since good philosophy always demands neutrality and therefore necessitates separation from faith and religious belief.[22] Indeed, since the philosophical endeavor is grounded in self-evident, natural reason, a philosopher cannot and must not, allow particular convictions to interfere with the prejudice free,

21. In my mind, Raphael's painting, "The School of Athens," is illustrative of the twin pillars of metaphysics of which I speak. There you have Plato pointing upwards toward "meta-world" of the Forms, and Aristotle with his hand lowered toward the physical world. To the extent that "God" or "Faith" are conceptually construed and directly accessible by way of reason alone, they can be considered "metaphysical."

22. Ironically enough, Descartes's famous *Meditations on First Philosophy* is a faith-inspired text, the profound religiousness of which is all but dismissed by well-meaning philosophers intent on maintaining a rigid separation between faith and reason. See especially Descartes's opening letter, "To Those Most Wise and Distinguished Men, the Dean and Doctors of the Faculty of Sacred Theology of Paris," 1–4.

universal domain of philosophy. In this economy, faith belongs to the province of theology, and reason to philosophy; and this, according to Descartes, is simply and self-evidently the way things are.[23]

But if, for Descartes, faith is external to reason, it is important to ask, for what lies ahead, to what extent the former is construed in terms of the latter. In other words, by definition, "knowledge" that is opposite to reason (ibid., 6) is not and cannot be rational knowledge since it is opposed to reason. As such, faith (non-knowledge) must be confined to a space other than reason (knowledge) where (at best) it is not subject to it's logic, strictly speaking, or, (at worst) where it is dismissed out of hand. Even if faith appears to enjoy honor in this economy, the honor is bestowed by reason, on reason's terms. If the Scholastic mandate was *fides quaerens intellectum,* a major part of which involved rationally demonstrating that faith was not incompatible with reason, this was yet another instance of the former being viewed through the lens of the latter.

Although Descartes's dualism appears to honor faith, as does the text of *Fear and Trembling* itself, things are not what they appear to be, as he rightly taught us. To be sure, rather than bring together the already strained Greco-Christian relation between spirit and flesh, Descartes's radical turn toward the subject ("I think, therefore I am," whereby essence precedes existence) drove a wedge between the invisible and the visible (mind/body) thus, creating the possibility for the triumph of reason and ultimately the reign of Hegelianism.

In this divided light, even questions such as, "what does faith have to do with reason?" implicitly prioritize the principle of rationality and therefore exclude questions of faith from philosophical discourse. Indeed, it assumes that philosophy must remain neutral, and this neutrality is achieved by separating itself from all things other than itself, including faith. But is philosophy as neutral as it thinks it is? Is it free of prior commitments, from particular, historical attachments and the natural prejudices intrinsic to them? Moreover, is not concrete particularity the condition of knowing what one claims to know? How one addresses these issues, particularly the relationship between faith and reason, reveal the philosophical and hermeneutical assumptions at work, which, in this case, indicates how one reads *Fear and Trembling* itself.

23. Ibid., 1.

3.3. EXORDIUM

With these things in mind, we proceed with cautious trust to the *Stemn-ing* where the tone is established and the mood is set for the story that has already begun. If it is true that Johannes de Silentio is a personage in his own story, then this adds yet another layer to an already multi-layered, complex, and tension-filled text. Thus, we note that the story begins with the "what is" caught in the crossfire between "what once was" and "what ought to be": "Once upon a time there was a man" who, with awe, remembered a story from childhood, "that beautiful story" of Abraham's trial and the near sac-rifice of his son Isaac; how the patriarch "kept the faith, and, contrary to expectation, got a son a second time" (*FT*, 9). But as the man grew older, the naïve simplicity with which he once believed gives way to complexity and consternation. Although he reads the story "with even greater admiration," the less he is able to understand it (ibid.).

In keeping with the Platonic rupture of time that necessitates the sepa-ration of passion and reflection, the older the man becomes the more he is torn. Thus, he experiences the tension between "child" and "man" as a tearing, or *fall* from the former to the latter; from perfection and innocence to imperfection and corruption; from the immediacy of full presence, to mediation and the dull pain of absence.[24] It is worth noting that the inno-cent awe of admiration here leads to obsessive "craving" that reaches beyond mere poetic representation and serves to highlight the horizon of the abso-lute unknown against which the man's desire pushes (ibid.). Although de Silentio quips that the "man" was no thinker who "did not feel any need to go beyond faith" (Ibid), the irony seems to be that his craving for immediate knowledge betrays an allegiance to the immediacy and certainty that reason promises. But since when did concrete existence ever deliver unmediated understanding? And since when were passion and reflection united in the pious immediacy of prelapsarian innocence?[25]

But de Silentio's already frustrated and conflicted exercise in poetic, imaginative understanding is only partly complete. As a logical extension of his concerns and preoccupations, he offers four dramatic and vary-ing accounts of how Abraham might have otherwise responded to God's command. Briefly, but to the point, in the first account Abraham *deceives* Isaac in order to protect him and thereby preserve his faith. In the second

24. My commentary here as it relates to Platonic metaphysics is consistent with the dualistic structure and Cartesian impulse of the text from which they emanate.

25. Ironically, de Silentio questions Hegel, Greek categories, and the possibility of rational mediation; but as I argue, he is also beholden to and ultimately complicit with metaphysics, albeit at higher level.

scenario, Abraham *conceals* his despair from Isaac so as to once again shield
him and his faith. In the third scene, Abraham *questions* God's command,
doubts himself and in the end *valorizes* duty. In the fourth and final variation, Abraham unwittingly *reveals* his despair to Isaac, causing him to lose
his faith. If it is true that inherent in all of these accounts is a frustrated desire for certitude, each of which is an attempt to suspend the call to sacrifice,
then the imaginative understanding that the man seeks to achieve here rubs
shoulders all too closely with rational understanding. But even if all four
"Abrahams" are comprehensible, de Silentio says that they are not admirable
in the way that he admires the "real" Abraham; and admiration, the author
believes, is separate from comprehension.[26]

Significantly, in the face of understanding, poetic or otherwise, and
true to his dualistic form, de Silentio contrasts the man's (his?) desire for understanding with a seemingly obscure weaning metaphor at the end of each
account. Arguably, these metaphors serve to highlight the very different,
indeed, opposite relationships between the man and Abraham, and between
a mother and her child. Whereas the man is motivated by a selfish desire
to mediate an understanding between himself and Abraham, the mother is
motivated by a selflessness, the desire for which is for a relationship rooted
in love.[27] If the man sacrifices connection and love on the altar of understanding (which he does not achieve), the mother sacrifices understanding
on the altar of love (which she achieves).[28] Whatever way one slices this
hermeneutically, de Silentio is caught in the frustrated tension of his own
drama, his own telling of a story that he interprets to great dramatic effect.

At the end of these four scenarios, the man finds that nothing the
imagination can stitch together is able to depict the *real* Abraham in a way
that he can be made sense of. In fact, the text clearly indicates that all his
efforts to somehow comprehend the patriarch's actions, coupled with the
passage of time, had the opposite effect.[29] Not so strangely, then, what de

26. For de Silentio, the category of "[t]he absurd does not belong to the differences
that lie within the proper domain of understanding. It is not identical with the improb-
able, the unexpected, the unforeseen" (*FT*, 46).

27. The juxtaposition of selfishness and selflessness is yet another example of the
many dualisms that the text takes for granted, one that could no doubt be fruitfully
explored in Kierkegaard's *Works of Love* (1998 ed.).

28. On my reading this is an example of the many ways the text hints at or otherwise points toward the critique of speculative philosophy and the logic of metaphysics
intrinsic to it.

29. In turn, this is an example of the many ways that the author is beholden to and
thereby complicit with the logic of metaphysics. In other words, if "the man" (de Silentio?) cannot ground his understanding in certitudinal thinking then all is ungrounded
and therefore lost. This way of thinking is also connected to the negative logic pervasive

Silentio does come to *understand* is that Abraham and his faith lie beyond any kind of understanding, imaginative or otherwise. Whatever dramatic representation is able to achieve, it does not and cannot, given the paradoxes involved, lead to apprehension or comprehension.

> Thus and in many similar ways did the man of whom we speak ponder this event. Every time he returned from a pilgrimage to Mount Moriah, he sank down wearily, folded his hands, and said, "No one was as great as Abraham. Who is able to understand him?" (Ibid., 14)

At the conclusion of this section de Silentio, the silent one, is brought to silence, if only for a moment, for he has not yet given up his attempt to give Abraham his due or otherwise bow the knee which must involve an understanding of some kind. If then an exercise in poetic representation is impossible, perhaps a hymn of praise or a eulogy would be appropriate. If de Silentio cannot understand Abraham or his faith, surely he can admire him, pay tribute to him, even eulogize him.

3.4. EULOGY ON ABRAHAM

Thus, the story that has already begun begins once again from a different, yet still lyrical or poetical vantage point. As the reader finds a seat in the sanctuary of the text, the dramatic and imaginative depiction of Abraham and his faith ends and a eulogistic oration begins with a view toward measuring or at least somehow gauging the patriarch's greatness. Although de Silentio here takes a slightly different tack resulting in a slightly different poetic twist, his strategy is consistent with the dual focus of the text. It is no surprise then to find de Silentio, on the one hand, still trying to comprehend Abraham, while on the other hand, confessing that he finds the patriarch wholly incomprehensible.

The author begins his panegyric with a few broad, brush strokes adding a cosmic dimension to the backdrop of his discussion of Abraham thus far. What he depicts is universal in scope, which, among other things, prepares the divided way for a meditation on the hero (Abraham) and the poet (de Silentio?). "If a human being did not have an eternal consciousness," writes de Silentio, and "if underlying everything there were only a wild, fermenting power that writhing in dark passions produced everything . . . if a vast, never appeased emptiness hid beneath everything, what would life be then but despair?" (*FT*, 15). If this were the cosmic state-of-affairs, if

---

throughout.

flux and movement were the very essence of things and "eternal oblivion" its end, "how empty and devoid of consolation life would be!" (ibid.). But for that precise reason—presumably for the self-evident reason that life is *not* "empty and devoid of consolation"—it is not and cannot be so. For in the same way that God created both man and woman in order that the human race, indeed, creation itself, might continue, he also made the hero and the poet so that there would always be greatness, and that greatness would live on in the collective memory of humankind. So if Abraham is the hero, Johannes de Silentio is the poet who will honor the patriarch's greatness and save faith from the forgetfulness and vicissitudes of finitude.[30] Thus, John, the silent one, who nevertheless speaks, finds himself an unwitting messenger/mediator who stands, or perhaps better, is caught between the two worlds of silence and utterance, a space between places where he cannot speak, but unlike Abraham, must speak. For the poet "is recollection's genius."

> He can do nothing but bring to mind what has been done, can do nothing but admire what has been done; he takes nothing of his own but is zealous for what has been entrusted. He follows his heart's desire, but when he has found the object of his search, he roams about to every man's door with his song and speech so that all may admire the hero as he does, may be proud of the hero as he is. This is his occupation, his humble task; this is his faithful service in the house of the hero. (Ibid.)

In keeping with the twin metaphysical pillars that support the text, Johannes continues his encomium with more contradictory claims and contrasts that constitute a negative logic he employs to great paradoxical effect. From the outset de Silentio struggles to articulate the greatness of Abraham, and the only way he can come close to doing him and his faith justice is poetically, paradoxically and *negatively*.[31] It is important therefore to witness this negative logic in action in order to ascertain what de Silentio hopes to achieve by employing it, which will in turn reveal something of the assumptions at work as we try to *read with* the conflicting textual currents. At issue is Abraham's greatness and the adequate measurement of and response to that greatness. Thus, the poet insists that "[n]o one who was great in the

30. It is worth noting de Silentio's inconsistency when he refers to Abraham as a "hero" in the same way that Agamemnon is a hero of ethics. In general, the patriarch is portrayed as a humble servant in contrast to the self assured hero.

31. Importantly, negative logic thrives on contradiction and ultimately makes sense only against the horizon of positive logic. De Silentio's consistent use of this logic and the significance of it for an adequate understanding of the text will become apparent as the chapters unfold.

world will be forgotten"; and since Abraham was no ordinary man, since his deeds reach beyond the pale of human understanding, his greatness is clearly beyond measure and his place in world history is therefore guaranteed (ibid., 16). Accordingly, a person's greatness is directly proportionate to what they love, what they expect, and with which they strive. The fact that Abraham loved God (the greatest possible being *beyond* being), expected the impossible, and strove with the creator himself, makes the patriarch great, a greatness that cannot be measured in any quantifiable way. The only way one can hope to measure such greatness is to do so negatively and paradoxically. Thus, the author concludes that "Abraham was the greatest of all," precisely by virtue of "that power whose strength is powerlessness, great by that wisdom whose secret is foolishness, great by that hope whose form is madness, great by the love that is hatred to oneself" (ibid., 16–17).

As if on the way to Mount Moriah himself, inviting the reader along on the journey, de Silentio begins again by drawing our attention to the specific context within which his concerns take place. The focal point here is the character of Abraham's faith that remained steadfast in the face of increasingly poor odds and ultimately unspeakable circumstances. Importantly, then, how de Silentio re-tells the story provides significant clues as to *what* exactly faith is, and is not, *how* Abraham's greatness is to be measured, and *why* negative logic is a necessary measuring stick.[32] "*By faith*" we are told, "Abraham emigrated from the land of his fathers and became an alien in the Promised Land. He left one thing behind, took one thing along: he left behind his worldly understanding, and he took along his faith" (ibid., 17; emphasis added). "*By faith*" Abraham became a stranger in a strange land where his soul was tempted to "sorrowful longing" as if banished from God's grace (ibid.; emphasis added). "*By faith* Abraham received the promise that in his seed all the generations of the earth would be blessed" (ibid.; emphasis added). But as the reader knows, time went by and that possibility became an impossibility, at least by any human, rational standard of understanding.[33] In such times of testing it is understandably and excusably human to

32. The subsequent paragraphs and sections in this chapter indicate 1) that faith is without doubt, unshakeable and therefore *extra*ordinary; and since it exhibits unquestioning trust in the object of its belief, faith exceeds rational explanation. 2) Since it is the opposite of reason, requiring as it does belief in the face of rational uncertainty and the tension that follows, faith is necessarily difficult, nay impossible to attain. 3) As such, if faith is to be measured it must be done so negatively and gauged paradoxically. 4) Since language is inadequate to describe faith, and since faith is unspeakable, it is part of a completely separate economy and therefore out of finitude's reach.

33. There too was another, indicates the poet, who will not be forgotten, one who also "had an expectancy" and did not forget it as "evening drew near;" and who, in the end, and "in the sweetness of his sorrow . . . possessed his disappointed expectancy"

sorrow, grieve and weep; and it is greatly human to sacrifice one's life, hope, and desire, "but it is greater to have faith, more blessed to contemplate the man of faith" (ibid.). For worthy is Abraham who fought valiantly and joyfully against ethics itself.

> We have no dirge of sorrow by Abraham. As time passed, he
> did not gloomily count the days; he did not look suspiciously at
> Sarah, wondering if she was not getting old; he did not stop the
> course of the sun so she would not become old and along with
> her his expectancy; he did not soothingly sing his mournful lay
> for Sarah. (Ibid., 17–18)[34]

Under the circumstances Abraham could have quite reasonably given up his hope and desire, and still influenced, even "saved many by his example, but he still would not have become the father of faith, for it is great to give up one's desire, but it is greater to hold fast to it after having given it up; it is great to lay hold of the eternal, but it is greater to hold fast to the temporal after having given it up" (ibid., 18). Not only did Abraham fight against the temptation of temporality, and against the temptation of ethics to do the right, honorable, and obligatory thing, he fought against the temptation of God himself. On all accounts Abraham's faith overcame the obstacle of worldly understanding (which is to say, reason or rationality) proving itself to be unshakeable and unsoiled by doubt.[35]

From the outset, then, de Silentio has been slowly, poetically, but methodically preparing the way for a very specific understanding of faith. It is as if the reader is standing in the middle of a frozen lake with both feet firmly planted on either side of a crack that is getting wider by the second. True to the negative logic that he employs throughout, Johannes the poet is out to demonstrate just how far faith is from "worldly understanding," not to mention how far Abraham was from the anxiety generated by doubt. So with the distinction now established between giving up the temporal for the sake of the eternal, and holding on to the temporal after having given it up, de Silentio attempts to clarify a notion of faith that he will more formally unveil in the next section. The contrast between giving up or sacrificing the temporal for the sake of the eternal, and holding on to the temporal after giving it up, then, sets up a key distinction, as we will see, between (the

---

(*FT*, 17). This may be a reference to "the Roman poet Ovid (43 B.C.–A.D. 17?), who in AD 8 was banished by Caesar Augustus to Tomi on the Black Sea" (ibid., 342).

34. Contrary to the picture of Abraham that de Silentio paints here, we know from the Genesis account that Abraham was a man who not only questioned and tested God (Genesis 18:16–33), but doubted him as well (Genesis 16:1–6).

35. But is *true* faith qualified by certitudinal logic and therefore without doubt?

knight of) infinite resignation and (the knight of) faith. While this imaginative construction seeks to honor faith by placing it beyond rational thinking, we will also see that even if faith is therefore purportedly other than reason, the former remains within the purview of the latter precisely because it is circumscribed by the very language and logic of rational thought.

In a significant step along the way, the author elaborates on what he sees as a unique characteristic of Abraham's faith, one that he has already alluded to and will continue emphasizing throughout. As we know, the patriarch had faith, but according to the poet his was *not* otherworldly, for he "had faith *for this life*" (ibid., 20; emphasis added). This emphasis is significant for a host of reasons, not the least of which is the obvious difference from the received notion of faith that exists for the sake of the eternal and breathes only the rarified air of the transcendent. The author makes it clear that Abraham's faith was not of the conventional kind, for such faith is not really faith at all "but the most remote possibility of faith that faintly sees its object on the most distant horizon but is separated from it by a chasmal abyss in which doubt plays its tricks" (ibid., 20).[36]

Continuing his exercise in contrasts designed, ostensibly to allow Abraham's faith to stand out in bold, temporal relief against the backdrop of the eternal, de Silentio insists that the patriarch had faith, real and relevant faith that had no room for doubt whatsoever. If Abraham had doubted, contends the poet, he would have done something entirely different, like sacrificing himself instead of his son. And while such a move would have been understandable, even admirable, in a tragic sense, he would not have "become a guiding star that saves the anguished" (ibid., 21). If Abraham had doubted, if he had hesitated before the knife was drawn and thereby opened the back door of indecision and irresoluteness, something altogether different would have happened.

> If Abraham had doubted as he stood there on Mount Moriah,
> if irresolute he had looked around, if he had happened to spot
> the ram before drawing the knife, if God had allowed him to
> sacrifice it instead of Isaac—then he would have gone home, ev
> erything would have been the same, he would have had Sarah,
> he would have kept Isaac, and yet how changed! For his return
> would have been a flight, his deliverance an accident, his reward
> disgrace, his future perhaps perdition. (Ibid., 22)

---

36. De Silentio rightly, yet ironically, believes that the received notion of faith (as intellectualized/rationalized) is inadequate to the task of explaining Abraham and his faith. In fact, he says, it is not faith at all but "a substitute for faith" (*FT*, 35, 46–53).

Is it not true, asks the author of his audience (you and me), that you or I would respond to the same test with fear, hesitation and doubt?[37] "Not so with Abraham. Cheerfully, freely, confidently, loudly he answered: Here am I. We read on: 'And Abraham arose early in the morning.' He hurried as if to a celebration, and early in the morning he was at the appointed place on Mount Moriah (ibid., 21). Abraham therefore "did not doubt, he did not look in anguish to the left and to the right, he did not challenge heaven with his prayers" (ibid., 22).

> He *knew* it was God the Almighty who was testing [*prøvede*]
> him; he *knew* it was the hardest sacrifice that could be demanded
> of him; but he *knew* also that no sacrifice is too severe when God
> demands it—and he drew the knife. (Ibid., emphasis added)

De Silentio takes great pains, therefore, to demonstrate that the patriarch's faith was without doubt, his courage unmatched, and his greatness beyond description. Faith such as this is surely worthy of admiration. But ultimately the measuring rod of language that he employs appears inadequate due to its limited reach. As such, it cannot help but fall forever short of the infinite glory that is Abraham. The poet's eulogy therefore begins grinding to a not-so silent halt, but not before de Silentio confesses his sin to the Father of faith, imploring his forgiveness. In keeping then with a negative logic which reasons that Abraham was great by virtue of a faith that is beyond reach, a "hope whose form is madness," and a "love that is hatred to oneself" (ibid., 17), Johannes then insists that Abraham does not require the panegyric of a poet to protect him from the piracy of time. Although he engages in precisely such an exercise, the poet nevertheless confesses that it is futile to do so, all the while insisting that Abraham is great beyond measure and that his faith exceeds value. Clearly, finite language itself is inadequate to the infinite task at hand and must bow the knee in reverent silence. But Johannes continues eulogizing, following his logic to its conclusion, all the while confessing his inescapable guilt to Abraham and the sin associated with the utter inadequacy of his efforts to sufficiently eulogize him.

> Venerable Father Abraham! Second Father of the race! You who
> were the first to feel and to bear witness to that prodigious pas-
> sion that disdains the terrifying battle with the raging elements
> and the forces of creation in order to contend with God . . . for-
> give the one who aspired to speak your praise if he has not done
> it properly. He spoke humbly, as his heart demanded; he spoke
> briefly, as is seemly. (Ibid., 23)

37. In drama this is known as "breaking the fourth wall," a device used since the time of the Greeks to involve or implicate an otherwise passive audience

It would appear that Johannes the poet has nothing left to say. His attempt to appropriately praise the greatness of Abraham (which would mediate an understanding of faith) has apparently come to naught.

We recall from the *Forord* that de Silentio began with an economic metaphor, his concern being that faith, like everything else in life, was up for sale and could be had at a bargain basement price (ibid., 5). More to the point, in nineteenth-century Denmark, faith and religion had become insignificant stepping-stones along the way toward the certainty of reason and reason's philosophy.[38] The text of *Fear and Trembling* in general, and the story of Abraham's near sacrifice of Isaac in particular therefore become the focal point of the author's concern to restore the *original* price of faith, which we have already seen is quite difficult, or more precisely, impossible to afford with mere human currency. Although de Silentio's overall strategy is perplexing for many commentators who have come up with their own strategies to right or otherwise harmonize the poet's misguided reason, his negative logic makes perfect, if paradoxical, sense when viewed, colliding as it must, against the horizon of positive logic. The implications of this are both fascinating and troubling for the hermeneutical reasons already alluded to, and, as we will yet see.

If cheapening the story of Abraham involves selling his greatness short by valorizing reason, thereby reducing faith, what of de Silentio's reverse logic? If, as the poet insists, that the true value of faith (along with Abraham's greatness) is itself beyond measure, how does this remedy the assumed divide that exists between the former and the latter? Even if Johannes employs a *reductio ad absurdum*, a strategy that necessitates the use of opposites (negative/positive) in order to generate "a higher" or truer view of faith, does this not confine his critique of metaphysics to the same metaphysical sphere, that is, the sphere of the same? While such a move serves to focus his readers' attention in opposite directions, to great dramatic effect, I contend that the poet's negative logic leads to the Emerald City of metaphysics and into the court of Reason. At the very least, the author's allegiances suggest that things are not what they seem which sends us back to the hermeneutics inherent in the issues, indicating as it does, the highly constructed character of de Silentio, de Silentio's Abraham, and the text itself.

This then begs the question: whose faith and which Abraham is the author talking about? For that matter, how are we to know? On this score, given the logic that it necessitates, the tension that it generates, and ethical implications that it suggests, the poet's depiction of the patriarch is, at best,

---

38. This is an allusion to de Silentio's many inferences and references to Hegel's "System" that requires the individual to move beyond or further than faith to the certainties and results that it guarantees. See, for example, *FT*, 32–33, 62–63, 123.

suspect.[39] On the one hand, for example, we find that Abraham's greatness is beyond comparison and his faith beyond value, not to mention without doubt. And yet, on the other hand, de Silentio insists that his greatness is to be somehow emulated, and his faith, which ostensibly is *for this life*, somehow appropriated.[40] This is quite curious since Abraham and his faith appear to belong to an entirely different economy, that is, unless one or the other—or perhaps both—assertions are meant to be true.[41] Whatever the case, what this means is that de Silentio's "real" Abraham is every bit as constructed as the Abraham(s) that he himself fabricates in the *Exordium*.[42]

Importantly, if Johannes is right about the stark relationship between faith and reason, then before he even gets started the cat is already out of the bag; the secret has already been (negatively) revealed. Even if the author has all along been hard pressed to say anything regarding the true or positive measure of Abraham's greatness or the true value of his faith, nevertheless, he appears to have uncovered the secret—paradoxical though it may be—[43] when he declares that the patriarch is "the greatest of all" by virtue of a faith that *is* beyond reason, "by that wisdom whose secret *is* foolishness . . . (ibid., 16; emphasis added). While it is true that the poet is reduced to silence as "Part I" (the lyrical) draws to a close, he has already uttered and thereby

39. In other words, I am suggesting that, although camouflaged with much lyrical flourish, de Silentio's poetical strategies are undergirded by dialectical, deeply philosophical assumptions.

40. This tension is also consistent with the one that exists between the author and Hegel. One gathers from the text that, unlike Hegel, de Silentio at least has the courage to think through a scary thought (i.e., Abraham and his faith), as well as the honesty to say that if such a thought were sufficiently shocking he would not think it (*FT*, 30). Not surprisingly, thinking about faith, yet resisting it at the same time, is precisely what de Silentio does best, confessing (no less than 10 times in this section) that he cannot perform the necessary movement. Whereas Hegel claims to have gone further than faith, de Silentio claims he cannot get as far as faith. While the author is proficient at praising, even *thinking* about what Abraham did, he cannot appropriate or *do* what Abraham did.

41. If this is the case, however, one has the torturous task of trying to negotiate the tumultuous waters between these two terms.

42. It is significant to note that de Silentio nowhere indicates that he is self-aware/critical of the fact that his reading of the Abraham story is an interpretation of interpretations that have gone before him, which is to confess that any reading is always already a re-reading. His literalist approach to the story is evident in the following passage: "Or perhaps Abraham simply didn't do what the story says, perhaps in the context of his times what he did was something quite different. Then let's forget him, for why bother remembering a past that cannot be made into a present?" (*FT*, 60 [Hannay]).

43. Even though de Silentio's negative logic is complicit with metaphysics, I maintain that there is also a self-critical logic or current at work later in the text, one that calls into question and therefore subverts the totalizing reach of the former.

revealed quite a lot. Be that as it may, with the poet's power to mediate the paradox of faith apparently broken, paradoxically, the divided way is clear for "Part II" (the dialectical) where the philosopher is set to take the stage, one whose specialty is dialectics and the tensions intrinsic to it.

INTERLUDE

Problemata
Preliminary Expectoration

AS THE SUB-HEADING SUGGESTS, there is something that Johannes needs to get off his chest before things get underway more formally. In this way, the *Foreløbig Expectoration* can be seen as a purgative exercise, one that functions as an interlude which prepares the philosophical ground for "Part II"—in a way not completely dissimilar from the *Stemning* that set the poetical tone for "Part I."[1] While it is true that the 'lyrical" first half of the text stands in evident contrast to the "dialectical" second half, their similarities are equally evident, indicating their mutual dependence.[2]

Having been reduced to silence, Johannes the poet leaves the platform only to return whilst donning the robes of a philosopher. If the poet's attempt to reach an understanding of the paradox ended in frustrated silence, perhaps the dialectical efforts of a philosopher can generate an explanation, or, at the very least, make some sense of it.[3] True to form, de Silentio begins by reinforcing the assumptions that have already been on display in the text. According to the poet-dialectician, two worlds or economies simultaneously exist which are governed by two separate orders respectively. On the one hand, there is the temporal or "visible world"; and on the other hand, there is the eternal, invisible "world of the spirit" (*FT*, 27). Whereas the former is imperfect and therefore "subject to the law of indifference," the latter is beholden to a "divine order" where perfection reigns (Ibid). Unlike

---

1. Mackey, "The View from Pisgah," 402.

2. If Part 1 (the "lyrical") of *Fear and Trembling* is an attempt to imaginatively understand Abraham and his faith, and if Part 2 (the "dialectical") is an attempt to philosophically explain the patriarch, I maintain that they represent both sides of the coin of reason. My hope is that this will become more evident throughout.

3. As we will see, however, the most that a philosopher can know is confined strictly to rational knowledge that stops abruptly at the horizon of faith beyond which lies non-knowledge, which is to say, the opposite of actual knowledge.

89

the temporal world where distinctions are blurred and injustice abounds, the eternal world operates on a completely different register.

> Here it does *not* rain on both the just and the unjust; here the sun does *not* shine on both good and evil. Here it holds true that *only* the one who works gets bread, that *only* the one who was in anxiety finds rest, that *only* the one who descends into the lower world rescues the beloved, that *only* the one who draws the knife gets Isaac. (Ibid., emphasis added)

For de Silentio, the problem is that the so-called (Hegelian) wisdom of the day "wants to introduce into the world of spirit the same law of indifference under which the external world sighs" (ibid.). The concern is that when human knowledge is inflated to a divine status[4] it inevitably results in the blurring, if not eradication of the necessary distinction between reason and faith. This reduction of the latter to the former is precisely what de Silentio sets out to rectify, since it is exactly this boundary blurring or crossing that has cheapened faith making it easy to obtain. The problem is that the ease fostered by such reductionism has had a soporific effect on the masses, lulling them into a false sense of security and comfort. Restoring the original difficulty of faith is therefore of utmost importance for de Silentio but also dangerous involving as it must the difficult task of separating and maintaining a clear line of demarcation between human and divine realities, or more specifically, between reason and faith. Indeed, the tension generated by maintaining this distinction is necessary if people are to be kept on their toes and ready for action.

When it comes to the story of Abraham and his faith, the amazing thing, observes de Silentio, is "that it is always glorious no matter how poorly it is understood . . ." (ibid., 28). Nevertheless, the question that makes all the difference is the extent to which "we are willing to work and be burdened" (ibid.). The idea here is that the harder we work, the greater the reward. The issue for de Silentio, the lyrical dialectician, is that few have the courage to meet the difficulty of faith head on. The truth is, he insists, most people choose the path of least resistance, insisting on cheaper versions of faith that come with insurance policies and money-back guarantees. This penchant to take the easy way out manifests itself in the way the Abraham story is told, re-told, and generally mishandled, resulting in neutered accounts that strip the original event of its potency, its anguish, and its ability to keep people

---

4. The fact that human rationality (ethics) is inflated to the level of the divine, reduces, cheapens, and in the end, dismisses faith as completely other. On my reading, this finds de Silentio (negatively) responding in a way that inflates the latter and thereby reduces the former.

awake at night. For example, says de Silentio, by simply interchanging the words "Isaac" and "best," one obscures both the existential reality, and the deeply ethical fact that Isaac was Abraham's son, his very own flesh and blood. He continues: to anything or anyone else "I have no ethical obligation, but to the son the father has the highest and holiest" (ibid.).

Although we do not hesitate talking about Abraham, the problem is that thinkers and hearers alike want to relax while doing so. The idea, observes Johannes, is to have things move along as swiftly as possible without interruption or discomfort. The same holds true of the well-meaning parson who sermonizes in a similar way with similar expectations, and then is taken aback when a lone insomniac in his midst actually takes him at his word! The man goes out intent on doing exactly what Abraham did, "for the son, after all, is the best" (ibid.). But as Johannes indicates, a "most profound, tragic, and comic misunderstanding is very close at hand," one that will involve the parson in a contradiction that finds him denouncing on Monday what he preached on Sunday (ibid.). For if the good pastor were to find out what the man intended to do, no doubt "he would muster all his ecclesiastical dignity and shout, 'You despicable man, you scum of society, what devil has so possessed you that you want to murder your son' [?]" (ibid.). At this point, if the preacher thought that he had any understanding at all, without a doubt he would lose it if the man, with quiet composure, replied: "But after all, that was what you yourself preached about on Sunday. How could the preacher ever get such a thing in his head," asks de Silentio, "and yet it was so, and his only mistake was that he did not know what he was saying" (ibid., 29).

The question then posed by de Silentio is this: how does one explain such a contradiction (ibid., 30)? Since the minister "did not know what he was saying," as Johannes suggests, one can only surmise that he was under the spell of his own assumptions that allow for such contradictions. Thus, by simply and unthinkingly interchanging the words "Isaac" and "best" the parson all too easily reduces the former to the latter resulting in a misunderstanding of near tragic proportions. In this way he becomes a pawn in the game of reason where a specific (individual ["Isaac"]) is subsumed under the general (description ["best"]); this is how and why he was able to denounce on Monday what he preached on Sunday. But is this the way things really are; does reason have the last word, should it?

De Silentio needs to insist, however, that reason simply cannot, indeed, must not, have the last word, otherwise, what are we to make of Abraham and his faith. In the face of this tension, its inescapability, and, in fact, its necessity, he concedes that the stark reality is that reason (ethics) dictates that what Abraham was prepared to do was murder, while faith deems it a

sacrifice—and therein lies the paradox. But rather than cover up this contradiction with easy answers provided by philosophy and its whore theology
(ibid., 32)—both of which, working in the service of reason, seek to bypass
the difficulty of faith, thereby dismissing it altogether—what is needed is a
certain courage that is able to own up to it and not be afraid to think such a
thing all the way through. For in this absolute contradiction lies the necessary anxiety that keeps people alert, without which "Abraham is not who he
is" (ibid., 30).

To speak or not to speak of Abraham then, is not so much the question
but rather *how* one is to speak. If the concern is that someone will be led
astray by actually (literally) following Abraham's example after hearing a
watered down, generalized version of the story, de Silentio's only recourse
is either to tell it like it is, or keep silent. Should Johannes take up the cause
and speak on Abraham's behalf, he would have to be agonizingly clear about
the paradox and allow its contradictions to stand out in bold, horrific relief.[5] But this would take time to do. Demonstrating Abraham's fear of
God and his love for Isaac alone would take at least a month of Sundays;
and that would be just the beginning. Depicting the pain of the actual trial
would take even longer. To be sure, it would be necessary to draw out the
three-day journey to Moriah so as to distill "all the anxiety and distress and
torment" from the story by describing in painful detail what Abraham actually suffered (ibid., 53).[6] The idea would be for his hearers to enter into the
bosom of Abraham's sufferings; to feel the weight of his heavy legs and heart
as he trudged step by agonizing step up that unrelenting, unforgiving trail;
to "smell the smoke of the sacrificial wood, feel the edge of the knife, see it
glint in the morning sun, hear the weeping of Isaac begging for his life on
behalf of the youthful promise still hidden in his loins."[7] The point in all
of this would be to highlight the severity and tension of the ordeal in order
to make certain that the story is not sold short and that its hearers are fully
able to count the cost of faith.

By speaking in this way, by conveying "an awareness of the dialectical struggles of faith and its gigantic passion," Johannes would not, among

---

5. Of course, this is precisely what de Silentio is doing, what he has done, and what
he will continue to do throughout the text.

6. Consistent as it is with the conflicted and contradictory currents at work in the
text, on the one hand, de Silentio highlights the need here to restore the inherent difficulty to the Abraham story, and yet on the other hand, he insists that the patriarch
"Cheerfully, freely, confidently, loudly . . . answered [God]: Here I am. We read on: 'And
Abraham arose early in the morning.' He hurried as if to a celebration, and early in the
morning he was at the appointed place on Mount Moriah" (*FT,* 21).

7. Mackey, "The View from Pisgah," 405.

other things, be guilty of setting himself up as one who actually has faith, let alone faith in a high degree (ibid., 32). Indeed, the last thing he wants is to have anyone claim to have faith, even by mere association to him. It is more than enough to speak on behalf of faith, since everyone, following Hegel's example, claims to have gone further than faith (ibid., 32–33). The difficulty of Hegel's philosophy is one thing, insists de Silentio, Abraham's faith and the difficulty of his trial are altogether different, deeply individual matters. Philosophy, no matter how rigorously it is applied, cannot penetrate the monstrosity that is the paradox. In fact, the harder rational thought thinks about it, the more it is repelled. Despite all his efforts to understand the paradox, then, de Silentio confesses that his best thinking is utterly insufficient for the task. It is as if thought hits a brick wall when it comes to faith. "I stretch every muscle to get a perspective, and at the very same instant I become paralyzed" (ibid., 33). Johannes maintains that he can "*think*" himself "*into* the hero," but not Abraham, the hero of faith (Ibid); and not because faith is the lowest and therefore inferior, on the contrary, it is because faith is the highest. In fact, faith is so high that it is completely out of reach.

For de Silentio, it is inappropriate and dishonest of philosophy to speak on behalf of faith and offer itself as a substitute or mediator between the two. "Philosophy cannot and must not give faith, but it must understand itself and know what it offers and take nothing away, least of all trick men out of something by pretending that it is nothing" (ibid.). The *heroic courage* it takes to think a difficult thought all the way through, then, is nothing like the *humble courage* necessary for faith. In fact, the former cannot even be compared to the latter because the two terms are incommensurable. And since de Silentio confesses, again and again, that he can neither understand faith nor make the necessary movement of faith, he has no difficulty admitting that he lacks the requisite courage for it. Faced with this tension, Johannes is nevertheless "convinced that God is love," at odds though it may be "with the whole of actuality" (ibid., 34). On these terms, de Silentio does not, indeed cannot, bother God with the minutia of life; all he can do is hold his love for God at an appropriate distance in order to "keep its virgin flame pure and clear" (ibid.). If de Silentio's logic appears inconsistent, even confusing, his overall strategy is not, for his posture follows from the need to keep faith and reason separate, which he does heroically and consistently to great paradoxical effect.

If, as we have seen, Johannes cannot comprehend faith or perform the necessary movement, there is enough to understand and accomplish on this side of reason, that is, before faith begins. What the author *is* able to think through and execute is a "preliminary expectoration," an "infinite movement" that he refers to as an "immense," or "infinite resignation" (ibid., 27,

35, 37). As it turns out, the distinction between the movement of resignation and the movement of faith is a major theme in this section of the text,
connected as it is with later similar themes and figures. Part of the significance here has to do with Johannes's literalistic handling of the Abraham
story which is more often than not credited to Kierkegaard himself. But
there is still some distance to travel before we can consider in greater detail
the hermeneutical importance of this literalist reading and its implications.
To be sure, a matter that concerns us greatly, in the final analysis, is the
inescapable significance of taking de Silentio at his authorial word, and *not*
attributing to Kierkegaard the views of the pseudonym.

Whether or not his contemporaries are capable of making the movement of faith, de Silentio does not know (although he does have his sus-
picions). What Johannes does know is that he himself cannot perform it,
and he does not pretend to be able to. If he cannot perform the necessary
movement of faith and therefore display its truth, the least he can do is
dialectically and negatively illustrate what faith is not.[8] Using himself as
an example, de Silentio tries to *imagine* himself in Abraham's situation, but
he can only do so "*in the capacity of the tragic hero*," for he cannot get any
further or higher than that (ibid., 34). If he was summoned to undertake
a similar journey, he knows exactly what would have happened. Because
tragic heroes or "knights of infinite resignation" as he later calls them (ibid.,
38 ff.), believe that the eternal world wholly transcends the temporal world,
de Silentio would be ready and willing to sacrifice the latter on the altar of
the former.

While Johannes knows that he would go forward with heroic courage
and determination, he also knows that the moment he sets off on the journey "all is lost" and everything would be over, temporally speaking, between
himself and God, "for in the world of time God and I cannot talk with each
other, we have no language in common" (ibid., 35). And if someone were
to consider such an act to be "even greater than what Abraham did," that
is, "more ideal and poetic," they would surely be mistaken and no doubt
misled. To be sure, declares de Silentio, "my immense resignation would
be a substitute for faith" (ibid.). While that kind of courage might illustrate
the pinnacle of human heroism, it does not in *any* way show that he came
close to Abraham's faith or his love for Isaac. For even if de Johannes went
through with the sacrifice he would be dumbfounded and at a total loss
if he received Isaac back again. Paradoxically, then, what Abraham found

---

8. But even in demonstrating what faith *is not*, negatively, such logic still manages to
show what faith *is*. In short, faith is the opposite of reason. In other words, the former
is non-knowledge and the latter knowledge. Put differently, faith *is not* what reason *is*,
an assertion dictated by reason itself.

easy, de Silentio finds infinitely difficult. The heroic courage necessary for the knight of infinite resignation to make such an immense movement can go no further than human effort will take it, and therefore "keeps Isaac only in pain" (ibid.).

Abraham, as the "knight of faith" (ibid., 38), however, is an entirely different, utterly perplexing matter. He obeyed the command (and thereby renounced the finite), but simultaneously and inexplicably he believed (and thereby received the finite back) on the strength of the absurd, which is to say by virtue of a power beyond himself and his ability to understand it (ibid., 35–36). If Abraham was at all taken aback by the final outcome, speculates de Silentio, it was by means of a "double movement" that he was able to come full circle, as it were, and receive Isaac back with unabated joy (ibid., 36).[9] Thus, Abraham was able to perform both movements simultaneously and seamlessly, all the while retaining the requisite tension inherent in such a move. For without the preliminary movement of renunciation whereby one "expectorates" the world in pain, faith is had all too quickly and thereby cheapened in the process. Even if Abraham had sacrificed Isaac, de Silentio insists that it would not have made any difference whatsoever because the patriarch had long since suspended (sacrificed) human reason, believing all along that his faith had relevance for this life (ibid). To be taken to the brink of uncertainty is one thing, but to confidently plunge headlong into a bottomless abyss and believe the impossible possibility (ibid., 44) is altogether beyond comprehension, something that leaves the author aghast (ibid., 36).

But this does not mean that faith is of no account and therefore worthless, on the contrary, it is priceless. The "dialectic of faith," says de Silentio, is a wonder, the most refined and remarkable jewel of all dialectics (ibid.). In fact, it exceeds any and all comparative scales and thus, can only be conceptualized. De Silentio understands that a "trampoline leap" is by all means possible, but "the next movement" whereby one comes to faith, can only been seen as a marvel (ibid.). At this extreme stands Abraham where he loses sight of infinite resignation and faith comes into view (ibid., 37).[10] If one is tempted along with parsons, philosophy professors, and theologians,

9. The famous "double movement" (resignation/faith) that de Silentio proposes in "part 1" of *Fear and Trembling* is not to be confused with the conflicting textual currents that I argue for. On my reading, the latter occurs on a different hermeneutical register that sees the "double movement" itself as complicit with the logic of metaphysics that, ironically and paradoxically, comes under critical fire later in the text.

10. As an exemplar of faith, *par excellence*, de Silentio reads Abraham as the Knight of Faith whose faith was without doubt and therefore absolute. But of course this means that either he was divine, or such faith was gifted to him providentially. This thorny dichotomy is yet another expression of the author's tension filled dualistic world that this present work attempts to wrestle with.

to think that a person can be moved to faith as fast and easy as it is to read
the Abraham story and know the outcome, one not only deceives oneself
and cheats God out of faith's first movement, but cheapens the account by
papering over its inherent difficulty (ibid.).

But why is it, asks de Silentio, that everyone wants to quickly move
beyond faith? Is it because of the penchant to erase the difficulty involved
in acknowledging the paradox, linked as it is to the path of least resistance?
Where on earth do such people think they are going when they ostensibly
leave faith behind? Is it to the supposed certainty and security that reason
promises? "Would it not be best to remain standing at faith" and resist the
temptation to go further (ibid.)? As one who talks much about faith, de
Silentio knows, at least intellectually, that "the movement of faith must continually be made by virtue of the absurd," in such a way "that one does not
lose the finite but gains it whole and intact" (ibid.). What he does not know
is how to perform the movement of faith (ibid., 38). But, as the honest poet-
dialectician that he is in this section, Johannes confesses that neither will he
grow tired of admiring the knight of faith who stands still in faith, nor will
he allow himself to be fooled by those who make similar, but ultimately false
movements beyond faith.

So rare is the knight of faith—and barely indistinguishable from the
knight of infinite resignation—that de Silentio would travel the world just
to witness, study and admire the movements of the former. A phenomenon
such as this, he imagines, would be like watching a dancer who, with pre-
cision and poise, performs the most difficult (impossible!) feat of leaping
perfectly "into a specific posture in such a way that he never once strains . . .
but in the very leap assumes the posture. Perhaps there is no ballet dancer
who can do it—but this knight does it" (ibid., 41). Impossible though such
a feat may be, the poet-dialectician remains amazed, stupefied, and all the
while intoxicated by its impossible possibility.

Because "this marvel can so easily deceive," de Silentio takes further
pains to describe the movements of both resignation and faith by illustrat-
ing their relationship to each other; and he proposes to do this in a specific
context in contrast to a general description that he believes always falls short
of the mark (ibid.). The author, therefore, tells the story of a young man's
love for a princess that ultimately cannot be realized, or, as Johannes puts it,
cannot "be translated [which is to say mediated] from ideality into reality"
(ibid.). For the knight of infinite resignation, only the (heroic) ideal will do.
Thus, once the lad convinces himself that this love "is the substance of his
life," he commits himself to that ideal, concentrating the whole of his existence into a single focus (ibid., 42–43). And when the "messengers of grief"
return, *as they must*, and tell him of the impossibility, that his love cannot

be realized, his resignation is sealed; "he becomes very quiet, he dismisses them, he becomes solitary, and then he undertakes the movement" (ibid., 42). Having infinitely resigned himself to the agony of unrealizable love, "he is reconciled with existence" by dint of the pain that he will always remember and *must* honorably carry with him (ibid., 42–43). The impossibility of love here highlights the absolute necessity of the tension involved, without which the lad cannot receive the eternal.

By sacrificing the finite on the altar of the infinite, a crucial (ex)change occurs for the young lad. For in renouncing the temporal he receives the eternal. In this way, his love

> would become for him the expression of an eternal love, would
> assume a religious character, would be transfigured into a love
> of the eternal being, which true enough denied the fulfillment
> but nevertheless did reconcile him once more in the eternal
> consciousness of its validity in an eternal form that no actuality
> can take away from him. (Ibid., 43–44)

In other words, the young man's love is "transformed" into a *spiritual* possibility and thereby takes on a religious dimension that finds comfort in the pain that resignation affords (ibid., 45). This comfort and the accompanying changes in relation to oneself and to the world are functionally linked to ascetic and thoroughly rational, theological beliefs whereby the imperfect must pass through the temporal portals of pain in order to be made perfect in the eternal image of an ideal (God). Importantly, then, the infinite resignation that de Silentio speaks of is closely aligned with faith and therefore can be easily misconstrued (*FT*, 48), especially so given its connection to the intoxicating allure and promise of salvation. Johannes recognizes that resignation requires immense self-discipline, involving as it does an attitude of utter self-sufficiency often enacted in the name of God. But in fact it is performed in the name of the self, for the self, by the self.[11]

Having exchanged his temporal identity for an eternal one, this ascetic-like movement produces a sense of radical detachment that makes the lad

---

11. Even though resignation is touted as a precondition for faith, and thus essential to and therefore inseparable from faith (*FT*, 46), de Silentio insists that: "By faith I do not renounce anything; on the contrary, by faith I receive everything exactly in the sense in which it is said that the one who has faith like a mustard seed can move mountains . . . By faith Abraham did not renounce Isaac, but by faith Abraham received Isaac" (ibid., 48–49). Once again, the penchant to penetrate the confusion and thereby resolve the contrasts and contradictions in order to make good rational sense of all this needs to be resisted in favor of a more patient approach that honors the text's ambiguities, pitfalls, and general unmanageability. But, as I have already alluded, I do not mean to suggest that the text does not or cannot mean anything, or that it potentially has an infinite number of equally valid meanings that stretch across an infinite spectrum.

impervious to emotional hurt, the kind normally connected with temporal love (ibid., 41; 43). In fact, the litmus test for infinite resignation, consistent as it is with a divided economy, is complete disconnection from worldly concerns. To the extent one is able to completely separate oneself from all things finite, and thereby maintain a detached insularity, one is said to be resigned. For example, asks de Silentio, what would happen if, after a certain amount of time, the princess married a prince (ibid., 44)? On such an occasion if the lad lost the resilience of resignation and showed concern for what the princess did, it would demonstrate "that he had not made the movement properly, for one who has resigned infinitely is sufficient to oneself" (ibid.). For the one who is truly resigned, then, *whatever* happens does not, indeed cannot, affect him. But if, on the one hand, by sacrificing the real (temporal) on the altar of the ideal (eternal) the knight of resignation *devalues* the former in the idealized name of the latter, on the other hand, the knight of faith, as Johannes insists, is said to, conversely and paradoxically, *honor* the finite even as he renounces it.

Caught as he is between two extremes, de Silentio's only recourse is to rigorously establish and vigilantly maintain an infinite distance between resignation (reason) and faith. Indeed, this is the focal point of his strategy. Unlike the knight of resignation who can *only* give up the finite (thereby devaluing it), the knight of faith is able to simultaneously and seamlessly both renounce and receive the temporal (thereby honoring it).[12] Whereas the former is great to the extent that he is able to achieve full resignation, the latter is great beyond measure because of his ability to perform the impossible. In these terms, the knight of infinite resignation can be rationally understood, made to fit the system; the knight of faith, however, defies understanding; which, for de Silentio, is both maddening and awe-inspiring.

> . . . I can perceive that it takes strength and energy and spiritual freedom to make the movement of infinite resignation; I can also perceive that it can be done. The next [movement] amazes me, my brain reels, for, after having made the movement of resignation, then by virtue of the absurd to get everything, to get one's desire totally and completely—that is over and beyond human powers, that is a marvel. (Ibid., 47–48)

12. If it is true, as I maintain, that the author's presenting logic is directly tied to the twin pillars of metaphysics on which the text's structure rests, then de Silentio strategy is *complicit* with metaphysics. This means that while part of his intention is to honor temporality by repeating the metaphysical gesture intrinsic to the "double movement," in fact, he achieves the opposite effect.

De Silentio therefore finds himself in perpetual tension. On the one hand, he admires Abraham and wants to take the marvel of faith seriously so as not to cheapen it; yet on the other hand, he confesses that none of it makes any real rational sense. In the face of such a paradox the author repeatedly expresses his frustration, confessing all the while that he cannot get as far as faith because it lies beyond his reach. This is a curious dilemma indeed, especially since even his admiration of Abraham unavoidably condemns him to guilt at the hands of the ethical universal.

If there is any doubt as to the infinite, absolute, and therefore tension generating difference that exists between faith and resignation (reason), the following highlights the abyss that the author claims he cannot bridge. Consider that,

1. Whereas resignation is perceivable, understandable, and measurable, faith cannot be perceived, understood, or measured (ibid., 47).

2. Whereas resignation renounces the finite on the strength of the possible, faith (both renounces and) receives the finite on the strength of the ("absurd" or) impossible (ibid., 47–48).

3. Whereas resignation is bound to the lower regions of finite knowledge, faith is something infinitely higher (ibid., 47).

4. Whereas resignation entails "human powers," faith entails divine power, something "over and beyond" the former (ibid., 48).

5. Resignation is not faith, does not require faith, and therefore ought not to be confused with faith (ibid.), yet, paradoxically, the former is a necessary prerequisite for the latter.

6. Whereas the movement of resignation finds comfort in the pain of renouncing the finite, the movement of faith finds joy in (both renouncing and) receiving the finite back—"by virtue of the absurd" (ibid., 50).

7. Whereas "the knight of resignation is a stranger and an alien" in a strange land, "the knight of faith is the only happy man, the heir to the finite" (ibid.).

8. Whereas resignation is a movement everyone has the will and ability to perform, faith cannot be performed (ibid., 49, 52).

9. Whatever resignation is (positive), faith is not (negative).

As the *Foreløbig Expectoration* draws to a close it is important to keep in mind that the specific issue of the relationship between resignation (reason) and faith is framed by the more general concern about faith being cheapened at the hands of the "System." And since Abraham is held to be the father of faith, epitomized in the story of the near sacrifice of his son, the biblical account of that event becomes the focal point of de Silentio's less than straightforward exploration. Importantly, as we will see, de Silentio's strategy, which assumes an infinite space between the two terms—ultimately necessitating a suspension of the rational, ethical universal—provides a remedy with a view toward reestablishing and maintaining the primordial tension intrinsic to that relationship. And this is precisely where the author turns his readers' attention as he begins to turn up the dialectical heat all the way.

For the last time in this section, de Silentio confesses that whatever might be involved, "I cannot make the final movement, the paradoxical movement of faith, although there is nothing I wish more" (*FT*, 51). If it was a simple matter of duty, Johannes insists that he could and would perform the necessary movement. But as he has already emphasized, faith is not something that one performs. But if faith appears to be another matter altogether, de Silentio says that it would be wrong to insist that it is "something inferior or that it is an easy matter, since on the contrary it is the greatest and most difficult of all" (ibid., 52). If one papers over this difficulty, and all too quickly praises Abraham, we have a contradiction of monstrous proportions, one that reduces the patriarch to insignificance, and at the same time forbids anyone from acting as he did (ibid., 53).

In the face of this problem de Silentio's posture is consistent with his overall position: "Let us then either cancel out Abraham or learn to be horrified by the prodigious paradox that is the meaning of his life, so that we may understand that our age, like every other age, can rejoice if it has faith" (ibid., 52–53). Choosing the latter, more difficult way involves, as we have seen, telling the story like it is. Only in this way can Abraham be given his due and the account itself done justice. To be sure, a sweetened, more palatable Abraham is no Abraham at all. So *if* de Silentio were to speak of Abraham, he would put the story's most painful foot forward. By emphasizing the immense difficulty of faith, its unreachable height, and its unaffordable price, Johannes wants his readers to count the cost of such a journey and thereby face the (unbearable) responsibility involved. The last thing he wants to do is "sell a cheap edition of Abraham" and then insist that no one can act as he did (ibid., 52).

If, in this Interlude, this "border territory," this lyrical-dialectical place between places, Johannes the poet-philosopher has attempted, among other things, to *determine* or measure the difficulty of the Abraham story, in the next three sections that constitute the Problemata, he proposes to *distill* its dialectical elements. He will do this "[i]n order to perceive the prodigious paradox of faith, a paradox that makes murder into a holy and God-pleasing act, a paradox that gives Isaac back to Abraham again, which no thought can grasp, *because faith begins precisely where thought stops—*" (ibid., 53; emphasis added).

4

The Complicity of Utterance
Making Dialectical Sense of Abraham's Faith

But here I stop; I am not a poet, and I go at things only dialectically.
—JOHANNES DE SILENTIO

4.1. PROBLEMA I: IS THERE A TELEOLOGICAL SUSPENSION OF THE ETHICAL?

AS WE HAVE SEEN, de Silentio is looking for an understanding of faith that does not sell it short thereby making it easy to obtain. The idea, he suggests, is "to jack up the price" so that people will count the cost and think twice about the purchase; and since faith has been selling at bargain basement prices for so long, he assumes that few will rise to such an increase (*FT,* 121). Paradoxical though it may be, Johannes wants people to rise to the occasion of faith even though the price he puts on it is infinitely out of reach. But if the depiction of faith thus far has pushed it over the edge of possibility, the strategy he proposes in this section follows through with his negative logic in an attempt to honor both Abraham and his faith, and ostensibly, ethics (reason) itself. As we will see, de Silentio achieves this by way of a "teleological suspension of the ethical."

Securing his philosophical robes, Johannes thus begins explicitly on dialectical grounds, describing as he does, "the ethical" in terms of the universal. It becomes evident in the second paragraph of Problema I that while the author is referring to Hegelian ethics, his concern is less with the specifics of Hegel's "System" and more with a general attitude or posture that would reduce the uniqueness and particularity of human experience to wholly universal terms.[1]

> The ethical as such is the universal, and as the universal it applies to everyone, which from another angle means that it applies at all times. It rests immanent in itself, has nothing outside itself that is its telos [end, purpose] but is itself the telos for everything outside itself, and when the ethical has absorbed this into itself, it goes not further. (Ibid., 54)

On these stark terms it is the *duty* of the particular individual to continually give himself to the universal by annulling (or "sacrificing") his particularity in order to conform to the universal ideal. To the extent that the individual resists this (exchange) in the name of his singularity, "he sins," and the only hope of reconciliation is to confess it as such and perform the necessary movement, enabling him to become an obedient son of ethics (ibid.).

De Silentio, however, is not convinced that this is the whole story, for if the ethical as the universal is all that can be said, and is therefore the highest that a person can reach, then it is on the same level as the divine, which means that it cannot be denied or suspended because it is absolute (Ibid). "If this is the case," asks de Silentio, "then Hegel is right" to qualify "man only as the individual" *[den Enkelte]*,[2] a qualification understood by contrast "as a moral form of evil" that must be nullified in the name of the universal (ibid.).[3] But if he is right, observes de Silentio, then there is no place for

1. Be that as it may, it is quite clear de Silentio believes that Hegel's ethics, in the final analysis, does precisely that.

2. Kierkegaard's texts employ a number of terms for the individual, terms that indicate possible levels of human development. Thus, the lowest category is *Exemplar* (specimen), then *Individ* (person), followed by *Individualitet* (individuality), and lastly *den Enkelte* (single individual) as the highest and most central of the categories. In sum, his texts everywhere suggest that human existence lies between "animality" and "spirit." See Kierkegaard, *Søren Kierkegaard's Journals and Papers*, vol. 2, #2004, 597–98. Having said that, I would also argue that Kierkegaard's texts everywhere indicate that all of existence is wholly religious and that faith is the highest passion. But because of the Fall and the resultant human brokenness, instead, we reach back toward the creaturely in a bid to create our own maps of meaning in order to find our way home.

3. In keeping with de Silentio's emphasis that true faith honors temporality, in this section it is clear that he wants to preserve the intrinsic goodness of singularity that for Hegel is always "on the verge of slipping into evil;" and therefore to be held in check by the universal. See Hegel, *Philosophy of Right*, 92 §139. But because Hegel's oppositional philosophical system dictates that evil is both necessary and not necessary, de Silentio recognizes that the single individual *[den Enkelte]* is at the mercy of a structure that condemns one to *necessary* guilt with no hope of salvation apart from the universal.

Abraham or his faith apart from the system itself, in which case, faith has never existed since the System is all that has ever been, all that is, and all that will ever be. "But Hegel is wrong," declares Johannes, dead wrong! On his own terms "he is wrong in not protesting loudly and clearly against Abraham enjoying honor and glory as a father of faith when he ought to be sent back to a lower court and shown up as a murderer" (ibid., 55).

In the same way then that the innkeeper had no room for the Holy family, so too the System has no room for the individual or for paradoxes. But if de Silentio is suggesting that the single individual is higher than the universal, precisely "by virtue of the absurd," it is no surprise that the faith required to suspend the universal in the face of all things right, true, and good, is an uninvited and unwelcome guest in the house of reason. If, however, there is nothing higher than the ethical universal, and if there is nothing in man that resists or otherwise exceeds that totality in a way that is not evil, "then no categories are needed other than what Greek philosophy had or what can be deduced from them by consistent thought" (ibid.). But for Johannes, clearly there *is* something more, and he puzzles over why Hegel would conceal such a thing, that is, the incommensurability between the singular (faith) and the universal (reason). Why would he hide the fundamental inadequacy of language and thought with the cover of reason? "Hegel should not have concealed this," insists Johannes with a straight face, "for, after all, he had studied Greek philosophy" (ibid.).

In an effort to both rescue Abraham from the judgment of ethics and save faith from being reduced to reason, de Silentio maintains that the sacrifice of Isaac must be understood paradoxically. It must necessarily be, therefore, that "the single individual is higher than the universal . . . in such a way . . . that the single individual as the single individual stands in an absolute relation to the absolute" (ibid., 55–56). It follows, says Johannes, that such a relationship, that is, a *direct* relation to the absolute, "cannot be mediated, for all mediation takes place only by virtue of the universal

---

The extent to which de Silentio's own strategy is successful at rescuing the individual and saving faith is a pivotal question to which we will return in chapter 5. But for now it is only important to emphasize that de Silentio understands that, rather than merely being "on the verge" of evil, Hegel's philosophy, by virtue of its absolutization of the universal, pushes the single individual (indeed, all of temporal existence) toward *necessary* evil. "With this facet of evil, its necessity," declares Hegel, "there is inevitably combined the fact that this same evil is condemned to be that which of necessity ought not to be, i.e. the fact that evil ought to be annulled. It is not that there ought never to be a diremption of any sort in the will—on the contrary, it is just this level of diremption which distinguishes man from the unreasoning animal; the point is that the will should not rest at that level and cling to the particular as if that and not the universal were the essential thing; it should overcome the diremption as a nullity" (ibid., 93 §139).

. . ." (ibid., 56). Faith therefore is always and forever a paradox that thought cannot penetrate or think all the way through. Indeed, it is *either* a paradox *or* it has never existed, in which case "Abraham is lost" (ibid.). If it is tempting to think of the paradox as a difficulty that one can eventually move beyond, nothing could be further from the truth. To be sure, faith cannot be rationally digested and therefore must not be made into pablum for weak stomachs. On the contrary, faith, like a good cognac, must be taken straight which is why de Silentio insists on telling it like it is, whether one can stomach it or not.[4] If Abraham and his faith are to be taken seriously, Johannes maintains that the account of the near sacrifice of Isaac, and the extremity that it entails, necessitates a positive answer to the question posed at the beginning. This means that there is, indeed, *must* be, "a teleological suspension of the ethical," otherwise, not only is Abraham lost but so too is the rest of humanity (ibid.).

While it is true that many people have found analogies to the story, capitalizing as they do on the many surface comparisons to be made, the fact remains that no example comes even close, save one or two, as Johannes notes.[5] Why? Because Abraham is unique, acting as he did alone, by virtue of the absurd in concert with the Absolute. Since his actions cannot be explained, understood or mediated, de Silentio maintains that the patriarch is no hero of resignation; he does not have a synthesizing or *mediating* "middle term" that saves the tragic hero (ibid., 57). As a hero of faith, he stands completely outside the universal, destined to walk alone against the cold winds of silence. Yet even in the face of absurdity and apparent irrationalism, de Silentio maintains a stubborn admiration for Abraham. Even if it is the case that the "ethical has various gradations," de Silentio emphasizes that there are no parallel stories that can help illuminate and thereby justify Abraham or his actions (ibid.). For the patriarch is neither a friend of the universal, nor the son of ethics.

Even examples from ancient Greek, Hebrew, and Roman literature find no substantial point of connection to the Abraham story (ibid., 57–59). Whereas Agamemnon, Jepthah, and Brutus all sacrificed something personal for a wider communal good, Abraham's sacrifice was a purely private

4. De Silentio's posture of "telling it like it is" in order to ensure that difficulty is maintained, is consistent with the literalist hermeneutic that is felt throughout the text. Early in the *Foreløbig Expectoration* we remember that a problem of tragic proportions arose when the well-meaning preacher interchanged the words "Isaac" and "best" thereby reducing the former to the latter, thus stripping the Abraham story of its literalness and the horror that follows from such a reading. Later in Problema II we will see once again that de Silentio insists on a literal interpretation of Luke 14: 26 so as to maintain the tension and difficulty necessary to the paradox of faith.

5. For example, Mary and the apostles. See p. 109.

matter and thereby disconnected from any public good or benefit. The fact that his sacrificial gesture was undertaken privately and in secret makes it not only publicly incomprehensible, but ethically reprehensible. The larger point being made here—whether or not one agrees with the justifications of each—is that, whereas the particular sacrifices of the three tragic figures are connected with and therefore mediated by a universal cause, the sacrifice of Abraham transcends the universal altogether in the name of the absolute (ibid., 59). This is something that the universal does not and cannot recognize. In other words, for tragic heroes, there are larger, concrete reasons for their actions that make larger rational/ethical sense, reasons that fit into a larger rational and social framework. But for the lone personage of Abraham, knight of faith that he is, there is no understanding because his actions are rooted in a private relation to the absolute, and as such completely divorced from any public sensibility (ibid.). If Agamemnon, Jepthah, and Brutus are tragic figures, Abraham can only be their comic counterpart. "The power in tragedy is the ethical power of infinite resignation," observers Louis Mackey, "but the religious power of faith is the *vis comica*, the spirit of comedy."[6]

Once again we are confronted with the fact that the chasm separating the tragic hero from the hero of faith cannot be bridged, otherwise there would be no paradox. Whereas the knight of infinite resignation sacrifices the love of son or daughter to "a higher expression of the ethical," the knight of faith "transgressed the ethical altogether and had a higher *telos* outside of it, in relation to which he suspended it" (ibid., 59). Since Abraham is always already guilty by dint of his silence, his inability to speak and thereby defend himself via language cannot and will not be heard in the public court of the ethical universal. What the patriarch did then can only be described as "an ordeal, a temptation," for he was surely tempted in a way unlike any other temptation (ibid., 60). "As a rule," says de Silentio, "what tempts a person is something that will hold him back from doing his duty, but here the temptation is the ethical itself, which would hold him back from doing God's will" (ibid.). But since what Abraham did cannot be mediated by rational ethical discourse, his very presence brings into question the divine attributes of the ethical as universal. If Abraham's actions cannot be mediated, he is rendered silent, for to speak is to express the universal, to play by the rules of language, and to employ rational resources for the purpose of ethical defense, justification, and ultimately emancipation (ibid.). But Abraham does not have recourse to any of these, which can only mean that he is guilty, ethically speaking. If he *were* to speak, the only thing he could say is "that his

6. Mackey, "The View from Pisgah," 413.

situation is a spiritual trial *[Anfægtelse]*," but even this would not register on any ethical scale (ibid.). In fact, ethics would only condemn him.

Caught as he is between colliding worlds, it comes as no surprise that Johannes says, at different times and in different ways, that he admires Abraham, but also abhors him (ibid.). The paradox is therefore either admirable or abhorrent, a site where everything is on the line. For if the hero of faith is right, then he gets everything back, but if he is wrong, everything is lost. In other words, whereas the tragic hero participates in an economy of investment and return, for Abraham, the hero of faith, there is no such safety net or security system. It is all, or nothing at all.

For Agamemnon, there is a point at which his task is finished, where he, and others like him achieve catharsis (ie., through the shedding of tears) (ibid., 61). But for Abraham, there are no tears to be shed and nothing at all can be said. He must walk the path of faith alone and in silence. If one were to approach him from the opposite direction, one would do so "with a *horror religiosus,* as Israel approached Mount Sinai" (ibid.). Even the poet is lost for words as he vainly reaches out with "the leafage of language" in order to conceal such silent nakedness (ibid.). Why is it, muses de Silentio, that even you, "great Shakespeare, you who can say everything . . . why did you never articulate this torment" (ibid.)? Why? Because he too is a tragic figure who achieves the heroic through what he does not (esthetically) say, "for with his little secret that he cannot divulge the poet buys this power of the word to tell everybody else's dark secrets" (ibid.). In this way, concludes de Silentio, the poet is by no means an apostle, but one who "drives out devils only by the power of the devil" (ibid.).

As the reader now knows, if there is such a thing as a teleological suspension of the ethical, then the particular individual exists *only* in opposition to the ethical universal. If there is no such relation, that is, if "Hegel is right," then even the attempt to suspend the ethical would be seen as unethical. Moreover, since "the ethical [universal] makes its claim" on everyone, everywhere, at all times, the single individual is always already guilty by dint of his finite particularity, which is to say his inability to do the right thing, at all times, in all circumstances. As such, the universal provides the only possible means of reconciliation (or salvation) for the single individual.[7] In this

---

7. According to the terms of de Silentio's argument, if there is nothing higher than the ethical universal then there is no means other than the universal by which the particular individual can be reconciled to the universal. If, however, there is something higher, as he continues to insist, then ethics does not have the power it purports to exert as the ethical universal. If it is true, however, that ethics is finite, as Johannes suggests, then it can do neither. But by concealing this fact, ethics only deceives itself, perpetuates fear and fosters guilt. Moreover, even though the terms of the argument at this juncture in the text are, strictly speaking, dialectical, it is clear that we are essentially

economy, no one is exempt from judgment, including Abraham. But if the patriarch is to be lauded as one who had faith, to the extent that he became the father of faith, "then he is justified not by virtue of being something universal but by virtue of being the single individual" (ibid., 62).

Precisely because Abraham, as the single individual, stands outside of a relationship to the universal, he cannot assure himself that he is justified. Of course, if he *had* this assurance, there would be no anxiety, no tension, and thus no story. As we have seen, these are the very things humans love to paper over on our way toward the happy endings and the results we love to create and promulgate (ibid., 63). Johannes is therefore concerned that an inordinate focus on the "results" perpetuates illusions of ease by stripping life in general, and the story of Abraham in particular, of their inherent anxiety. It is not 'what happened' that is important, insists de Silentio—for Abraham did not see the result—but rather the 'happening,' or the moment (ibid.).[8] The focus on calculated results that will never be, is not only cowardly, but dishonest; and the penchant to do so has nothing whatsoever in common with greatness or the true hero of faith. Nevertheless, says de Silentio, "we are curious about the result, just as we are curious about the way a book turns out. We do not want to know anything about the anxiety, the distress, the paradox" (ibid.). But who would deny mystery in this way; who would demand that she reveal her secrets? As it is with holiness, the only way to honor greatness, and the mystery intrinsic to it, is to stand in awe of it and tremble at its feet. To explain a secret is to contain or otherwise reduce it, that is, reduce the tension; and to do so, insists de Silentio, is to act inhumanly towards oneself and the other, a move that "violates everything" (ibid., 64).

But since the hero of faith cannot be reconciled with the universal that he violates, and since the greatness of faith cannot be reduced without violation, de Silentio has no recourse but to drive a wedge between faith and reason, posit the single individual, and suspend the ethical in the name of absolute duty to God. In this way, he is able to maintain the tension that he contends is necessary to life and faith. Although what Johannes asserts is

---

talking about a system of ethical salvation that has a concealed, deeply religious impetus, yet one whose reach is limited and therefore impotent to deliver on the lofty promises that it makes.

8. It has been rightly suggested (in personal conversation) by Old Testament scholar Richard Middleton, that, if we are to think of the story of Abraham and Isaac as a test, it seems more consistent with biblical testimony that the patriarch deserved a "C," rather than the "A" that tradition (and de Silentio) loves to confer on him. The fact that Abraham did not question the command at the outset, in the way he doubted, appealed to, and questioned God in the past, can be seen as a relinquishment of the responsibilities of faith.

filtered through a negative dialectic, let us bear in mind that things *do* make a certain rational sense, even though he insists on the absurdity of it all. If it is true that the author is offering "a 'dialectical corrective' to the traditional view of faith as mental assent, in order to, by means of a *reductio ad absurdum*, call attention to the *true* character of faith," the logic he employs is not so absurd as we have seen and will continue to examine more closely in the pages that follow.[9] For de Silentio, to deny or otherwise *forget* anxiety is to *erase* its necessity, a move that leads to soporific ignorance. But to *remember* anxiety is to *embrace* it, which highlights the greatness of faith.

De Silentio further illustrates this logic by referring to Mary and the apostles as the only worthy comparisons to Abraham. While it may be comfortably tempting, for example, to think that the mother of Jesus lived her blessed life untouched by pain, anxiety and suffering—after all, she, like Abraham was chosen of God—nothing could be further from the truth, insists Johannes. Is it not true that no woman has ever faced the difficulty and anxiety that Mary did; "and is it not true . . . that the one whom God blesses he curses in the same breath (ibid., 65)? Moreover, declares de Silentio, a woman such as Mary "needs worldly admiration as little as Abraham needs tears, for she was no heroine and he was no hero, but both of them became greater than these, not by being exempted in any way from the distress and the agony and the paradox, but became greater by means of these" (ibid.). It was the same way for the apostles was it not? Is it not true that the enormity and difficulty of being an apostle is something we would rather not even talk about?

> Sweet sentimental longing leads us to the goal of our desire, to see Christ walking about in the promised land. We forget the anxiety, the distress, the paradox . . . Was it not terrifying that this man walking around among the others was God? Was it not terrifying to sit down to eat with him? Was it such an easy matter to become an apostle? But the *result,* the eighteen centuries—that helps, that contributes to this mean deception whereby we deceive ourselves and others. (Ibid., 66; emphasis added)

The difficult, paradoxical answer to the opening question, then, is that the story of Abraham *must* entail "a teleological suspension of the ethical,"

---

9. Gill, "Faith Is as Faith Does," 204; emphasis added. As I alluded to earlier, Gill appears to be caught in a rational web that he helps spin when he insists that "Kierkegaard's" "intended meaning" is to reveal faith as it really is. "Thus he [Kierkegaard] juxtaposes an irrationalist view of faith, through de Silentio, to the rationalist view in order to give rise to a *higher* view" (ibid., 204; emphasis added). What appears to be a commitment that flies under (or before) the reflective radar serves to highlight the insidiousness and all-pervasiveness of a rationalist, metaphysical worldview.

a truth (or, secret) that cannot be mediated and thereby understood in any straightforward, which is to say, rational, way (ibid.). While faith is a wonder that leaves one awestruck, speechless, and without understanding, de Silentio insists that "no human being is excluded from it; for that which unites all human life is passion, and faith is a passion" (ibid., 67).

4.2. PROBLEMA II: IS THERE AN ABSOLUTE DUTY TO GOD?

Problema I anticipates Problema II, shifting as it does from the question of the ethical as universal to the related question of duty. If, in Problema I, the ethical is the universal, that is, as opposed to the particular individual, it follows in Problema II that it is also the divine (ibid., 68). In other words, if ethical obligations are universal in scope, and therefore constitute one's whole duty, then the ethical as the universal is the divine, since the resulting duties represent ultimate or absolute duty (ibid.). But if this is all that can be said, if, in fact, the ethical universal is the end toward which all duties must ultimately conform, then it follows that there is no duty to God, since God and the ethical are essentially the same thing (ibid.). But by collapsing these terms, by reducing the former to the latter, de Silentio rightly reasons that life itself becomes "a perfect, self-contained sphere," a place where God is reduced to "an impotent thought" in the omnipotent, all-revealing light of the ethical (ibid.). In this economy, it would be ridiculous for anyone to express love and devotion other than to the ethical since even God is beholden to it! In fact, it would be ethically wrong to resist doing so (ibid., 54, 69–70).

    If this way of thinking is accurate, surmises de Silentio, that is, "if there is nothing incommensurable in a human life, and if the incommensurable that is present is there only by accident from which nothing results insofar as existence is viewed from the idea, then Hegel was right" (ibid.). As de Silentio already concluded in the first part of Problema I, however, Hegel is wrong to think of Abraham as the father of faith. Since it is clear in Hegel's philosophy that "*das Aussere (die Entäusserung)* [the outer (the externalization)] is higher than *das Innere* [the inner]," and that accordingly, the particular (individual) must be stripped of his interiority in the name of the universal (ethical), he ought not to have thought of Abraham in an exalted way (ibid., 69). In fact, he ought to have condemned him. If, however, Hegel is wrong, as de Silentio maintains, then faith is a paradox, which is to say that incommensurability between interiority and exteriority does exist, a paradox whereby the former cannot be subsumed by the latter. Moreover, faith cannot without detriment be put "in the rather commonplace company of feelings, moods, idiosyncrasies, *vapeurs* [vagaries], etc. (ibid.). On the contrary, says de Silentio, faith lies beyond reason, something he claims to understand without claiming to have faith (ibid.).

For Johannes, then, faith is *either* a paradox, *or* it does not exist at all. That faith is a paradox, means, contrary to the dictates of the ethical universal, that there *is* an absolute duty to God, "that the single individual . . . determines his relation to the universal by his relation to the absolute, not his relation to the absolute by his relation to the universal" (ibid., 70). But, as de Silentio insists, this does not mean that the ethical is rendered null and void, rather, it is simply given a more human or humane status in the face of its limitations. Consequently, this may lead the knight of faith to express his duty paradoxically, which may find him performing an absolute duty (to God) that is contrary to his ethical duty. If there is no excess of the kind that makes room for faith and the object of its devotion, "then faith has no place in existence . . . and Abraham is lost, inasmuch as he gave into it" (ibid.).

But de Silentio contends that faith does exist in the form of a paradox, a paradox that "cannot be mediated" and therefore depends on the absolute singularity of the single individual. But since the single individual, who, as the single individual in relation to the absolute, does not and cannot have an absolute obligation to the universal, he is damned if he performs his duty (to the ethical universal) and damned if he does not perform it. If he performs his duty, he fails the absolute, if he does not perform it, he fails the ethical and therefore transgresses the ideal. Importantly, even if he performs his duty to the ethical, he can never satisfy it in any ultimate sense (which leaves him always and everywhere guilty) since his reach is finite and the ethical as universal is infinite (ibid.). In the face of such a paradox then, de Silentio's only recourse is to posit a third category, that of the single individual *[den Enkelte]* who, at least theoretically, is capable of making the movement of faith. But it is assumed that this category ought not to be confused with Hegel's mediating third term since singularity and faith transcend the universal by virtue of the single individual's absolute (direct) relation to the absolute. If there was such a mediating link, de Silentio tells us that faith would not exist in its absolute otherness.

Although reducing the ethical universal to the relative does not reduce ethics to relativism, says de Silentio, it does relegate the single individual to silence, and therefore subjects him to public misunderstanding (ibid., 71). While it is tempting to think "that the single individual can make himself understandable to another single individual in the same situation," even this is impossible, says de Silentio, lest anyone "sneak slyly into greatness" (ibid.). The hard truth is that the single individual is condemned to the full weight of silence and solitude (not to mention, guilt), and this, according to the author, is as it should be. But as we have seen, silence, that is, the absolute silence of faith—linked as it is to absolute singularity and absolute duty—follows from the absolute paradox. This stark treatment of the issues is further evidenced not only by Johannes's rendering of Abraham's sacrifice in Genesis 22 as an absolute duty to God, but also in his treatment of the notion of devotion in Luke 14 which also deals with the issue of duty. In terms of the latter, New Testament passage, de Silentio tells us that its meaning is self-evident, and thus to be taken at face value, in all its starkness and horror. He assures his reader that verse 26 of chapter 14 is simply, but essentially, "a remarkable teaching on the absolute duty to God: *If anyone comes to me and does not hate his own father and mother and wife and children and brothers and sisters, yes, and even his own life, he cannot be my disciple*" (ibid., 72).

In its shocking literalness, it is easy to see why the harshness of such a verse is, more often than not, played down, or altogether dismissed. De Silentio is confident, however, that the zealous student of theology, who, with the help of theological and exegetical resource books, finds that the uncompromising use of language in the passage is not to be taken literally, is sorely mistaken and sadly misled. If, per chance, this "pious and accommodating exegete is able to convince anyone that a softened, more palatable rendering reflects the real meaning of the verse, Johannes insists he will have succeeded in convincing them "that Christianity is one of the most miserable things in the world" (ibid.). To be sure, by papering over the terribleness of the passage in this way, one is left with nothing whatsoever to believe in or stand for. Even though such "words are terrible," de Silentio emphasizes "that they can be understood without the necessary consequence that the one who has understood them has the courage to do what he has understood" (ibid., 73). If one is sufficiently honest about his lack of courage, he can still participate in their paradoxical beauty, providing, as they can, a certain comfort that distance affords.

For de Silentio, the bottom line here is that there is no escaping the starkness of such words or the implications involved in meeting them head on. To embrace the difficulty is to understand the paradox as only the paradox can and must be understood, that is, that "absolute duty can lead one to do what ethics would forbid, but it can never lead the knight of faith to stop loving" (ibid., 74). In fact, according to de Silentio, Abraham's (near) sacrifice of Isaac is, paradoxically, the highest expression of love.[10] But of course

---

10. The very idea that the sacrifice of Isaac is actually the highest expression of love is for Jack Caputo "the first sign of trouble in *Kierkegaard's* project, the first sign that the power of eternity might abolish the significance of time." *How to Read Kierkegaard* (New York: Norton, 2007), 51; emphasis added. While it is precisely my argument that *de Silentio's* strategy, from the outset, militates against time and temporality, I am not

the ethical can only conclude that Abraham is guilty of at least attempted murder, which can only mean that he despises his son. However, nothing could be further from the truth, since, as de Silentio reasons, if Abraham in fact despises Isaac, one can be sure that God would not require such a thing, "for Cain and Abraham are not identical" (ibid.). The truth is that Abraham loves his son with a supreme, even divine love, "for it is indeed this love for Isaac that makes his act a sacrifice by its paradoxical contrast to his love for God" (ibid.).

The point of contrast and contradiction is that the knight of faith cannot say anything that would allow him to be understood, let alone justified. Only at the point of absolute contradiction—when sacrifice collides with murder, when duty to God crashes against ethical duty—does Abraham sacrifice his son. Having left behind the ethical, there is no higher, external expression by which Abraham can be saved. This includes, perhaps most especially, the Church, since, according to Johannes, it is not qualitatively different from the State (ibid.). As soon as the idea is externalized, made public, there is mediation, and mediation only produces heroes, heroes of the State or heroes of the Church. And make no mistake, even the latter is no hero of faith, for even the hardship that a hero of the Church endures cannot be compared to the trial a true knight of faith must undergo (ibid.).

"As a rule," observes de Silentio, if passages such as Luke 14 or Genesis 22 are quoted at all, one can be sure that their teeth have been removed. For Johannes, the underlying, all-pervasive fear is that the single individual would in fact become the single individual. In other words, if people were left to their own responsibility, the fear is that they "would abandon themselves like unmanageable animals to selfish appetites" (ibid., 75). Apart from this fear, however, is the assumption that it is easy to become the single individual, since following the path of least resistance appears to be the only requirement. In truth, says de Silentio, "the person who lives under his own surveillance alone in the big wide world, lives more stringently and retired

---

willing to concede that this is Kierkegaard's own strategy, otherwise one slides all too easily towards authorship as authority and the thorny hermeneutical problematics that attend to it. Of course Caputo understands this, but since even he uses Kierkegaard's name often interchangeably with de Silentio's, the threat of collapsing the necessary distinction between the two is a little too close for comfort. For since when is the "portrait of the knight of faith [in *Fear and Trembling*] the paradigm of *Kierkegaardian* faith" (ibid.; emphasis added)? If Caputo took the use of the pseudonym as seriously as I believe Kierkegaard asks his readers to do, he (and Derrida) would have to rethink his conclusions about *Kierkegaard's* view of faith in general. While this particular text of Caputo's is obviously a primer of sorts, it seems all the more reason to problematize these distinctions from the start.

than a maiden in her virgin's bower" (ibid.). To be sure, anyone who says that it is easy to live as single individual is proof that he is no hero of faith.

While it is easy to articulate the differences between the hero of faith and the tragic hero, the lived anxiety that separates them highlights an infinite difference that cannot be articulated, for it is a difference between two absolutely separate economies. One might say that whereas the former knows two things (between which lie tension and anxiety), the latter knows only one thing. On the one hand, the knight of faith knows too much. He knows all too well how much it pays to become the favored son of ethics, one who "produces a trim, clean, and, as far as possible, faultless edition of himself, readable by all.

> He knows that it is refreshing to become understandable to himself in the universal in such a way that he understands it, and every individual who understands him in turn understands the universal in him, and both rejoice in the security of the universal. (Ibid., 76)

But the knight of faith also knows of another, higher path where the wind is cold and the air is thin; he knows the terror of walking alone, separated from the universal, from any human understanding. "Humanly speaking, he is mad and cannot make himself understandable to anyone. And yet 'to be mad' is the mildest expression" (ibid.). On the other hand, the knight of infinite resignation (tragic hero) knows too little. He knows only the glory of belonging to the universal, and nothing whatsoever of the horrors and responsibilities of faith and the freedom intrinsic to it. From a human standpoint, Abraham, in fact, accomplished nothing for the universal. What we do know is that he persisted in his faith to become a father in his old age, only to have his son ripped from his bosom. Is this not madness, asks de Silentio?

Of course, Abraham too knows "that it is glorious to express the universal, glorious to live with Isaac. But that is not his task" (ibid., 77). He can only wish that his task was "to love Isaac as a father would and should, understandable to all, memorable for all time . . . that the task were to sacrifice Isaac to the universal, that could inspire fathers to laudable deeds" and not to madness (ibid., 76). But such a wish underscores the absolute gap between the two economies, the very existence of which gives rise to the anxiety and the resultant trial that is central to de Silentio's understanding of faith. This space within which worlds collide is precisely what the knight of faith cannot articulate, let alone explain, and also why Abraham's "life is like a book under divine confiscation and never becomes *publice juris* [public property]" (ibid., 77). This absolute secret and the silence that follows highlight the tension that is necessary for the paradox to be what it is, and for Abraham to be who he is. Indeed, we remember that the hero of faith is always in tension and always kept awake, while the tragic hero ultimately finds rest and repose in the arms of the universal (ibid., 78).

Thus, it is consistent with the logic of the paradox that only the single individual, isolated and alone as he is, is able to decide for himself whether or not he is a knight of faith. But even though one is not in the paradox and therefore not a knight of faith, de Silentio maintains that there are indications that allow for a certain understanding. Chief among them are silence and isolation. "The true knight of faith is always absolute isolation, the spurious knight is sectarian" (ibid., 79). Even though the latter always finds a way out, there are no short cuts when it comes to the paradox of faith. Weaklings that they are, the sectarians know nothing about the dreadfulness of the paradox and the silence that haunts it. Instead, they

> deafen one another with their noise and clamor, keep anxiety away with their screeching. A hooting carnival crowd like that thinks it is assaulting heaven, believes it is going along the same path as the knight of faith, who in the loneliness of the universe never hears another human voice but walks alone with his dreadful responsibility. (Ibid., 80)

And make no mistake, the weight of this responsibility rests solely with the knight of faith, and along with it the anxiety of not being able to explain himself enough to be even remotely understood. The hero of faith, therefore, does not and cannot have any desire to teach others. "The true knight of faith is a witness, never a teacher," one who believes that no one requires another to achieve greatness (ibid.). Since the knight of faith is suspicious of bargain hunters and bargain basement prices, he would not think to sell what he has for anything less than its infinite worth.

"Therefore," concludes de Silentio, once again, "either there is an absolute duty to God . . . or else faith has never existed because it has always existed [in the form of the "System"], or else Abraham is lost, or else one must interpret the passage in Luke 14 as did that appealing exegete and explain the similar and corresponding passages in the same way" (ibid., 81).

4.3 CONCLUSIONS

The starkness evident in this last sentence epitomizes the text's dualistic structure, its tension filled figures and themes, and the strategy employed by the author to somehow navigate the absolute distance between faith and reason, between the divine and human. But if something is not quite right with de Silentio's strategy, and if we are thereby tempted to save "Kierkegaard" from himself in the way that many commentators have attempted to do, we would do well to remind ourselves that the author is *not* Kierkegaard.[11] As I have emphasized throughout, this means that we must judge and evaluate both the text and the author's strategy based on wider hermeneutical concerns that present themselves, particularly the issues of authorship and authority. In so doing we are able to see that Johannes' strategy (involving as it does a philosophical gesture that suspends ethics in the name of absolute duty to God) is a complex but fundamentally rational gesture.[12] Let's consider this a little more closely as a way to conclude chapter 4, and prepare for chapter 5.

Although the author depicts Abraham as one who does not suffer from a conflict of duties in the strictly ethical sense, that is precisely the question worth probing. If, as I maintain, that the teleological suspension of the ethical is ultimately a rational gesture then this changes everything, which among other things would mean that the Abraham interpreted by de Silentio is but an extreme version of Agamemnon. As we know, however, Johannes insists that there is no comparison between the two economies. Indeed, according to the negative logic at work in the author's strategy, there cannot be.[13] When held against the blinding light of *absolute* duty de Silentio believes that even universal duty must concede to *the former*. In this dualistic state-of-affairs it makes perfect sense to praise Abraham as the ultimate (*necessarily* sinless) exemplar of faith, since he is bound by what Joe Westfall calls a "non-universal duty," which is to say, an absolute duty unique only to him.[14]

"In a teleological suspension of the ethical," says Westfall, "Abraham is raised higher than the ethical, so that the ordinary constraints of the ethical

---

11. Even if Evans admits that de Silentio is not Kierkegaard, thereby claiming that the view of ethics found in *Fear and Trembling* does not belong to the latter, the fact that he attempts to sand the sharp edges off faith and bring it in line with "Kierkegaard's" own view, indicates a collapse of the personalities and the rise of a universal principle of authority meant to precisely determine who said what and why.

12. In the still ongoing debates about whether "Kierkegaard" is a rationalist or an irrationalist (itself a rationalistic construction that assumes Kierkegaard is the author of, in this case, *Fear and Trembling*, and therefore has final authority over that text), the question of authorship and authority asserts itself.

13. As Caputo rightly contends, since "negative theology . . . goes under the name of God, and that which calls forth speech is 'God,' it operates as a kind of "hyperessential-ism" which sneaks in the back door of metaphysics. See Caputo, *The Prayers and Tears of Jacques Derrida*, 3–4, 6.

14. Westfall, "Saving Abraham," 280.

do not apply to him."[15] And this is precisely how and why de Silentio is able to justify Abraham and in the end praise his actions, all the while paying lip service to a suspended, relativized ethics. But if, as it was for Agamemnon, that Abraham had a "good (read, absolute) reason" for what he proposed to do, in what sense does the teleological suspension of the ethical escape the confines of ethics and language, indeed, the language of ethics? On my reading, far from escaping it, de Silentio's strategy is dictated by such language and the mediating impulse that drives it. Nevertheless, he insists that the patriarch is in a religious category all by himself; and for Johannes, this means that "Abraham does *not* have the [mediating] middle term that saves the tragic hero" (*FT*, 57).

But if de Silentio's "absolute duty" is a product of a particular time, and a particular place, entailing as it does a particular belief system and philosophy articulated in a particular language by a particular person, then, as Westfall argues, we are talking about a radicalized universal duty dressed in absolute, non-universal robes. In this case, such duty and the faith required to support it are not absolute after all since they belong, inescapably, to the finite sphere of the same. In this way, we might suggest that, like the merman portrayed in Problema III, de Silentio too is self-deceived, which means that in his self-deception he is hidden from himself. In his apparent resistance to the uncompromising demands of the ethical universal, the author, in fact, reveals that his allegiance, nevertheless, lies with reason. By dint of divine duty, which is to say, absolute duty to God, de Silentio is able to posit the single individual and thereby elevate him above the universal. And it is precisely an absolute faith that enables the single individual to enter into an absolute relation with the absolute. In this way, however, the author deceives "himself and his readers into believing that a justification of the faith of Abraham is possible . . . He claims to be within the ethical, but this is precisely the concealment by which Johannes de Silentio is evicted from the ethical.[16]

De Silentio and his attempts to negatively reveal the truth of Abraham, his relationship to the patriarch, not to mention the relationship between faith and reason, in the end, reveals that his strategy is not what it appears to be, least of all to himself. In his concealment we witness a desire (hidden to himself?) "to reveal to thought that which cannot be thought: the

---

15. Ibid.

16. Ibid., 284. Put differently, de Silentio believes that the "teleological suspension of the ethical" sufficiently honors both ethics and faith. If that gesture is meant to honor faith, but such a move is rationalistic at its core, it necessarily excludes the former. By virtue of his Cartesian-like posture, de Silentio transgresses (Hegelian) ethics and is therefore evicted from it.

praiseworthiness of faith."[17] In this way, the shape and function of the text reveal that the desire to *praise* Abraham, *justify* his actions, and ultimately *save* faith are symptoms of silence and concealment that de Silentio painstakingly and ironically teases out in the context of Agnes and the merman. In a way that parallels the relationship between Agnes and the merman the author attempts to justify and thereby save Abraham and his faith by way of the ethical universal (ibid., 97).

My general concern in this section, as in all previous sections, was to highlight the main textual themes/figures and their connection to the text's dualistic structure, and to the author's overall (negative) strategy, both of which work to keep faith absolutely separate from reason. My specific, somewhat more complex, hermeneutical concern was to underscore the importance of taking the author, de Silentio, strictly at his authorial word. This is important, nay crucial, because if the author's strategy is *not* Kierkegaard's, then, among other implications, this puts the reader in a position to wrestle with the text's conflicting currents in a way that opens the question of *how* the text functions rather than simply or exclusively trying to determine *what* the text means by looking through the interpretive lens of Kierkegaard's later, signed works. If the latter invariably fixates on harmonizing or otherwise mediating textual differences in order to unearth and display a hidden meaning, the former works to keep the text from closing in on itself even as it reaches toward its meaning and significance.

In the face of the absolute distance between faith and reason (ethics) we saw that de Silentio elevates the single individual (over the universal) enabling him to posit a "teleological suspension of the ethical" in the name of absolute duty to God. If the problem that Johannes wrestles with involves an incommensurability that ostensibly exists between (divine) faith and (human) reason, and if his solution necessitates a strategy that entails, what we might call, unmediated mediation, it seems clear that both the textual structure and the strategy itself are built on the twin foundational pillars of metaphysics. While it is still too early to draw conclusions as to the significance of this, as we move into chapter 5, I will argue that whereas Problema I and II are *complicit* with the logic of metaphysics, in Problema III a current emerges that is more explicitly *critical* of that logic, specifically as it connects with de Silentio's treatment of sin in the context of Agnes and the merman.

If appearances are deceiving, then the text of *Fear and Trembling*, with its subversive use of language, its creative employment of the pseudonym, and its treatment of sin, conceals the truth with one hand and reveals it with the other in a never ending shell game that problematizes precisely where

17. Ibid.

the truth lies. Since texts, à la Hale, are mere fragments conditioned by their inherent incompleteness, this means that whatever specific meanings one derives from the text can only be held in an open hermeneutical hand. Nevertheless, *Fear and Trembling,* like all texts, has very specific meaning contours, and we can know those contours, and the meanings they entail, with a knowledge that knows otherwise than reason, that is, without the promise of rational certainty, which is to say, a knowledge that knows what only faith as trust can know.[18]

But even as Problema III begins, the reader is easily distracted by and caught up in de Silentio's continued dialectical attempt to make sense of the Abraham story, and he does this, as he has all along, by keeping faith and reason separate using a negative logic.[19] As we have seen, if the patriarch's actions are to be (ethically) explained, and ultimately justified, thereby saving him and his faith, but there exists a necessary disjunction between faith and reason, the author's only recourse, or so it appears, is to employ a negative logic that maintains this tension. And he accomplishes this by suspending the ethical universal and positing the single individual in the name of faith and absolute duty to God. But as we will see with greater clarity, and not without a little irony, things are not as they appear to be.

18. I contend that *Fear and Trembling* ultimately reaches toward a phenomenological understanding of faith that resists reduction to an either/or rationalistic structure, which is to say, one that dictates: *either* one has faith, *or* one does not (as if one has a choice, the final arbiter being reason); *either* one believes, *or* one has knowledge. Since the text of *Fear and Trembling* takes the biblical worldview seriously, there is a concrete, lived dimension to faith, arising from particularity that is distinguishable from, but not separate from, faith as trust. This focus not only recognizes the inextricable and delicate linkage between faith and knowledge (and that the former precedes the latter), but that this relationship is deeply and fundamentally religious in character. My strong sense is that Kierkegaard would confess with Anselm: "I do not seek to understand that I may believe, but I believe in order to understand. For this I believe—that unless I believe, I should not understand." See Anselm of Canterbury, *Proslogium,* chapter 1.

19. I maintain that like the machinations of the merman in Problema III, the elaborate strategy employed by the author functions as a distracting and distancing mechanism that separates him from true self-knowledge, enabling him to hide (in the illusion of self-sufficiency) from the painful truth of his own lack, finitude and vulnerability to sin, from what he cannot, but desperately desires and attempts to, understand.

PART III

Critique

5

Silence, Sin, and the Critique
of Reason in Problema III

The tragic hero, who is the favorite of ethics, is the purely human; him I can understand, and all his undertakings are out in the open. If I go further, I always run up against the paradox, the divine and the demonic, for silence is both. Silence is the demon's trap, and the more that is silenced, the more terrible the demon, but silence is also divinity's mutual understanding with the single individual.

—JOHANNES DE SILENTIO

IF PROBLEMA I SEES the ethical as the universal, it follows in Problema II that it is also the divine (*FT*, 54, 65). As the ethical universal, we discover in Problema III, that it is necessarily the disclosed. In keeping then with the dialectical structure of the Problemata, Johannes here focuses on an essential characteristic of the ethical, that is, the "disclosed" or the "revealed" *[Aabenbare]*. But since Abraham is silent and ethics demands disclosure, we have an obvious problem if we are to take faith, and the Father of faith, seriously. De Silentio must therefore fill out his argument and follow through with his attempt to somehow justify the patriarch's actions and save faith. In order to accomplish this Johannes sets out in Problema III to distinguish between aesthetic (human) silence and the (divine) silence of faith in the same way that he distinguished between ethics and faith in Problema I and

II. In this way he will reinforce yet another philosophical dualism that is consistent with the text's overall structure, themes and figures.[1] But even as the author unpacks his argument in order to keep divine silence absolutely separate from human silence, he finds that the issue of the demonic/sin, asserts itself.

According to de Silentio, aesthetic silence has different sounds that need to be distinguished from each other, an effort that takes up a significant part of his task in Problema III. However, the one sound of silence that concerns him the most is the sound of demonic silence. Since it is closest to divine silence (or, the silence of faith), and often indistinguishable from it, he takes great pains to differentiate the two, detailing their differences by scrutinizing the notion largely, and most significantly, through the poetic personages of Agnes and the Merman.[2] The result is a focused and complex look at the philosophical, phenomenological, and psychological dynamics of the demonic and the sin intrinsic to it, a consideration that, I contend, is the focal point of the text's critique of rationalistic logic.[3] Not without profound, ironic significance, we will see that this critique points to de Silentio's own negative logic and its connection with both deceitful and demonic concealment for reasons we will explore.

Thus, like the faith/reason dichotomy, the divine silence emphasized in Problema III, linked as it is positively to Abraham and juxtaposed negatively with demonic silence (and ethical utterance), is yet another symptom of the metaphysical malaise that infects both the author and his text.[4] Combined with its sheer length, its meandering structure, and its complex, confusing, even convoluted argument, the sounds of silence in Problema III can distract even the most alert reader. But this makes it even more crucial to find our way through this section in order to witness for ourselves the

1. Here I am referring to the fact, assumed throughout, that faith requires absolute silence, while ethics (reason) demands utterance, which is to say, absolute disclosure.

2. Johannes does contrast the demonic with the divine in the story of Sarah and Tobias, although his treatment of it there is less extensive and penetrating.

3. Although the author does not make a clear distinction between the "demonic" and "sin," and in some sense employs them interchangeably, the overall sense of the text (specifically in Problema III) suggests that the latter is the consummation of the former.

4. Thus, it is important, as we move forward from here, to keep in mind that the innumerable couplets on full display are symptoms of a malaise that Johannes's text exhibits, even as he attempts to treat those symptoms dialectically and negatively. As the text moves even closer to its treatment of demonic silence, it is crucial to remember that these dualisms, in the end, hamstring de Silentio's overall efforts. In this way, they are part of the problem, even as he attempts to employ them as a necessary part of the solution. The dualistic terms of which I speak include, but are not limited to: immediacy-second immediacy; merman-Abraham; and demonic silence-divine silence.

self-critical dynamic at work in the remote corners of the text, and how it functions.

5.1. PROBLEMA III: WAS IT ETHICALLY DEFENSIBLE FOR ABRAHAM TO CONCEAL HIS UNDERTAKING FROM SARAH, FROM ELIESER, AND FROM ISAAC?

Problema III begins stylistically in much the same manner as the first two Problemata. After the second paragraph, however, the similarity ends, followed as it is by a lengthy and meandering excursus that seems to be more personal, anecdotal, and therefore peripheral to the central concerns of the text.[5] But in keeping with its tensions, dualisms, and paradoxical reversals throughout, things are not quite what they appear to be. In fact, a close consideration of Problema III reveals key notions that have lain dormant throughout the text, the significance of which would be entirely missed if this third and final problem were not given due attention.[6] Thus, it is imperative that readers resist the drift into soporific distraction just when de Silentio begins to move silently but steadily toward the veiled entranceway at the end of the sanctuary as if drawn by forces outside of himself.

In the form of a question that gets Problema III underway, the author posits the ethical problem facing Abraham: *Was it ethically defensible for Abraham to conceal his undertaking from Sarah, from Eliezer, and from Isaac?* Since, as we have seen, that there is both a teleological suspension of the ethical (Problema I) and an absolute duty to God (Problema II), we can only conclude that Abraham's actions are not *ethically* defensible. Of course, this is consistent with the author's split philosophical worldview which draws a thick line of demarcation between faith and reason. This means that even though de Silentio's negative strategy is meant to resist metaphysics as a way to honor Abraham and save faith, in the end, it is bound between its twin pillars. And as we look more closely at Problema III it is important that we keep this mind.

As we have seen, the first two Problemata see Johannes link the ethical universal with disclosure, the latter following from the former. Note that ethics is distinguished from esthetics by the ethical imperative that has

5. To conclude this, however, is far too rash, missing as it does the significance of the central question in Problema III (intrinsic to which is concealment) on its hurried way toward the answer (intrinsic to which is disclosure).

6. I am referring here to the central notion of silence (concealment, hiddenness, secrecy), and more specifically to the notion of sin and the hermeneutical role that it plays in the larger textual drama.

every man disclose himself publicly; and this is only possible by employing the universal resources of language that are in principle accessible to all
rational beings. According then to the dictates of the ethical universal, it is
every man's duty "to annul his singularity in order to become the universal" (ibid., 54). Of course the main reason why the darkness of concealed,
inward night must be exposed to the external light of ethical duty is that
if moral community is to be realized, then open communication between
moral individuals is necessary, indeed, crucial. Since internality, and the
silence intrinsic to it, cannot be comprehended by reason, it can only be
seen as an affront to rational intelligibility and therefore dismissed as its
opposite.[7] Thus, in keeping with the oppositional structure throughout, we
know that if the individual maintains silence then communication between
moral agents is not possible. Only if the private is dutifully sacrificed on the
altar of the public is community possible, the basis of which is open and
forthright communication.

In these stark terms, then, how does de Silentio attempt to rethink
the Hegelian relationship between the ethical universal and the particular
individual? Based on the remedy proposed in Problema I and II, we know
that his "teleological suspension of the ethical" involves a reversal, a kind of
negative logic that upends the positive logic of Hegel's System and relativizes it. In this way, simply put, instead of annulling or otherwise sacrificing
one's singularity in the name of the ethical universal, the latter is sacrificed/
suspended for the sake of singularity. In these reformulated terms, how are
we able to rethink Abraham and his faith? What is the difference between
Abrahamic (or religious) silence and esthetic silence? How are we to ultimately judge between what the author calls "divine" silence and "demonic"

7. Even though de Silentio rails against reason for overstepping its boundaries in
matters of faith, his strategy for negotiating those boundaries reveals that his own assumptions about language, thought, and communication are rooted squarely in Enlightenment sensibilities, conforming as they largely do to an amalgam of Hegel's and
Kant's views. The text everywhere indicates that, although he may resist it, Johannes
is beholden to the idea that it is every person's ethical duty to be revealed in the public square of language. How he attempts to renegotiate the relationship between faith
and reason therefore takes off from wholly rationalistic assumptions that function as
infinitely separate bookends for his strategy. If ethics dictates that human beings are
morally obligated to wholly divest themselves of their particularity, then the reason that
it opposes *all* forms of silence is that morality (moral obligation) is defined, à la Kant,
strictly in terms of universality. Since it is assumed that all humans are fundamentally,
which is to say, essentially rational and moral, it follows that the particular individual
must, in the end, conform to the universal law. The suggestion here is that if individuals
are left to their own naturally selfish desires and devices, all hell would break loose.
Inevitably, as Mark Taylor suggests, "a Hobbesian war of all against all would result"
Taylor, "Sounds of Silence," 180.

silence? These are the central questions motivating Problema III and why de Silentio believes that "[i]f there is no hiddenness rooted in the fact that the single individual . . . is higher than the universal, then Abraham's conduct cannot be defended . . . But if there is such a hiddenness, then we face a paradox, which cannot be mediated . . ." (ibid., 82). This being the case, however, de Silentio observes that Hegel would find himself in quite a bind if he wanted to give faith its due, and praise Abraham as the father of faith, since his own philosophy "assumes no justified hiddenness, no justified incommensurability" (Ibid).

Thus, it is de Silentio's task in Problema III to let the question of esthetics guide his inquiry. And he will go about it "dialectically to pursue hiddenness through esthetics and ethics, for the point is to have esthetic hiddenness and the paradox [of religious hiddenness] appear in their *absolute* dissimilarity" (ibid., 85; emphasis added). In order to accomplish this, de Silentio sets out to transition from ethics (Problemata I and II) to esthetics (Problema III); but since his "examination must constantly wander into the territory of ethics," he will find himself in a hidden land, "a *confinium* [border territory]" between the two (ibid., 83). And since ethics is a sphere unto itself, we already know that it has neither the room for such a category nor the time that Johannes will give to it, dialectician though he purports to be.

But even while Greek tragedy reminds us that there is no revelation without concealment, de Silentio says that the unseen face of fate at the center of its imagination "lacks the potency of the eye," which is to say that it cannot see (ibid, 84). Our self-enlightened age, however, has no need of this kind of tragedy and has therefore jettisoned any notion of fate or destiny in favor of its own sightedness and salvific ability that drinks destiny in, absorbing it into it's own consciousness (ibid.). Contrary to Greek tragedy, observes Johannes, where fate sees all and determines all, in modern drama *both* revelation and concealment are the responsibility of the hero (Ibid).[8]

---

8. The text here puts it its finger on yet another connected, indeed, fundamentally significant dualism: Greek tragedy and modern drama, representing the pivotal notions of fate and freedom respectively. This dualism is significant because we are able to see that to the extent the latter has absorbed the former, nothing is really new under the western philosophical sun, since the same economy is at work in both worldviews which achieve similar results. Whereas in Greek tragedy the unseen face of fate sees all and decides the outcome, in modern drama, the all-seeing eye of (rational) freedom determines the result, having seen all things, past, present and future. At issue here in both instances is a metaphysical, sacrificial economy of exchange, the necessary tension that lies at its center, the fear that drives it, and the violence that often results. The motives and assumptions that give rise to an economy such as this seem clear enough: that unmediated access to the "truth" is not only desirable and possible, but essential.

That modern rational consciousness dismisses, excludes, or otherwise absorbs silence, is one thing, the different faces of silence are something different. And this is the difference between ethics (as the universal) and esthetics. If, as we will see, that not all silences are created equal, it will be de Silentio's job to begin at one end of the esthetic spectrum and work his way to the other end and back again with a view toward indicating just how far every instance of silence is from religious silence, or the silence of faith.[9] According to de Silentio, there is silence, and there is silence. Thus, he takes great pains to distinguish between the sounds of silence.

∼

The first two kinds of silence that he highlights are examples of what Mark Taylor calls "playful silence":[10] one comedic the other lightly dramatic. Johannes first tells of a "bald male" who "is eager to make a hit with the fair sex and is sure of success with the aid of . . . makeup and wig, which make him altogether irresistible" (ibid., 84–85). The long and short of the story is that the man gets the girl and everyone is happy. But if the man, with honest intentions, decides to confess his deception to his beloved, there is little doubt that he would lose her, for esthetics "is no friend of bald hypocrites and abandons him to laughter" (ibid., 85). Indeed, esthetics does not reward open and forthright confessions after the manner of ethics. Aside from immediate silence, comic silence and the fickleness attached to it, therefore, is the furthest removed from Abrahamic silence, and as such, says

9. Although the notion of esthetic immediacy and the silence intrinsic to it is not explicitly dealt with in *Fear and Trembling*, it is important to make mention of it since it represents the other side or opposite pole of esthetic silence assumed throughout Problema III. As Mark Taylor points out, this extreme end of esthetic concealment is represented by yet another pseudonym's portrayal of Don Juan, whose "prereflective" life is an endless erotic adventure, a quest to satisfy an insatiable appetite. "Sounds of Silence." 168. He is "so driven by the power of passion that he cannot be properly called an individual. Rather, his life is a reflex of desire, a concrete expression of the natural force of sensuousness: 'Here we do not hear Don Juan as a particular individual, or his speech, but we hear a voice, the voice of sensuousness, and we hear it through the longing of womanhood'" (ibid.). The writer of *Either/Or*, notes Taylor, "makes this point more graphically when he describes Don Juan as 'flesh incarnate, or the inspiration of the flesh by the spirit of the flesh'" (ibid.). Significantly, "Don Juan neither thinks nor speaks . . . The *prereflective* character of Don Juan's existence makes it impossible to express his essential character in words" (ibid.; emphasis added). At the other extreme end of esthetic concealment sits Johannes the Seducer whose *reflective* posture involves endless plotting and torturous reflection. Whereas the prereflective whirlwind Don Juan seduces 1003 women, the reflective, sedate Johannes (the Seducer) seduces only one.

10. Taylor, "Sounds of Silence," 172.

de Silentio, it cannot be the focal point of his exploration (ibid.). But there are other forms of esthetic silence/concealment that need to be teased out, all of which will allow divine silence to stand out in bold relief against the negative backdrop of Johannes' project.

Other than straightforward comedy, the second form of "playful silence" might be found in a light, romantic drama. The example de Silentio uses is of a young woman and man whose love for each other has gone unconfessed. As the story unfolds, the young woman, out of parental duty, marries another and therefore "keeps her love hidden 'in order not to make the other unhappy, and no one will ever find out what she suffers'" (ibid.). And so too the young swain keeps his love hidden so as not to bring ruin to all parties concerned. But lest this be confused with "heroic silence," the kind that saves another in the name of a higher ideal, one only has to see that their silence was decided freely, a *free act* on their part. As de Silentio points out, "esthetics is a courteous and sentimental branch of knowledge that knows more ways out than any pawnshop manager. What does it do? It makes everything possible for the lovers" (ibid.). So it is that by "a coincidence" the lovers get wind of each other's "magnanimous decision"; and following appropriate explanations "the lovers get each other and also a place among authentic heroes, for even though they never had time to sleep on their heroic resolution, esthetics regards them as having bravely battled their intention through over a period of many years" (ibid, 85–86). But of course this is the furthest thing from ethics and what ethics demands. At best, observes John Lippitt, the silence depicted here "plays a role in an entertaining yet undemanding evening at the theatre."[11] As such, stories like this merely imitate the true ethical hero and therefore know nothing of the seriousness and depth of ethics. Indeed, ethics knows nothing at all of silence and the secrets it harbors.

> Ethics does not lend itself to debate, for it has pure categories. It does not appeal to experience, which of all ridiculous things is about the most ridiculous; far from making a man wise, it makes him mad if he knows nothing higher than that. Ethics has no room for coincidence; consequently, there is no eventual explanation. It does not trifle with dignities, it places a heavy responsibility on the hero's frail shoulders, it denounces as arrogant his wanting to play providence with his act, but it also denounces his wanting to do that with his suffering. It enjoins believing in actuality and having courage to do battle with all the sufferings of actuality, especially those anemic tribulations that he on his

11. Lippitt, *Kierkegaard and* Fear and Trembling, 112.

own responsibility has brought upon himself. It warns against
having faith in the cunning calculations of the understanding,
which are less to be trusted than the ancient oracles. (Ibid., 86)

In a way that further illustrates the fecklessness and pretense of esthetics, de Silentio indicates that there are times when it suits esthetics to
demand disclosure. Thus, it is important for him to make a further distinction, lest anyone confuse the esthetic hero with the ethical hero, neither
of whom of course can be compared to the hero of faith. The reader will
remember that the tragic hero Agamemnon was called by the prophet Cal-
chas to sacrifice his daughter Iphigenia for the ultimate good of the nation,
which is to say, to a higher ideal. In order to have it both ways (esthetically
and ethically) esthetics sets out to make the most of the dramatic tension
by *both* demanding Agamemnon's silence (having him suffer in solitude)
and by tempting him to speak (having him seek release in consolation).
But whereas esthetics is only interested in the path of least resistance in
order to maximize pleasure all around—and perhaps even save another in
the process—and thereby have everyone live happily ever after, ethics knows
nothing of the sort; it knows only the suffering, sacrifice, and the rigor involved in a commitment to a higher universal cause. In the end, esthetics
looks for an exit where it finds catharsis; "it has the old servant in readiness
to disclose everything to Clytemnestra. Now everything is in order" (ibid.,
87). And in this way esthetics has its illusion; it gets to have its cake and eat
it too, as it were. But of course, ethically speaking, it is only an illusion since
no one can have it both ways. Indeed, ethics knows only the hard way of
ethical obligation and duty. According to the ethical universal, esthetics is a
contradiction, a house divided against itself. And to be sure, a house divided
is an unstable house that will surely fall.

Whereas the esthetic hero is a waffler, the ethical hero is courageous
because he faces up to the hard responsibility of telling Iphigenia *himself*
of her fate. In so doing, "the tragic hero is ethics' beloved son in whom it is
well pleased" (ibid.). By remaining silent the ethical hero fully realizes that
doing so would universalize his particularity, as it were, a responsibility that
his frail shoulders are not able to bear. What he *is* called to bear, however, is
the loss of his particularity (everything finite) in the name of universality.
But whether the esthetic hero sacrifices either disclosure or concealment,
it is always in the interest of particularity at the expense of universality. By
contrast, the ethical hero is called to sacrifice the particular on the altar of
the universal; and in this way, although he loses the finite, he gains the infinite. Thus de Silentio concludes: "Esthetics demanded disclosure but aided

itself with a coincidence; ethics demanded disclosure and found fulfillment in the tragic hero" (ibid., 87–88).

Even if the ethical universal represents the veritable apex of human achievement, de Silentio also insists "that secrecy and silence make a man great simply because they are qualifications of inwardness" (ibid., 88). If the demand of esthetics is easy, based as it is on the *internal* whims of the individual, and if ethics is difficult because of the *external* demands placed on him by the "system," the divine paradox of faith (the religious) is impossible because it demands the *eternal*. De Silentio readily confesses that he understands the human (esthetics, even ethics), but to go beyond that is something altogether different.[12] "If I go further, I always run up against the paradox, the divine and the demonic, for silence is both" (ibid.). Johannes here formally introduces a new and pivotal category of silence (the demonic) that we will see is quite different from the other forms of silence that he has already dealt with and will continue dealing with throughout this section.

If Johannes thus far has considered two examples of "playful silence" (comic and dramatic)—the latter also being an example of simple "heroic silence"[13]—having contrasted them with the seriousness of ethics and its demand for complete disclosure, he will move circuitously in the direction of more serious forms of silence. In the sections below de Silentio will probe yet three more variations of heroic silence, the second of which he juxtaposes with demonic silence that arises from a source other than individual agency. But it is not until the story of Agnes and the Merman that we will closely consider his treatment of "deceitful silence" and much more so his preoccupation with "demonic silence."[14] Since demonic silence is the most serious, and since it can be deceptively similar to divine silence, "for silence is both," says de Silentio, he will take great pains to distinguish them.

By turning his dialectical attention then to a series of four stories and the personages involved in each, Johannes intends to negatively demonstrate just how far esthetic silences are from the silence of faith. He does this, ostensibly, to achieve a better understanding of Abraham by juxtaposing him with other personalities, examples that appear similar to the patriarch but are quite literally opposite to him and his uniqueness. The idea is to

12. But precisely because the demands of the eternal are impossible, de Silentio understands that this is beyond understanding. In other words, since possibility and impossibility represent both sides of the same coin, one can only understand the latter in terms of the former. In this way, the unknown is forced into the box of the known.

13. "Heroic silence," we remember, might save another, but its primary concern is the esthetical *not* a truly universal, ethical ideal.

14. See Taylor, "Sounds of Silence," 172–78.

have these examples utterly pale by comparison to Abraham. In fact, in the end, de Silentio will go so far as to say that *nothing* he has said "contains an analogy to Abraham;" whoever or whatever was described or explained was done so "in order that in their moment of deviation they could, as it were, indicate the boundary of the unknown territory" (ibid., 112). And although this appears, at least on the surface, to be an exercise in head scratching futility, the negative logic de Silentio employs will work, paradoxically, he believes, to mediate his cause.

Along with a few brief narrative asides, de Silentio focuses on four stories involving legendary poetic personages that, subject to imaginative revisionings, will serve his overall strategic purposes. The first story involves Aristotle's account of the Delphic Bridegroom; the second story centers on the Scandinavian myth of Agnes and the Merman; the third story is drawn from the book of Tobit 6–8; and in the last story Johannes employs the German legend of Faust. As de Silentio then transitions to the next section, he emphasizes that by employing "the power of dialectics" he plans to hold the personalities that follow "at the apex, and by disciplining them with despair . . . prevent them from standing still, so that in their anxiety they may possibly be able to bring something or other to light" (ibid., 88).

Since, on my reading, the story of Agnes and the merman is the critical fulcrum of the text, the reader will note that it will appear last in my treatment of the four stories.

5.1.1. The Delphic Bridegroom

The first in a series of four short stories involves a bridegroom who faces a dilemma of heroic proportions, the bare bones of which is taken from Aristotle's *Poetics* and used in the service of Johannes's negative project. The basic structure of the story is all that he needs to get started: *"The bridegroom, to whom the augurs prophesied a calamity that would have its origin in his marriage, suddenly changes his plans at the crucial moment when he comes to get his bride"* (FT, 89). At the last minute the bridegroom backs out of the marriage. Unable to resist the impulse to wax poetically, Johannes begins by attempting to imaginatively identify with the situation in general and with the bride in particular. If there was ever a circumstance that evoked sympathy, suggests de Silentio, this would certainly be it. If it is generally true that it is the difficulties intrinsic to earthly existence that cause all the problems, in this case we have a disturbing exception. "Here it is heaven itself that separates what heaven itself, after all, has brought together. Who would have suspected this? Least of all the young bride" (ibid.). Who would have dreamed that another kind of veil enveloped the bride, one that kept her from seeing the truth as the bridegroom passed by on his way to the temple (ibid., 90). Thus it happened that at the very moment when the bridegroom sees the bride in all her beauty and comes to his decision, she does not see him since "she . . . dropped her eyes in maidenly modesty and did not see that his countenance was disturbed, but he saw that heaven seemed to be envious of the bride's loveliness and of his happiness" (ibid.). A mere coincidence then veils the young bride's eyes, hiding her from the tragedy that will follow.

But as if catching himself in a fit of poetic forgetfulness, de Silentio asserts: "But here I stop; I am not a poet, and I go at things only dialectically" (ibid.). Waking from his poetic slumber Johannes quickly rearranges his philosophical robes, clears his throat, and insists that, while this is the stuff of good story telling, in the larger ethical scheme of things, that is, where things really matter, there are no coincidences, there is no easy way out of life. Since the bridegroom is not technically married, and since a prophetic pronouncement weighs heavily on him, de Silentio surmises that his motive to halt the marriage comes from somewhere other than the fickleness of self-opinion the way lovers often are.[15] Moreover, such a pronouncement makes him unhappy, perhaps even more so than the bride herself since "he is the occasion" for both his and her unhappiness (ibid.).

In the form of a question, the dilemma facing the bridegroom is this: if the prophesied calamity was for *him*, will it *necessarily* affect the bride and their mutual happiness? According to de Silentio there are at least three, perhaps four options open to him. He could: 1) go through with the marriage but keep *silent* on the matter with the thought that the calamity might not happen immediately, in which case the couple might be able to experience a brief period of marital bliss. In this way would he not be keeping silent for the sake of the bride and the marriage? We remember, however, that ethically speaking, one cannot have it both ways, which is to say, satisfy both esthetics and ethics. So rather than honoring the bride and fulfilling the ideal (his marital duty), de Silentio insists that keeping silent constitutes an offense to the girl since she is made guilty by his silence. For had the bride known of the prophesy she would have never given her consent to marry the bridegroom in the first place. In other words, his silence makes the bride guilty by virtue of the marriage bond through which she is complicit, since the prophesy was for him and him alone (ibid.). In this case, says de Silentio, "in his hour of distress, he will have to bear not only the disaster

15. The most immediate example is the "lightly dramatic" story of the young lovers and the "playful silence" that they represent in the text.

but also the responsibility for remaining silent and her righteous anger over his remaining silent" (ibid., 91). Of course central to this option is silence, which ethically speaking is never appropriate because there is only the hard way of open, public confession.

If then the idea of getting married, but remaining silent implicates the girl and is therefore an offense against her, perhaps the bridegroom could: 2) *not* get married and remain silent. But this option, concludes Johannes, involves him in a ruse whereby he, in effect, destroys himself for the sake of the girl. However noble such action appears to be, this too, concludes de Silentio, is "an offense against the girl and the reality of his love" (ibid.). Even if it is true that this option does not implicate the bride-to-be in whatever might befall the bridegroom, the important thing is that it only pretends to be tragedy. When the tragic veil is lifted we find esthetics pretending to be ethics. Although esthetics would attempt to use this situation to great tragic advantage, it would no doubt culminate "in a last-moment explanation" (ibid.). Anything less than forthright honesty, therefore, is an offense not only against the bride and the bridegroom, but against ethics itself, to which they are ultimately beholden.

If options 1 and 2 are unacceptable, the question is this: 3) should the bridegroom speak? Of course the implicit answer here is yes! For if both options are deemed unacceptable the only option left is a straightforward confession, a conclusion that ethics approves of and de Silentio implicitly accedes to.[16] Only in this way do we approach a bona fide tragedy "in the same style as Axel and Valborg" (ibid.). In a footnote de Silentio does entertain another alternative, a fourth option whereby the bridegroom could

> dispense with getting married without therefore giving up the girl; he could live in a romantic alliance with her, which would be more than adequate for the lovers. This, however, implies an offence against the girl, for he is not expressing the universal in his love for her. (Ibid.)

Taking his cue from the ethical universal, Johannes concludes that the bridegroom should speak (ibid., 92). The bottom line here is that since he is not an exception to the demand of ethics (as is Abraham) his only recourse is to speak. Why is the bridegroom and his tragic circumstances *not* an exception? Because the augur's prophesy, while religious in nature, is understandable *both* privately *and* publicly by the community at large. To be sure,

16. This is not to say, however, that de Silentio is not also committed to overcoming the dilemma that this poses for faith and its Father. Indeed, suspending ethics in the name of absolute duty to God is his remedy for the problem. The question is, what of the remedy? What does it at once reveal and conceal?

there was no secret message sent to him alone. But if the prophecy had come to the bridegroom in a personal way, says de Silentio, then it would have changed everything. Only under utterly private, religious circumstances would he be an exception; only then would he be in the presence of the paradox, in which case *he could not speak* (ibid., 93).

So what is the point of this sketch, asks Johannes, if, in the end, "I still get no further than the tragic hero? Because it was, after all, possible that it could throw some [negative] light on the paradox" (ibid., 92).

The third story is taken from the book of Tobit in the Apocrypha and involves the plight of Sarah and Tobias.[17]

5.1.2. Sarah and Tobias

Once again de Silentio needs only the basic structure of the story to get things under way; and as it is with all the stories, he finds that a variation on the received version is necessary. In the original account we discover that the young Tobias is set to marry Sarah, the daughter of Raguela and Edna. But as it happens she has a profoundly tragic past. In fact, a tragedy times seven! It turns out that Sarah has been given in marriage seven times to seven different men, all of whom died on their wedding night at the hand of an evil, jealous demon. Since in the original story the emphasis is on Tobias's heroic character in the face of unspeakable tragedy and overwhelming odds, Johannes wishes to put the spotlight on Sarah for reasons that will become apparent. In order to accomplish this shift in focus de Silentio will seek to minimize the comic element, and he does so by making this her first betrothal (*FT*, 102).[18]

Here again we find Johannes indulging his penchant to wax poetic by attempting to imaginatively identify with Sarah and her predicament. "I have read about many griefs," he muses, "but I doubt that there is to be found a grief as profound as the one in this girl's life" (ibid.). It is one thing if there is an explanation or a clear reason for such misfortune, perhaps a misstep or some kind of obvious guilt, witting or unwitting. But it is another thing entirely, indeed an altogether unthinkable grief to be guiltless and thrown to suffering without explanation or consolation.[19] Even in his

17. The second story involves the account of Agnes and the Merman but as I have already mentioned, it will be dealt with last for the sake of the larger argument.

18. Apparently, de Silentio finds the high number here quite comical to the extent that it obscures the tragic dimension of the story that he wants to tease out,

19. The distinction between innocence and guilt—and for that matter, predestination and freedom—and the necessary tension involved is crucial for the reversal that de

reworking of the story de Silentio recognizes that "Tobias behaves gallantly and resolutely and chivalrously," what man would do otherwise? (ibid., 103). Nevertheless, Sarah is the one that Johannes focuses on, attributing to her the heroic characteristics normally conferred on Tobias.

> For what *love for God* it takes to be willing to let oneself be healed when from the very beginning one in all innocence has been botched, from the very beginning has been a damaged specimen of a human being! What *ethical maturity* to take upon oneself the responsibility of permitting the beloved to do something so hazardous! What *humility* before another person! What *faith* in God that she would not in the very next moment hate the man to whom she owed everything! (Ibid., 104; emphasis added)

Now, if the shoe was on the other foot, if the roles were reversed and one imagines Sarah as a man, then everything would be different since the "demonic is immediately present" (ibid.). De Silentio maintains that the "proud, noble nature" which is the hallmark of the demonic, can, in its pride, endure almost anything except sympathy and the humiliation one must inevitably endure (ibid.). This it cannot bear. For the self-sufficient man who holds his proud head high, no sacrifice is too great, and no price is too high. And since guilt is ever before him, since this is his natural element, the more he endures the better. In this economy guilt is necessary and amounts to an "easy difficulty" for the demonic nature. But it is something else entirely "to be without guilt from his mother's womb and yet to be destined as a sacrifice to sympathy . . . this he cannot endure" (ibid.).

And this is Sarah's lot for she is without guilt from the start and yet, miracle of miracles, we witness her love, maturity, humility, and her faith. In the same way that de Silentio applauds Abraham, even as he struggles to explain, indeed, understand him, he admires Sarah almost as much, and is astounded by her capacities. Nevertheless, says Johannes, "even I cannot mention her name without saying: The poor girl!" (ibid.). One thing is certain for de Silentio: let Sarah be a man, let him discover that his beloved will be murdered on his wedding night, and most assuredly things would be different. No doubt he would withdraw and become enclosed within himself, insisting on the secrecy that is intrinsic to demonic silence. Speaking in secret the way demonic nature speaks, the man Sarah would secretly say: "Thanks, I'm no friend of ceremonies and complexities; I do not demand the delight of love at all, for I can in fact be a Bluebeard and have my delight in seeing maidens die on their wedding night" (ibid., 105).

Silentio proposes. Namely, that it heightens tension.

While one is hard pressed at this point to know anything about the demonic, de Silentio observes that it has been inimitably depicted in Shakespeare's *Richard III* in the form of Gloucester. Johannes observes that Gloucester himself had endured the weight of unbearable sympathy since he was a child, and his inability to bear it, along with the inherent guilt, in essence, excluded him from being saved by ethics or otherwise *mediated* into the idea of society. In this way, by his deformed physicality, that is, by nature, Gloucester is "in the paradox," (ibid., 106). Significantly, de Silentio says that Gloucester's "monologue in the first act of *Richard III* has more value than all the systems of morality, which have no intimation of the nightmares of existence or of their explanation."

> I, that am rudely stamp'd, and want love's majesty / To strut before a wanton ambling nymph; / I, that am curtail'd of this fair proportion, / Cheated of feature by dissembling Nature, / Deform'd, unfinish'd, sent before my time / Into this breathing world, scarce half made up, / And that so lamely and unfashionable / That dogs bark at me as I halt by them—. (Ibid., 105)

Consistent with his view of Abraham, de Silentio's point is that ethics, as a purportedly self contained system, cannot account for that which exceeds its boundaries, which is why it insists that there is nothing it cannot explain and therefore contain. In this way one can readily see why there are no exceptions to the rule of ethics. Indeed, if the Father of faith cannot escape its judgment, since he cannot speak in order to explain his actions, then there is little hope for Gloucester, or for that matter, Sarah, heroic though her character is.[20] Natures such as these, that is, natures that are aboriginally outside the universal "are either lost in the demonic paradox or saved in the divine paradox" (ibid., 106).[21] Like the genius who is also aboriginally in the paradox, and therefore caught between the demonic and divine, he must either in pride seek "demonic reassurance" or in humility and love find religious reassurance in the divine (ibid., 107).

---

20. But of course in the end Abraham and his faith are saved from judgment by way of de Silentio's "teleological suspension of the ethical."

21. If, as we have seen, that it is the duty of the single individual to "work himself out of his hiddenness and to become disclosed in the universal," but there are some who are "aboriginally in the paradox" and therefore "outside the universal" from the start, how is it possible to choose between the demonic and the divine, since, unlike Abraham, they are not chosen and are therefore primordially guilty? (*FT*, 82, 131 [Hannay], 106). And if they cannot choose, since they were not chosen, how are they not doubly damned and predestined so? Once again we find ourselves up against de Silentio's tension filled negative logic. In the context of Sarah and Tobias, the tension is between free will and predestination.

5.1.3. The Legend of Faust

In the fourth story de Silentio invites his readers to imagine with him some-one who, through silence, aims to save the universal (*FT*, 107). In order to accomplish his purpose of depicting this kind of "heroic silence" Johannes employs the legend of Faust, and as we have come to expect a little change in the story is in order.[22]

In the author's retelling, Faust "has a sympathetic nature" since, ac-cording to Johannes, even Goethe's version of the story lacks a certain depth, a certain "psychological insight into doubt's secret conversations with itself" (ibid., 108). Only a more poetic Faust, says de Silentio, can embrace the travail of doubt within. Indeed, a more sympathetic Faust "knows that it is spirit that maintains existence, but he also knows that the security and joy in which men live are not grounded in the power of the spirit but are easily explained as unreflected bliss" (ibid.). In this way, no one can convince the doubting Faust "that he has passed through doubt" and moved beyond it as if passing thorough one room into another (ibid., 109). And since Faust takes his doubting seriously, knowing as he does what other men do not, he knows that doubt, if unleashed, has the power to wreak havoc in the world and thereby lead men to despair. It follows that he is "too ideal a figure" to believe that if he were to speak, discussions would break out without nega-tive consequences (ibid., 110). No, this Faust knows that he cannot stem the tide of inevitable chaos that would wash over the hearts and minds of the masses if he spoke. Consequently,

> He remains silent, he hides doubt more carefully in his soul than the girl who hides a sinful fruit of love under her heart, he tries as much as possible to walk in step with other men, but what goes on inside himself he consumes and thus brings himself as a sacrifice for the universal. (Ibid., 109)

So our (esthetic) hero either keeps silent, and offers himself as a sacrifice to the sufferings of doubt on behalf of others, or he speaks knowing full well that chaos will ensue (ibid., 110).

In these familiar terms, Faust is caught between a rock and a hard place, damned if he keeps silent and damned if he speaks. If he chooses the former and remains silent he is ethically culpable and judged accordingly. To make matters more agonizing, ethics will taunt him saying: "You should have spoken. How are you not going to be sure that your resolution was not prompted by cryptic pride?" (ibid., 111). If he chooses the latter, if he

---

22. If not a doubter, Johannes could have chosen "an ironist," a re-imagined "Aristo-phanes," or "a slightly altered Voltaire" (*FT*, 107–8).

speaks, then all hell will break loose for which he will be wholly responsible. The only way out of this predicament and thereby achieve justification, according to de Silentio, is to have his silence authorized; and the only way this can happen is to leave behind the illusions of esthetics and the demands of ethics in order to "become the single individual who as the single individual stands in an absolute relation to the absolute . . ." (Ibid). In an interesting bit of salvific business, de Silentio suggests that in order for Faust to become "the single individual" who stands within the divine paradox, his doubt must be transformed into guilt; and this is accomplished only by recognizing his guilt in doubting, accepting it as sin, and confessing himself as a sinner. However, given what we have already been told, clearly this must be the sort of confession that ethics cannot hear and certainly would not sanction.[23] Nevertheless, on these terms, the single individual does receive "authorization for his silence"; but such "authorization" can only work if ethics is suspended which de Silentio's negative strategy purportedly achieves (ibid.).

Importantly, Johannes contends that this kind of silence need not have the approval of ethics. Summoning the authority of the New Testament, he insists that religious silence is a more profound silence, especially when one considers the intrinsic irony and the subversiveness involved. When, for example, in the Sermon on the Mount, Jesus says: When you fast, anoint your head and wash your face, that your fasting may not be seen by men," we are witnessing not only the reversal of the subjectivity/actuality dualism, but the necessary deception involved (ibid., 111–12). Much like the "powers-that-be" that rejected Christ and the truths he spoke, de Silentio says the following:

> Our age does not to know anything about this; on the whole, it
> does not want to know more about irony than was said by Hegel,
> who, curiously enough, did not understand much about it and
> bore a grudge against it, which our age had good reason not to
> give up, for it has to guard itself against irony, (Ibid., 111)

Along the way toward more serious forms of silence and their implications, juxtaposed explicitly at every turn with the ideal of ethics and its tragic hero, and more implicitly with the religious and its hero Abraham, de

---

23. The healing of doubt, then, and the subsequent salvation of the doubter as the single individual who stands in an unmediated relation to the absolute, connects us with the assumptions that de Silentio laid out at the beginning of the text in the context of his discussion of Descartes. As the opposite of faith (belief), doubt (unbelief) can only be seen as sin. In such an economy it follows that the only way for a doubter to be cured or otherwise saved from his doubt is to become a believer; and only as a true, which is to say, predestined, believer can he be made into an exception to the rule of ethics.

Silentio has sought to demonstrate that there are many instances of silence, that they have different sounds, and that they are not all created equal. But while the reasons for these vary greatly, each instance of silence is freely chosen. Already we have seen examples of *"playful"* silence involving the sorts of secrecy that comedy and light drama might employ.[24] But silences such as these, says Taylor, are not confined to the theatre; indeed, they are integral to the drama of everyday existence.[25] As we might expect, however, ultimately they are concerned with either pleasure for all or some form of explanation that in the end allow secrets to be finally told. And with the revealing of secrets there is release, everything is explained, laughter erupts, and everyone lives happily ever after.

While heroic silence is more serious, de Silentio shows, by way of his three poetic examples, that although there are distinctions to be made here, the results are the same.[26] Whereas the story of the Delphic Bridegroom concerns a complex situation involving choices between silences and the ethical tension intrinsic to them, and the account of Sarah and Tobias elaborates on the important distinction between the demonic and divine silences, both of which lie beyond the reach of ethics, in the reworked legend of Faust we discover that doubt, and the silence that follows, can only be truly overcome by it's ostensible opposite, faith.

Details aside, the larger, more explicit point being made is that while they all suffer the agony of heroic silence, there is always an end in sight: the bridegroom suffers for the sake of his bride; Sarah suffers for the sake of Tobias; and Faust suffers for the sake of the universal. But since the agony of heroic silence ultimately comes to an end, Johannes emphasizes that there is no comparison to be made with the silence required by faith and the ongoing suffering intrinsic to it. Whereas the ethical hero *must* speak, and the esthetic hero *can* speak (but does not), the religious hero of faith *cannot*

24. Taylor, "Sounds of Silence," 172.

25. Ibid.

26. It is important to point out that even within "playful silence" there is a heroic element, especially when one considers de Silentio's second example of the young lovers and the sacrifices made on behalf of each other in the name of parental/familial duty. See *FT*, 85–86. Moreover, though such sacrifices are on behalf of someone else, at least on the surface, the esthetic hero is not without benefit. Indeed, from an esthetic point of view, heroic identity is contingent upon remaining silent. Silent suffering is a trial through which the hero must pass. When this is recognized, it becomes apparent that heroic silence can easily slip into demonic silence. The misery that one silently endures can become a strange source of pleasure and ultimately the basis for one's self-understanding. The very act by which one seeks to spare another person unhappiness brings a form of suffering that is not unsatisfying to the silent individual. Taylor, "Sounds of Silence," 177.

speak; and therein lies the pain and the perpetual agony intrinsic to the paradox of faith (ibid., 112–14).

5.1.4. Agnes and the Merman

The Danish folk legend of Agnes and the Merman, embedded as it is in the thicket of Problema III is on my reading, the critical fulcrum of *Fear and Trembling*. It is here where the rationally charged tensions in the text reach a breaking point and give way to a critique that resists and ultimately destabilizes the binary logic pervasive throughout. In the face of the author's complicity with that logic I will highlight the fact that the exploration of sin in this section interestingly and ironically calls into question his negative strategy and the twin metaphysical pillars that support it.[27] In so doing the text puts its critical finger on the poverty of reason and its futile attempt to mediate the problem of sin.[28]

If, as I contend, that the presenting, textual strategy employed by the author draws its motivation and strength from Greco-Cartesian metaphysics, then de Silentio's attempt in Problema I and II to *keep* faith separate from reason, *posit* the single individual, *suspend* ethics, and ultimately *save* Abraham and his faith, are in fact symptoms of his allegiance to that logic. Designed as it is to negotiate the divine paradox, I maintain, therefore, that the author's negative strategy here conceals even as it reveals his desire to mediate the absolute difference between Abraham (divine) and the merman (demonic).

On my *reading with* the text, de Silentio's negative strategy is a misguided attempt to reach beyond the limits of human finitude, the motives of which are exposed in his exploration of sin below. As the text suggests, concealment becomes demonic when the self crosses the boundary between the human and divine in a bid to know itself, be itself, and establish itself in

27. According to Vanessa Rumble, "[t]he mere mention of sin in *Fear and Trembling* razes the conceptual edifice that was to separate knights of faith from their murderous alter egos, just as sin is understood to thwart both Judge Wilhelm's struggle for autonomy and Constantin's pursuit of repetition. Whether the suggestion arrives in a package from Jutland or in the unmotivated pronouncement, 'upon this concept [sin], . . . [ethics] is shipwrecked,' Kierkegaard's readers soon recognize that the vanity of the intellect and its distinctions, as well as the dizzying vacillations in the identity of his narrators (of pseudonymous and veronymous texts alike), are linked by Kierkegaard to the reality of sin." See Rumble, "Love and Difference," 169.

28. If, as I argued in the last chapter, that de Silentio's "teleological suspension of the ethical" is a rational gesture in the face of the infinite divide between faith and ethics (reason), in the context of Agnes and the merman, and the challenge of sin, the rational gesture is implicit and negatively expressed.

itself, by itself, and for itself. The positing of absolute faith, linked as it is to the implicit promise of direct access to the divine, are therefore symptoms of demonic silence that de Silentio ironically puts his critical finger on. If it is true that the author's dilemma parallels the merman's, then it is fair to suggest that de Silentio's strategy can be seen, at the very least, as an exercise in self deception.[29] But let's back up to the beginning, tease this out, and make a case for it.

5.1.4.1. Deceitful and Demonic Silences

As it presents itself in Problema III, de Silentio's negative strategy is designed to show that the divine silence of faith has *absolutely* nothing to do with any other form of (esthetic) silence, including, as we have seen, playful and heroic silences. Accomplishing this would mean that there is, in fact, a paradox, that Abraham is not lost, and that faith is real and relevant for this life.[30] But thus far, Johannes has yet to the deal explicitly with the most difficult and dangerous forms of silence, namely, deceitful silence and demonic silence, the latter following from the former. Dealt with as they are primarily in the context of Agnes and the merman, these silences are difficult largely because of the complex levels of self deception involved, as the self, in fear, ultimately gives way to its own deceit in a bid to know itself and establish itself in itself. These silences are dangerous, particularly the demonic, because of the implications that they entail for the self as it relates to itself and to the other. As I have already indicated, the story of Agnes and the merman is the hidden fulcrum of the text as it attempts to deal with the fly in the ointment of reason and ethics: sin (along with faith and love). But in negatively doing so, the author backs himself into a corner and thereby subjects his overall strategy to a critique of that strategy.

Although deceitful silence wears a variety of faces, it is most often undertaken in order to glean as much pleasure as possible for the perpetrating individual. "But unlike playful silence," notes Taylor, "deceitful silence involves the enjoyment of only one of those concerned, and this at the expense

29. If scholarly consensus has it that the pseudonymous writings in particular were meant to "deceive readers into the truth," perhaps the text's structure and the concomitant binary logic at work throughout Kierkegaard's *corpus,* are themselves a cunning deception meant to confound the notions of (textual) meaning and truth, and the very idea that they can be attained, or otherwise contained, via Kierkegaard's proper name, or any other principle of authority.

30. Since for de Silentio the poet, Abraham is a hero, worthy of admiration, it is not surprising that de Silentio the dialectician finds a way to explain and ultimately justify that admiration.

of the other."[31] Taylor elaborates: "Despite its various forms, deceitful silence usually springs from selfish sources and issues in the violation of other persons . . . But reflective silence can fall to still greater depths."[32] In the story of Agnes and the merman we see early on, how and why, if left unchecked, deceitful silence can slip all too insidiously toward demonic silence.

As it was in the earlier accounts of the three other poetic personages, de Silentio needs only the skeletal structure of the original story to get his sketch of the demonic—his primary focus—underway. In de Silentio's words:

> The merman is a seducer who rises up from his hidden chasm
> and in wild lust seizes and breaks the innocent flower standing
> on the seashore in all her loveliness and with her head thought-
> fully inclined to the soughing of the sea. (*FT*, 94)

Not surprisingly, Johannes deviates from the standard version of the story and spins it to serve his own strategic purposes. In fact, before he is finished, he will propose three variations, two of which he employs in the service of each other.

In the first variation, Johannes proposes a reversal of sorts. In sum, he tells the story of a merman who is himself seduced by the presence and "power of innocence" (ibid.). Whereas Agnes of the original version is seized, taken against her will, and ultimately crushed by the merman, in de Silentio's re-telling she willingly, and in absolute trust, gives herself to him, a posture that emphasizes her innocence and makes the merman's deceit easier and more obvious. Thus, we read that the merman, who *by nature,* is a seducer, calls to Agnes from the hidden depths, and through his deceptive "wheedling words" elicits that which lies hidden within her. As a result, Agnes submits to the merman, and all is in place as he takes her in his arms and prepares to plunge into the sea with his prize. But at that very moment Agnes glances up at the merman one last time. She does so "not fearfully, not despairingly, not proud of her good luck, not intoxicated with desire, but in *absolute* faith and in *absolute* humility . . . and with this look she entrusts her whole destiny to him in *absolute* confidence" (ibid.; emphasis added). At that point the dramatic happens, something changes fundamentally. In a way that pictures the merman's loss of power, the wild, violent, and turbulent sea suddenly becomes still; "nature's passion, which

---

31. Ibid., 173–74.

32. Ibid., 174. As we noted above, Taylor here distinguishes between reflective silence and pre-reflective, or immediate silence. As I have pointed out, the two seducers, Johannes (the Seducer) and Don Juan, represent the two poles of the aesthetic stage (ibid., 171–74).

is the merman's strength, forsakes him, and there is a deadly calm . . . Then the merman breaks down" (ibid.).

Confronted by *absolute* innocence and the purity of *absolute* love, the merman's power is broken. Consequently, he cannot carry out his initial plan of seduction and destruction. Succumbing as he does to deceitfulness, the merman takes Agnes home explaining "that he only wanted to show her how beautiful the sea is when it is calm, and Agnes believes him" (ibid.). Thus, having kept his true intention hidden from her the merman returns home alone. And as the sea gives way to it's original turbulence the merman's despair grows equally turbulent, and even more so, since not only did the merman love Agnes with a multiplicity of passions, but also, in his anguished concealment, he now possesses a guilt that he did not have before, that is, his original intention to seduce Agnes.

In the next main variation de Silentio will add an important, indeed, pivotal dimension to the merman's profile. As a quick aside, however, Johannes goes on to suggest that the story could be treated quite differently. Perhaps preparing the way for the one to come—this second, side version emphasizes that the merman can only respond in one of two ways—de Silentio describes a merman who "is reluctant to seduce Agnes" (ibid., 95). Such a merman, says de Silentio, "is no longer a merman . . . he is a poor miserable merman who for some time now has sat down there at the bottom of the sea and grieved" (ibid.). But since the merman knows "that he can be saved by the love of an innocent girl" and since he is taken by the girl's loveliness and "her quiet self engagement," he "takes courage, approaches Agnes, wins her love, and hopes for her salvation" (ibid.). But the Agnes in this rendering is no passive wallflower. On the contrary her own "internal storm" matches the turbulence of the sea that rages on ever more violently.

> She wants to be off and away, to storm wildly out into the infinite with the merman, whom she loves—so she enflames the merman. She distained his humility and now his pride awakens. And the sea roars and the waves froth, and the merman locks Agnes in his embrace and plunges into the abyss with her. Never had he been so wild, never so full of lust, because in this girl he had hoped for his salvation. (Ibid.)

If, as a mere merman, he can only seduce and destroy, Johannes proposes, in a third version, to give him "a human consciousness" in order to fill out his character with a depth, complexity, and mystery that only human freedom entails (ibid., 96). Now, says de Silentio, there is nothing stopping him from becoming "a hero" in the truest, most ethical sense; nothing is standing in his way from doing the *right* thing. Other than the addition of human consciousness, the details of the story remain the same as the first retelling: the seducer, confronted with innocence and awakened by the purity of love, submits to their power. But this new human dimension changes everything, and "immediately two forces struggle over him: (1) repentance, [and], (2) Agnes and repentance" (ibid.). If the former holds sway, de Silentio tells us, the merman remains concealed or closed; if the latter has its way, he is revealed or disclosed. In other words, in the context of de Silentio's larger concerns, "repentance alone" entails—according to ethics—the easy way, the (hidden) path of least resistance that, as a self-serving gesture, only esthetics would endorse. "Agnes *and* repentance," however, necessarily entails the hard way of ethics that few are able to follow. Whereas the concealed is enclosed in aesthetic silence, the revealed is disclosed in the rational speech of ethics.

5.1.4.2. *Demonic Enclosure and Heroic Disclosure*

The notion of (1) "repentance alone" here proves to be crucial for what follows, involving as it does two possible directions that the merman can take. Concealing from Agnes what the merman repents of is important because here we witness deceitful silence being pushed further inward toward what de Silentio calls demonic silence. But even as the merman attempts to soothe his conscience in the cathartic waters of the former, having been confronted by innocence and apprehended by love, a more dangerous silence crouches at the door of freedom as he now wrestles not only with the *loss* and *guilt* associated with his original intention to seduce and destroy Agnes, but also with *vulnerability* and *fear* in the face of his exposure. And in his profound despair, the demonic enters the scene and explains that anything he suffers is well deserved and "that this is indeed his punishment, and the more it torments him the better" (ibid.). Should the merman fully succumb to the temptation to indulge the demonic side of repentance ("alone"), what would it look like, and how is it significant as it connects with the text's critical current?[33]

Human consciousness, which entails human freedom and the responsibilities intrinsic to it, allows for the possibility of repentance. No longer

---

33. In terms of deceitful silence, seized with horror and confronted by the guilt at his capacity for violence against the innocent, the merman, as we have seen, "breaks down" (*FT*, 94). But instead of opening up to Agnes and confessing his original intention, the merman ushers her home and "explains that he only wanted to show her how beautiful the sea is when it is calm, and Agnes believes him" (ibid.). It is important to note that while the merman is depicted as being on the cusp of sin, the text nowhere indicates that he fully succumbs to the demonic.

is the merman simply a one-dimensional creature destined to seduce and destroy; the introduction of consciousness awakens him to the possibilities of other ways of being-in-the-world, as it were, namely, to the possibility of loving and being loved.[34] But having been apprehended by love and innocence he is simultaneously confronted with, and appalled by, his former self and his capacity for violence and the evil of sin. And it is precisely this awareness, made possible by reflection, as well as the experience of suffering occasioned by his corruption, that paves the way for demonic silence and the tug-of-war within. If the merman chooses to speak openly and frankly, there is of course the possibility that Agnes will forgive (save) him. But in the face of mere possibility and the felt risk of exposure, the temptation, as we have already seen, is to hold back and remain enclosed in concealment and self-protection. To be sure, the demonic voice is quick to remind him that he must pay for his sins, and that real salvation awaits him through the greater suffering of silence and concealment. Strange and paradoxical though it may appear, observes Taylor, the misery that silence generates and perpetuates, much like the draw of addiction, "can become attractive, and suffering one's *raison d' être*."[35] But even if the merman chooses silence, his relation to the suffering that it entails is strangely divided. "On the one hand," says Taylor,

> he is *repelled* by it and wants nothing more than to be free of it, while on the other hand, he is *attracted* to it and refuses to part with it. The attachment to one's own corruption and suffering that leads a person to guard silence and turn his back on the possibility of forgiveness, is what *Kierkegaard* means by the demonic.[36]

If the merman surrenders to demonic silence ("repentance, alone"), it is perhaps the most tortuous path to traverse, one on which he will "attempt to save Agnes just as in a sense one can save a person with the aid of evil" (ibid.).

Convinced as he is that Agnes loves him, the merman's demonically inspired plan would be to "tear this love away from Agnes," in order to 'save'

---

34. The introduction here of consciousness and the awakening of the self to the responsibility of love, for love, in the context of love, can be fruitfully and critically compared to Derrida's discussion of the "genesis of responsibility" that, along with "nonresponsibility," "belongs to a space that does not yet resound with the injunction to *respond,* a space in which one does not yet hear the call to . . . respond to the other and answer for oneself before the other" (*GD,* 5). At issue is the context for the condition of possibility for hearing and responding to the other.

35. Ibid., 174–75.

36. Ibid., 175. Emphasis added.

her (from himself) (ibid.). He would achieve this by violently pushing her love away from him, in effect, treating her appallingly. Since "a frank confession" would not likely inspire in her sufficient contempt toward him, the merman "will endeavor to incite all the dark passions in her, to belittle her, to ridicule her, to make her love ludicrous, and, if possible, to arouse her pride" (ibid.).[37] Pivotal to this posture is the extreme anguish and torture the merman is willing, nay hoping, to suffer by way of repentance alone, since, in essence, it promises salvation through extreme purgation.[38] But while his torment appears self-sacrificial, directed as it is towards Agnes and her own good, nothing could be further from the truth.

By way of comparison, de Silentio then considers the delusion and self-deception involved in demonic silence, explaining that it has an analogous but ultimately misleading, indeed antithetical, relationship to the divine silence of Abraham. "The demonic has the same quality as the divine, namely that the single individual is able to enter into an absolute relation to it" (ibid., 97). What then is the connection between the merman's deception towards Agnes and the single individual who enters into an absolute relation to the absolute; and in what sense is the demonic analogous to the divine? The short answer is that both the merman (demonic) and Abraham (divine) sacrifice the beloved, and both do so by transgressing the ethical; in doing so, both remain silent. Harking back to Taylor's description of the demonic, the longer answer seems to be that in turning his back on love, the merman would go beyond mere self-deception, and beyond unethical behavior. In other words, this would *not* be an example of aiming at the ethical mark and missing. The issue here is the conscious *will* in the service of itself at the mercy of it's owns fears and self serving desires. In this case, the merman would *choose* silence, *refuse* to part with it, and ultimately *turn* his back on forgiveness and the possibility of love.[39] A posture such as this, suggests John Lippitt,

> demonstrates a *self-absorbed embrace* of his (demonic) hiddenness. In this respect . . . the merman might appear to resemble Abraham, whose God-relationship is also hidden from view.

37. While it may be true that Kierkegaard adopted a similar posture as it relates to his broken engagement with Regine Olsen, any commentary that attempts to link such biographical details with the text of *Fear and Trembling* as a hermeneutical hint to the text's true meaning and significance is, on my reading, misguided. See the first section of the Introduction (Beginnings) where, following Hale's lead, I discuss Authorship, Authority, and Kierkegaardian Commentary.

38. To be sure, the one who is given over to the demonic is *fully* invested in the belief that his suffering is on behalf of the other.

39. Ibid.

> But this resemblance is only superficial, 'misleading': precisely
> because the merman's hiddenness is 'demonic' [self-focused]
> rather than 'divine' [other focused]. And whereas the former is
> entirely self-absorbed, the latter is premised on a relationship to
> another: God.[40]

In the merman's mind, then, the torment he suffers is tangible proof that
self-enclosure is justified since he has paid dearly for it (ibid.).

Unlike Abraham, however, the merman *can* speak which means that he
is poised to become not merely a tragic hero but "a grandiose hero" (ibid.).[41]
Much like the young lad who falls in love with the princess (Preliminary
Expectoration), a relation that "cannot possibly be realized," the merman
will have the courage to sacrifice the real on the altar of ideal (ibid., 41–45);
"he will have the courage, humanly speaking, to crush Agnes" (ibid., 97).
At this juncture, says de Silentio, the merman "stands at a dialectical apex"
(ibid., 98). If he resists demonic temptation, one other possibility remains,
connected as it is to the hiddenness of "repentance alone"—that being the
"counterparadox" (ibid.). In this way, the merman holds himself back and
remains hidden but does not depend on himself or his own shrewdness,
mired as it is in self-deception. While "he does not as the single individual
enter into an absolute relation to the demonic . . . he finds peace of mind in
the counterparadox that the divine will save Agnes" (ibid.). For de Silentio,
this is essentially a monastic movement whereby the merman would, in effect, retreat to the monastery.

(2) "Agnes and repentance" is the second of two possibilities that
struggle for primacy as a result of the emergence of human consciousness
(ibid., 96). This possibility is as complex as is it important since it involves
disclosure or revelation as the main contrast to hiddenness ("repentance
alone")—linked as it is to the contrast between faith/sin and reason/ethics.
As such, it involves being "saved by Agnes" and disclosed through marriage—the ethical (ibid., 98). While this possibility entails taking "refuge
in the paradox" (ibid.), something is not quite right here. According to de
Silentio, "when the single individual by his guilt has come outside [is separated from] the universal, he can return only by virtue of having come as the
single individual into an absolute relation to the absolute" (ibid.).[42] But, à la
Hegel, if the single individual is always already guilty by virtue of his

40. Lippitt, *Kierkegaard*, 122; emphasis added.

41. In keeping with Johannes's economy of opposites, whereas the merman *can*
speak and Abraham *cannot* speak.

42. On my reading, what precisely constitutes being lost and how salvation (mediation) is achieved is a primary issue as it connects with de Silentio's discussion of sin in
Problema III.

singularity (ibid., 54–55, 353 n33), and is therefore absolutely separate from the universal, his only hope of salvation is to become a Knight of Faith as one who has perfectly fulfilled the law.[43] In other words, the single individual can return to the universal only if an absolute relationship with the absolute is achieved. But by insisting that the merman "must . . . take refuge in the [divine] paradox," it would appear that de Silentio has painted himself into a corner because he has prescribed the *impossible*. On his own terms, the movement of faith can only be made by the Knight of Faith, and this is only *possible* by the likes of Abraham, since he was chosen by God (ibid., 99).[44]

The significance of this dilemma, followed as it is by enigmatic comments about sin, dropped into the text, cannot be understated. Connected as it is to the impossible dilemma facing the individual, the emergence of sin highlights problems and contradictions involving ethics, one of which demands perfect adherence to an ethical standard from an imperfect individual who is inherently incapable of meeting that standard. This problem exposes both the inadequacy of ethics and its pretense, that is, to the extent that it functions as end in itself.[45] But not only is the ethical incapable of rescuing the individual, it condemns him to perpetual guilt, all the while dangling the carrot of "salvation" just beyond his reach. If ethics can only perpetuate guilt and foster futility, and if it is finite, and therefore *not* the universal, what does this mean for ethics and how are we to think about it

43. On de Silentio's own terms, this is *impossible*. But for Abraham, as the Knight of Faith, this is possible because he was *chosen* by God to be the Father and exemplar of faith.

44. In her fine contribution to recent scholarship, Clare Carlisle recognizes that de Silentio has painted himself into a corner. In other words, if the individual (the merman, and the rest of humanity) is in sin, and therefore *necessarily* outside of ethics, he cannot return to the ethical by way of repentance (as a movement of resignation), since this is achieved through self-effort. See Carlisle, *Kierkegaard's* Fear and Trembling, 151. Carlisle also recognizes that "Johannes de Silentio does not provide a *direct* answer to this question" (ibid.; emphasis added). Although her attempt to "construct one" is laudable enough, which suggests that there is an *indirect* answer—based as it is on construing the merman's "own act of disclosure" as a venture of faith (ibid.)—it stays neither with the inherent difficulty of and tension in the text, nor with the hermeneutical implications they point to. As we will see, while de Silentio provides neither a direct nor indirect, positive answer to the problem of sin, he does provide a negative one.

45. "The ethical is the universal," observes de Silentio, "and as such it is also the divine" (*FT*, 68). "As soon as the single individual asserts himself in his singularity before the universal, he sins, and only by acknowledging this can he be reconciled again with the universal . . . If this is the highest that can be said of man and his existence, then the ethical is of the same nature as a person's eternal salvation . . ." (ibid., 54). In this way, de Silentio interestingly and rightly highlights the functionally and inescapably religious character of the ethical universal.

in relation to the individual and to sin? While exposing ethics to the fact of sin makes it quake,[46] what comes to the fore is the plight of the individual, including the merman, and humanity itself. If sin is the fly in the ointment of ethics that exposes its finitude and pretentious posturing as the universal, where can the individual turn in his need for forgiveness, acceptance, and ethical standing? But even as de Silentio draws on the negative logic that he has employed throughout *Fear and Trembling* (particularly in Problema I and II) to address this challenge, we find that when it comes to the problem of sin in Problema III, that logic is brought up short and its own linkage to and complicity with ethics is highlighted.

5.1.4.3. *The Problem of Sin and the Limits of de Silentio's Logic*

De Silentio knows enough to realize that sin is a serious problem that needs to be addressed. But as we will see with greater clarity, his own logic is inadequate to the task. In fact, in the end, his overall negative strategy is brought face to face with its own insufficiency, and more. But let's back up a little and follow that logic to its conclusion where it slowly grinds to a halt even as he attempts to follow through with it.

Because Johannes has all along trafficked in "immediate categories" he has been able to side-step the issue of sin as it relates to Abraham, which, together with faith, constitute a "later immediacy," which is to say, the religious (*FT*, 98). But since the emergence of human consciousness is the condition of possibility for both sin and repentance from sin, de Silentio must find a way to deal with it not only dialectically (P.I.–II.) but existentially (P.III.), in the context of the relationship between Agnes and the merman. Thus, based on previous observations and assumptions (ibid., 54, 68), de Silentio concludes that "[a]n ethics that ignores sin is a completely futile discipline, but if it affirms sin, then it has *eo ipso* exceeded itself" (ibid., 98–99). In other words, as a self-contained sphere, ethics is blind to the other and therefore cannot, indeed, will not, make room for faith, sin, or the plight of the individual.[47] If ethics acknowledges sin, however, it would become more than itself, which presumably means that it would include and somehow be able to address faith, sin and the individual.

---

46. In this way, de Silentio follows the logic he employed in Problema I and II by which ethics was relativized in the face of absolute duty to God. But here, the emergence of sin, which along with faith is a "later immediacy" (ibid., 98), poses a greater challenge as Johannes moves from theoretical to the existential/relational problematics in Problema III.

47. Interestingly, and ironically, ethics, as a self-contained sphere that refuses to include the other (of faith and sin), fits de Silentio's description of the demoniac.

In the same way then that de Silentio's "teleological suspension of the ethical" was a remedial attempt to make room for Abraham and his faith, he wants to do something similar here. But dealing with Abraham (faith) and ethics (reason) in Problema I and II by way of "immediate categories" is one thing, dealing with sin (in Problema III), however, is an altogether different challenge, at least on the terms de Silentio has set for himself (ibid., 98) "As soon as sin emerges," he says, "ethics founders precisely on repentance; for repentance is the highest ethical expression, but precisely as such it is the deepest ethical self-contradiction" (ibid.). As we have already seen, for Johannes, repentance represents the pinnacle of human achievement, and as such it can be closely aligned with ethics and its demand for public performance. But even if the individual/merman repents of every wrongdoing, and thereby reaches for the highest ethical expression, he is destined to always fall short of the mark by virtue of his particularity, that is, in relation to the universal. The contradiction that ethics is a part of here lies in the fact that repentance is fundamentally a religious gesture that highlights one's profound need in the face of profound lack, which is to say, lack of ability (or even desire) to do the right ethical/moral thing.[48] While ethics is in the business of conditioned and rationally calculated responses to ethical/legal transgressions, it knows nothing of unconditional forgiveness that follows from the unmerited favor of grace; and as the natural response of love, the latter is province of the religious. But the sharp line of distinction between ethics and the religious is part of the problem as de Silentio attempts to bring the former into proximity with the latter, even as he works to maintain that distinction.

But to be clear, sin, for de Silentio, is not an instance of aiming at the ethical mark and missing the target. We remember from both Taylor and Lippitt, that sin is something far deeper, involving as it does an "attachment to one's own corruption and suffering that leads a person to guard silence and turn his back on the possibility of forgiveness," a posture that displays a wilful, "self-absorbed embrace" of demonic hiddenness (sin). So even if ethics was able to grant temporary reparation for wrongdoing, it is ill-equipped to address the radical character of sin. While de Silentio's attempt to bring the religious to bear on ethics is important, ironically enough, it falls short of the mark because his logic stays squarely within the ethical. More on that in a moment. Nevertheless, Johannes's negative logic is meant as a remedial exercise in absolute contrasts that juxtaposes the patriarch (divinity) and

48. See Romans 7 where the Apostle Paul, in the context of a discussion of the law, sin, and grace, says: "For the good that I would, I do not, but the evil which I would not, that I do . . . O wretched man that I am, who shall deliver me from the body of this death?" (Romans 7:19, 24, KJV).

the merman (humanity).[49] But as the author nears the end of his treatment of Agnes and the merman, both de Silentio and the merman himself are caught in a rational paradox with no exit other than the rational itself, albeit negatively construed.[50] Given the logic that has come full circle, Johannes considers what options the merman has as he comes to the end of his own understanding on the matter. "As long as I move around in these spheres," he says, "everything is easy, but *nothing* of what has been said here explains Abraham, for Abraham did not become the single individual by way of sin—on the contrary, he was a righteous man, God's chosen one" (ibid., 99).

But by emphasizing that the patriarch was a sinless exemplar of faith chosen by God, Johannes once again draws a thick theological line of demarcation between Providence (divine/faith) and free-will (human/reason). Of course this all but confirms the textual fact that the merman (and the rest of humanity itself) can do nothing to save himself from sin, since he/we are "outside the universal" (ibid., 98). Theologically speaking, birthed as we are in Original sin, humanity is inherently sinful and therefore destined to sin with no hope of salvation, unless chosen by God. As de Silentio goes on to emphasize, unless the single individual is chosen or otherwise "brought to a position where he is capable of fulfilling the universal," there is no comparison to Abraham whatsoever, at which point, "the paradox repeats itself" (ibid., 99). And this is humanly impossible, otherwise the author's entire exercise in absolute contrasts is pointless. True to his logic, de Silentio says that he is able to grasp and understand the movements of resignation and repentance, but the movement of Abrahamic faith is another matter altogether. Of course this means that the paradox *must* repeat itself, otherwise the merman/humanity would be able to entertain the idea "of wishing to realize the universal" (Ibid). In these terms, says Johannes, if the merman remains self-enclosed, or hidden, "he becomes a demoniac and as such is destroyed . . . If he becomes disclosed, if he lets himself be saved by Agnes, then he is the greatest human being I can imagine . . ." (ibid.).[51] We are not surprised then when de Silentio summarizes his and the merman's dilemma as a paradox.

49. We remember that the whole point of the exercise here in Problema III "is to have esthetic hiddenness and the paradox appear in their absolute dissimilarity" (ibid., 85). In other words, de Silentio does not want any confusion between the absolute (religious) silence of Abraham and, in this case, the absolute (esthetic) silence of the merman. Consistent as it is with the absolute terms of the text, Abraham and the merman are absolutely dissimilar.

50. I maintain that the paradox of the "double movement" (ibid., 36) is a thoroughly rational gesture. I am not, however, against the need for an existential paradox in matters of faith.

51. That is, ethically speaking.

> The merman, therefore, cannot belong to Agnes without, after having made the infinite movement of repentance, making one movement more: the movement by virtue of the absurd. He can make the movement of repentance under his own power, but he also uses absolutely all his power for it and therefore cannot possibly come back under his own power and grasp actuality again. (Ibid.)

While the merman can make "the infinite movement of repentance," on de Silentio's own terms he cannot make the movement of faith because, with the rest of humanity, he is originally "outside the universal" by virtue of sin (ibid., 99, 98, 106). If the merman cannot make the "double movement" (ibid., 36) of resignation and faith, then along with the patron of ethics, there is no hope of salvation from sin, no hope of entering "into an absolute relation to the absolute," that is, unless he is saved by the divine paradox, which is to say, "chosen" by God (ibid., 98–99). Consistent as it is with the paradox, it would appear that de Silentio has nowhere to go other than the house of ethics.

5.1.4.4 Complicity and Critique

In keeping with both Derrida's critique of "Kierkegaard" in the latter part of chapter 2 (2.2.), and my argument at the end of chapter 4, de Silentio's attempt to *keep* faith separate from ethics/reason, *posit* the single individual, *suspend* ethics (in the name of absolute duty to God), and thereby *save* Abraham and his faith, effectively reduces the religious to the ethical and faith to "absurdity" or irrationalism. While de Silentio's attempt to bring the religious to bear on ethics is important, ironically, it falls short of the mark. This is because, other than "an absolute relation to the absolute" made possible by the absolute, there is absolutely no humanly possible way to access faith or the religious. This means, à la Derrida, "that ethics is also the order of and respect for absolute singularity, and not only that of the generality or of the repetition of the same" (*GD*, 84). In this way, it makes little sense to separate the ethical and religious in the stark manner that de Silentio does since there is no *actual* way to access the latter.

According to the dictates of the author's negative logic, in the face of the infinite chasm that necessarily exists between Abraham (divine) and the merman (demonic), all that the individual/merman can do, indeed, the very least that he can do, is to give up everything by way of repentance and resignation. Like the patron of ethics, however, the single individual/merman is destined to fall forever short of the mark. But although de Silentio insists that the movement of resignation is not to be confused with faith, the tension it generates is a necessary prerequisite for faith, to the extent "that anyone who has not made this movement does not have faith . . ." (*FT*, 46). In light of my argument, what might this mean? If the author's logic is unavoidably tied to the language of ethics, on my reading, he cannot avoid mediation, albeit of the negative variety. While negative mediation is the flipside of positive mediation, and takes place "by virtue of the absurd," "all mediation," says de Silentio, even if it seeks to achieve unmediated mediation, "takes place only by virtue of the universal" (ibid., 56).

If, as I am suggesting, that de Silentio's efforts, directed as they are toward highlighting the infinite chasm between Abraham (divine) and the merman (demonic), involve remediation in the form of negative mediation it exposes the author as the (ir)rationalist that he is. In this case, ironically enough, he is subject to his own critique of reason as one who reaches for an understanding of faith on wholly rational terms, that is, by way of negative ascent. And doubly ironic, it is the author's treatment of sin that exposes the gesture itself as sinful. In this way, the text is brought to the end of itself by demonstrating the utter futility, even idolatry of every human attempt to pull itself up by the bootstraps, as it were, and affect its own salvation. In the face of futility and frustration, however, the text indicates that a remedy *is* necessary. And while it does not provide any rational answers, definitive solution, or final formula for the problem of sin, there are enough textual hints to suggest that love provides the condition of possibility for forgiveness from sin.[52] As *Fear and Trembling* indicates throughout, without love as the condition for both awakening to and receiving the gift of love's responsibility, we are truly lost. If, in the face of sin, ethics demands perfect obedience (which cannot be achieved), and if the religious requires the "double-movement" of faith (which cannot be made), love invites forgiveness (which is accomplished for us, unconditionally). This suggests that love, received by grace through faith, is the mediating link between the divine (Abraham) and the demonic (merman/humanity).

52. Although one might be tempted to draw on the personage of Agnes as a point of textual critique, and thereby employ her as a paradigm of Christian love that transcends the dual*isms* of the text, I think it is more fruitful to leave her as the text presents her, that is, as an expression of ethical disclosure (through marriage). On my reading, employing her as a mechanism of critique is to be used by the very terms that de Silentio employs to mediate his negative logic.

5.1.4.5. *Concluding Comments*

> Everyone shall be remembered, but everyone became great in
> proportion to his *expectancy*. One became great by expecting
> the possible, another by expecting the eternal; but he who ex-
> pected the impossible became the greatest of all. (Ibid., 16)

If Silentio's coattails are caught in the divided logic of his own making, there
are enough penetrating hints and textual indications to keep the hot-air bal-
loon of rationality from flying too high. Even if notions such as "the absurd,"
and "the impossible" are too closely aligned with the stabilizing impulse of
rationality, the entire project of *Fear and Trembling* works to destabilize any
system (including its own) that would claim unfettered access to the truth.
Apart from the critical notion of sin, the author's use of irony, comedy, and
the excess, even profligacy intrinsic to them, for example, keep things on the
move, highlighting as they do the absurdity of faith in reason. In fact, embedded in a later journal entry, Kierkegaard says that the absurd is a sign of
excess, "a category that can exercise a restraining influence."[53] Importantly,
he goes on to say that, as a believer, "neither faith nor the content of faith
is absurd . . . [B]ut I understand very well that for the person who does not
believe, faith and the content of faith are absurd . . ."[54] This suggests that
only a rationalist would conclude that faith is absurd (irrational), since from
the perspective of faith, faith itself is not absurd at all. Moreover, we might
further suggest that, from the perspective of the faith, the very (rational)
conclusion that faith is absurd, is itself absurd.

Toward the end of his lengthy treatment of Agnes and the merman,
de Silentio, ironically enough, lampoons those who believe they have ar-
rived at the truth, when he says that such a feat "is of small concern in our
generation, which believes it has attained the highest, whereas in fact no
generation has been so much at the mercy of the comic as this one" (ibid.,
101). Times such as this, he continues, are at terrible risk of heroizing "the
demon, who ruthlessly puts on a dreadful theatrical piece that makes the
whole generation laugh and forget that it is laughing at itself" (ibid.).

After Johannes's treatment of the Tobit narrative, and the Legend of
Faust, both of which we looked at earlier, and before his final consideration
of Abraham, Johannes once again emphasizes the extravagance, and even
irony involved in the passion of faith and the silence intrinsic to it. Even the
New Testament, he says, recognizes the excess of existence that, along with

---

53. See *Søren Kierkegaard's Journals and Papers*, vol. 6, #6598, 301.

54. Ibid. See Carlisle's treatment of this same entry, in Carlisle, *Kierkegaard's* Fear
and Trembling, 20, 95.

irony itself, highlights the fact "that subjectivity is higher than actuality" (ibid., 111). An excerpt from the Sermon on the Mount, argues de Silentio, underscores the incommensurability between the two: "When you fast, anoint your head and wash your face, that your fasting may not be seen by men" (ibid.). A posture such as this might even be considered a righteous deception, which is to say, "that it has a right to deceive" (ibid., 112). For de Silentio, like Descartes before him, the point is that 'deceptiveness' is woven into the fabric of experience which is why faith lies beyond the pale of existence where it is difficult, nay, impossible to attain. And it is precisely the impossible certainty of faith, and the uncertainty of existence, that de Silentio's generation "does not want to know anything about . . ." (ibid., 111).

5.1.5. The Return to Abraham

The long, circuitous, and negative route that de Silentio has taken into esthetic territory (bordering on ethics) finally comes full circle back directly to the figure of Abraham, his faith, and the challenge they pose for both esthetics and ethics. If esthetics requires *either* hiddenness *or* disclosure, depending on what provides maximum pleasure for the esthete, if ethics necessitates disclosure, and if faith demands absolute concealment, the question Johannes has been entertaining is this: in the face of what Abraham cannot rationally justify, how do we know that his actions are not simply another example of, or a reversion to the silence of esthetics? The purpose of de Silentio's lengthy excursus has been to show that what Abraham did has *nothing whatsoever* to do with esthetics; and he does this by juxtaposing the patriarch's silence with superficially similar instances of esthetic silences. We remember that the author's reason for taking this negative route was "to pursue hiddenness through esthetics and ethics, for the point is to have esthetic hiddenness and the paradox [of religious silence] appear in their *absolute* dissimilarity" (*FT*, 85; emphasis added). This "absolute dissimilarity," therefore, involves the pivotal and *necessary* silence of faith, and one might say the *accidental* silence of esthetics.

As we have seen, such distinctions are the necessary ingredients in the author's overall strategy in order to make things more difficult and thereby save Abraham and his faith from easy accessibility, which is to say, mediation by reason. Johannes reminds the reader that the finer point of his excursus was "to make that subject an obstacle, not as if Abraham could thereby become more comprehensible, but in order that the incomprehensibility could become more salient, for, as I said before, I cannot understand Abraham—I

can only admire him" (ibid., 112).[55] Thus, in keeping with the author's negative strategy throughout, the above stories and personages were employed
"in order that in their moment of deviation they could, as it were, indicate
the boundary of the unknown territory" (Ibid). This "unknown territory"
of course is the realm of faith, the religious, or the kingdom of silence about
which speaking is impossible because it is absolutely other than the "known
territory" of reason. And Abraham is the king of this realm because in his
silence he *cannot* speak. He simply has no choice in matter. On these terms,
demonic silence is antithetical to the patriarch and the divine silence he
inhabits (ibid.). But while demonic silence and divine silence are completely
and absolutely separate from each other, according to the author's scheme
of things, they are also, paradoxically, so close that de Silentio goes to great
lengths in order to keep them utterly distinct.

   We remember that esthetics requires silence of the individual if, by
doing so, it might be able to save someone else. But while such a gesture
appears heroic, this alone sufficiently demonstrates that the hero of faith has
nothing whatsoever in common with the hero of esthetics since Abraham's
silence is for no one but himself and God alone. Of course this is an affront
even to esthetics "because it is able to *understand* that I sacrifice myself but
not that I sacrifice someone else for my own sake" (ibid.; emphasis added).
Nevertheless, the esthetic hero is subject to the judgment of ethics because
his silence is not for the sake of the ethical universal, in which case he would
have to speak. Rather, says de Silentio, his silence was for the sake of particularity rooted in "human prescience" which ethics "cannot forgive" since
"human knowing of that sort is only an illusion" (ibid.).

   Unlike the esthetic hero who is driven by his own particularity, the
hero of ethics is compelled by the universal; and because everything he has
and is belongs to the universal, because his every motive and emotion are
in the open, "he is the beloved son of ethics" (ibid., 113). On these terms,
Abraham, as the hero of faith, is an offense to both aesthetics and ethics, and
necessarily so. As such, faith necessitates an altogether separate category:
the religious. If then we are to take Abraham and his faith seriously, once
again we are in the presence of the paradox, in which case "[e]ither the
single individual . . . can stand in an absolute relation to the absolute, and
consequently the ethical is not the highest, or Abraham is lost; he is neither
a tragic hero nor an esthetic hero" (ibid.).[56] If one is tempted to think that

55. Yet, as we have seen, by way of his negative dialectic, the author achieves the
very thing he sets out to avoid, that is, mediation by way of reason.

56. Based on the given, dualistic terms of the text, de Silentio's strategy, from the
very outset, is structured in a way that keeps reason separate from faith, which ultimately necessitates the positing of absolute singularity and the suspension of the ethical

the paradox somehow represents the path of least resistance, de Silentio insists that such a person is not a knight of faith, for, as we know, the tension and the resultant difficulty are the necessary means of justification without which the paradox is rendered null and void (ibid.).

So Abraham cannot speak since he cannot avail himself to the public resources of language that ethics extends to him in order that he might be relieved of his distress and anxiety. But even if Abraham did speak, even if he were to speak incessantly day and night but is not understood when he speaks, in what sense is he truly speaking? This is precisely the predicament that the patriarch finds himself in. He can surely utter words, but if he cannot be comprehended, that is, speak in a way that he is understood, then he is not actually speaking. But to speak the language of the universal is to be beholden to and thereby dependent on the universal. "The relief provided by speaking," says de Silentio, "is that it translates me into the universal" (ibid.).

> Now Abraham can describe his love for Isaac in the most beautiful words to be found in any language. But this is not what is on his mind; it is something deeper. That he is going to sacrifice him because it is an ordeal. No one can understand the latter, and thus everyone can only misunderstand the former. (Ibid.)

Once again the issue here is *mediation* or access to the "truth" of what is said. Dialectician that he is here, de Silentio maintains that speaking provides catharsis, an exercise that relieves the individual of his particularity and thereby "translates" him "into the universal" (ibid.). This translation, exchange, or conversion, involves a transformation from one way of *thinking* to another and purportedly reveals the individual as he truly is, thus allowing him to speak, and in turn, understand, the whole truth, and nothing but the truth. In theory, this movement ostensibly saves him from himself and the "sin" of his particularity, allowing the individual to disclose himself to the ethical universal and thereby meet its impossible demands.[57]

---

in the name of absolute duty to God.

57. As I have already alluded, the ability of ethics to follow through on such lofty promises rests on a view of language rooted squarely in Enlightenment assumptions and the binary logic intrinsic to it. But even in the face of de Silentio's *complicity* with these assumptions and the "either/or" demand of ethics that follow, he confesses, out of the other side of his mouth, that not everything is said in the saying, Abraham, of course, being the case in point. Johannes recognizes, however, that in order to maintain this divided position, an exception to the rule of ethics must be made (and along with it, the positing of the single individual). But of course, at best, this relativizes ethics, and at worst completely undermines its purported universal scope. As we have seen, the very possibility of an exception requires the positing of another sphere outside of

But Abraham has no such recourse. Anything he says can and will be used against him in an open court of law; and without a doubt the gavel will fall heavily, and ethical judgment will surely be swift. Although Abraham can and ultimately does speak, as we will see, there is "something deeper" that cannot be expressed and therefore cannot be understood by anyone, not even himself. In language, there is simply no way to comprehend that what Abraham did was an expression of love because such a thing exceeds rational understanding and thereby resists the comfort that ethics affords.[58] As tragic as his situation is, "the beloved son of ethics" knows nothing of Abraham's distress and the ongoing anxiety that he must endure. The tragic hero is one thing, says de Silentio, "he has the consolation that he can weep and lament with Clytemnestra and Iphigenia—and tears and cries are re-lieving . . ." (ibid., 114). The hero of faith, however, is altogether different since there is no catharsis, no relief, only the ongoing torture of "groanings that cannot be uttered" (ibid.).

> Speak he cannot; he speaks no human language. And even if
> he understood all the languages of the world, even if those he

---

and beyond reason, an "unknown territory" (*FT*, 112) of faith that is not only opposite to reason, but necessarily antithetical to it. While de Silentio's desire is to ostensibly restore the difficulty of faith made easy by reason, reflected as it is in his attempt to *question* its reach, and thereby *honor* Abraham (as the father of faith), *save* faith, and *highlight* its relevance for this world, his negative approach and the tension inherent to it reveal a thoroughly rational impulse at work. Indeed, framed negatively in this way, an argument for an exception to ethics begins and ends on rationally divided grounds. Thus, by proposing a means to save Abraham and his faith in a way that escapes ethical judgment, de Silentio repeats the rational way of salvation that he wants to redress, and in so doing he reinscribes faith in the sphere of the same, one that maintains the traditional hierarchy of and necessary tension between reason and faith.

58. As we have seen, that the text of *Fear and Trembling* is for Jack Caputo a red flag "in *Kierkegaard's* project," focusing as it does, approvingly, on Abraham "to proceed [in faith] 'in virtue of the absurd'" with the sacrifice of Isaac, indicates that he attributes de Silentio's argument to Kierkegaard, calling it "not only false but dangerous" (Caputo, *How to Read Kierkegaard*, 51–52; emphasis added). Although Caputo draws on Kierkegaard's "journals and signed writings written before and after 1845," arguing that they "confirm that *Kierkegaard* held the views here expounded by de Silentio" (ibid., 54; emphasis added), his conclusions are not so compelling since the only thing they really confirm is a tension that virtually all of Kierkegaard's writings inhabit and set out to ad-dress, including the unresolved tension between the pseudonymous and signed works. It is almost impossible to imagine that the many voices heard throughout Kierkegaard's corpus are ultimately reducible to his own voice. See *H.KEL*, 1–36. See also Vanessa Rumble, where in the context of her reading of *Works of Love*, she argues that the unre-solved tensions in Kierkegaard's texts are not "restricted to the pseudonymous works" ("Love and Difference," 164). In fact, Rumble contends, "[u]ndermining the authority and coherence of the narrative voice . . . is a tactic common to both pseudonymous and veronymous works" (ibid.).

> loved also understood them, he still could not speak—he speaks
> a divine language, he speaks in tongues. (Ibid.)

For the tragic hero there is always comfort, always relief, always a way out. Not so for Abraham, for divine language cannot be heard by human ears or comprehended by human reason. The torture of silence and the misunderstanding that follows are his constant companions.

Even though de Silentio argues that Abraham cannot speak, he must account for the fact that a few words were spoken in reply to Isaac's query in Genesis 22:7–8.[59] In keeping with the tension filled character of his argument, Johannes emphasizes that even though Abraham did say a few brief words (nay, "one word"), how and why they were spoken were necessary and appropriate (ibid., 115). "First and foremost," says de Silentio, "he does not say anything, and in that form he says what he has to say. His response to Isaac is in the form of irony, for it is always irony when I say something and still do not say anything" (ibid., 118). This is not unlike Socrates whose use of irony was no "game" but "a world power" (ibid., 117). And although even his final words before he died are not directly analogous to Abraham's reply to Isaac, they highlight the responsibility inherent in language and the caution with which one must proceed.

Whereas for Agamemnon, the meaning of life is wholly external, and as such expressed ethically, and for Socrates it is wholly intellectual, Abraham's life is wholly spiritual/religious which is why he remains silent even in his speaking, and why his words are necessary even as silence necessarily inhabits his speech. Although what he utters is shrouded in mystery and is therefore hidden from Isaac, in these few words "we see, as described previously, the double-movement in Abraham's soul" (ibid., 119). And with this we remember the important distinction between *relinquishment* and *resignation*. Johannes argues, in other words, that if Abraham had merely given up Isaac, then his reply would have been untrue and his movement relinquishment, rather than resignation. Of course Abraham knew that God required his son as a sacrifice, and that he was willing to go through with it; and since we know that he was ready and willing to carry it out in that moment, we also know in that same moment of resignation that he simultaneously made the next movement of faith "by virtue of the absurd" (ibid.). This is how we know that Abraham is speaking the truth, "because by virtue

---

59. The biblical text reads as follows: "Isaac spoke up and said to his father Abraham, 'Father?' 'Yes, *my son?*' Abraham replied. 'The fire and wood are here,' Isaac said, 'but where is the lamb for the burnt offering?' Abraham answered, '*God himself will provide the lamb for the burnt offering, my son.*' And the two of them went on together" (Thompson, NIV, 20; emphasis added). Other than his reply to God on two other occasions ("*Here I am*"), these are Abraham's only recorded words in Genesis 22.

of the absurd it is indeed possible that God could do something entirely different. So he does not speak an untruth, but neither does he say anything, for he is speaking in a strange tongue" (ibid.). Once again, in the face of all that has been (un)said, Johannes characteristically confesses that the only way he can understand Abraham is paradoxically, which is to say, negatively, "by virtue of the absurd" (ibid., 119–20).

But if, as we have seen, that it is possible for Johannes the poet to *praise* and *admire* Abraham for what he did (the lyrical); and if it is possible for Johannes the philosopher to *think* about, and perhaps even *understand* the patriarch (the dialectical),[60] Johannes the author finds it impossible to *live* or otherwise *do* as Abraham did (ibid., 48–51 [Preliminary Expectoration or "Interlude"]). This leads to the now familiar refrain: "Thus, either there is a paradox, that the single individual as the single individual stands in an absolute relation to the absolute, or Abraham is lost" (ibid., 120).

5.2. EPILOGUE

De Silentio begins his ending as he began his beginning, that is, with an economic metaphor. "Once when the prices of spices in Holland fell," he says, "the merchants had a few cargoes sunk in the sea in order to jack up the price. This was an excusable, perhaps even necessary, deception" (*FT*, 121). If, on a specific, textual level, this has to do with the deception that Johannes deems necessary in order to drive up the price of faith and in turn make it more difficult, nay, impossible, to afford, on a more general, hermeneutical level, the issue of deception begs the question of the author's own strategy and just how deep the rabbit hole of deception runs here. On the surface of things at least, two things seem clear for de Silentio: (1) in the face of the reduction of faith to reason, the present age is self-deceived about the true value of the former and its relationship to the latter; and (2), something needs to be done about it. The last thing this age needs is to be encouraged in its deception. Has it not already developed deception into a fine art, he asks? (ibid.). Faced with such a challenge, what is necessary is not only an honesty that is not afraid to point out the fact that existence, faith being its highest passion, is an ongoing task of a lifetime, but also a fearlessness that does not paper over the difficulty of life, and the faith required for living it (ibid.).[61]

---

60. In the closing paragraphs, de Silentio all but admits that, at the end of the day, he "can understand Abraham" (*FT*, 119).

61. If my reading holds true, a large part of de Silentio's task is to problematize faith by making it (infinitely) out of reach, something that cannot be reduced to mere

Faith, says de Silentio, as life's highest passion, is therefore "essentially human," something that cannot be taught to the next generation and is not learned from the previous one (ibid.). But if a given age assumes the role that belongs only to the spirit, and as such are privy to the whole truth, they are not only dead wrong but deadly, even demonically deceived. What this generation lacks, suggests Johannes, is "the endearing earnestness belonging to play" (ibid., 122). Since faith is the highest passion, even if one does not come to faith, he is still in faith, in which case he has not gone further than it. So even if one does not come to faith, de Silentio maintains that the passion of life is a lifetime task, inherent to which is faith, whether one acknowledges it or not. If one is sufficiently impassioned by life, says Johannes, if he loves deeply, passionately, and honestly, "his life will not be wasted, even if it is never comparable to those who perceived and grasped the highest" (ibid.). Just as one cannot come to a standstill in life or reach the bottom of love, so too, faith beckons us always forward.[62]

5.3 CONCLUSIONS

But the "urge to go further," the push to finally arrive at a point where one can go no further, the point at which one comes to a complete stop at the truth, "is an old story of the world" says de Silentio (*FT*, 123). In other words, there is nothing new under the philosophical sun. The quest for truth and the accompanying desire to find stasis, a place where we experience freedom from the flux and anxiety of existence, has been with us at least since the time of Heraclitus. In fact, says Johannes, this quest is the veritable hallmark of Greek metaphysical speculation, one that finds Heraclitus arguing the following: "One cannot walk through the same river twice. Heraclitus the obscure had a disciple who did not remain standing there but went further—and added: One cannot even do it once" (ibid.). Thus, adds de Silentio, "the Heraclitean thesis was amended into an Eleatic thesis that denies motion," and yet in the end did the disciple go any further than Heraclitus; did he not in fact go back to where Heraclitus had begun, to what he abandoned in the first place? (ibid.). If de Silentio's concern is to underscore the impossibility of coming to a standstill in existence, and if the philosophical gesture is itself part of existence, we must conclude that it is

intellectual assent.

62. While the text may certainly be read in a way that sees Kierkegaard working through his own tragic love story, I have attempted throughout to avoid any reference to biography so as to keep the focus primarily on questions of hermeneutics and methodology.

impossible to determine precisely where the truth lies. Thus, once again we see that even as the text is complicit with the presenting logic throughout, one that unwittingly promises to still the flux of existence and finally reveal where the truth lies, it is also, paradoxically, critical of that logic.

If Silentio's concluding comments reach back to the beginning of *Fear and Trembling* and meet the reader anew in the Epilogue we note that, in the face of its self-evidence, the economic metaphor employed by Johannes to illustrate his strategic intention "to jack up the price of faith," opens up all manner of concerns and questions. For example, if his point (like the merchants) is to raise the price of faith, he does so artificially. Is this in fact the point, or is this the true value of faith as de Silentio sees it? Pushing the hermeneutical envelope even further, we could say that since *all* pricing is artificial, at least in a fundamental, philosophical sense, the rabbit holes of deception here run deep and labyrinthine, highlighting as they do the finitude of language and the impossibility, even the sin involved in trying to pin the truth of faith down. If then all pricing is artificial, which means that there is no *true* value of faith, no way to define or otherwise confine it, then every attempt to pin it down and put a *definitive* price on it, even one of infinite value, as the author attempts to do here, is an exercise in frustration, futility, and ultimately self deception—if not demonic concealment. As it relates to truth in general and to the truth of faith in particular, it seems clear that the tension filled function of the text brings any and all attempts up short.

6

Conclusions

Where the Truth Lies—The Conflicted Sense
of Fear and Trembling

IN THE BROADEST POSSIBLE sense, I have attempted to show that *Fear and Trembling* is fundamentally about relationships. In a very general but important sense the text is about the relationship between the human and the divine (God), and in a more specific sense between the author and Abraham. As a way to explore those relationships and their connections, the text's arguable focus is on faith and reason, and how that relationship is negotiated. As such, *Fear and Trembling* concerns itself primarily, if implicitly, with the question of *mediation* which de Silentio explores in the context of the biblical story of Abraham and Isaac. But, in truth, the text is less about Abraham and the near sacrifice of Isaac and more about the author's attempt to relate himself as a poet, then as a philosopher, to the patriarch, understood as a paradigm or exemplar of faith. *How,* then, the author accomplishes this, *why,* and to *what* end are questions that bear heavily on more probing questions such as the relationship between pseudonymity and veronymity and how that bears on textual meaning and its relation to the truth. But if truth (à la Constantius) is always on the move, when one considers this in concert with both the conflicting currents at work in *Fear and Trembling*, and its conflicted sense, we are able to see a relational, one might say incarnational, logic at work.

So, far from a blunt reading of *Fear and Trembling* that effectively collapses the distinction between Kierkegaard and his pseudonyms, *reading with* the text takes the reader down a different, less travelled hermeneutical path where differences abound and the quest for the truth of his texts gives way to questions of the conditions of its possibility. Thus, *reading with* the text of *Fear and Trembling*, with its emphasis on the integrity of the pseudonym and other literary devices, highlights a textual strategy that draws the reader into an ironically straight and sophisticated rationalistic discussion about the ostensible antithetical relationship between faith and reason. By dialectically constructing a remedy for that inherently disjunctive relationship in Problema I and II, the capstone of de Silentio's project is all but complete, and on my reading, his complicity with metaphysics is all but confirmed.

But the story does not stop there and neither should we as readers. This means that it behooves us to resist concluding that "Kierkegaard" was either a misguided rationalist or an irrationalist in need of harmonizing help. Indeed, to do so is to miss the integral character of the pseudonym, linked as it is to the richness of a critique of that complicity as it unfolds in Problema III; and it is precisely here where the proverbial rug is pulled out from under speculative philosophy with de Silentio's exploration of sin in the context of his discussion of Agnes and merman. With that exploration, the textual currents carry us to the ends of language, highlighting as it does its finitude. But even more significantly, it brings us up short as it probes the notion of sin and its implications for understanding the issues at hand, particularly as it relates to ethics and its inability to deliver on the lofty, indeed, salvific promises it holds out for its devotees. In so doing, it puts the text of *Fear and Trembling* itself in question and destabilizes its complicity by holding up the mirror of self-critique.

I maintain then that a large part of the text's significance connects with the notion of sin which is explored in Problema III. Indeed, the author's compelling and complex phenomenological treatment of it in the context of the story of Agnes and the merman underscores the impossibility of philosophically sidestepping its significance on the way to the truth. If Evans embraces the theological notion of (Original) sin itself but does not see it as central to the overall significance of *Fear and Trembling*,[1] Derrida eschews the notion altogether, yet, ironically enough, must deal with it in the context of finitude and human desire when it transgresses the boundary between the finite and the infinite in its bid for the truth.[2]

1. Other than the attempt to round out the sharp edges of de Silentio's distinction between faith and reason, Evans essentially agrees with "Kierkegaard's" methodological approach to the issues. But if my reading holds, this means that Evans is subject to the text's critique—since, for all practical purposes, there is no distinction between the pseudonymous voice and the voice of Kierkegaard.

2. See *GD*, especially 3–5.

If, as I have suggested, that the text is explicitly concerned with questions of how the author and Abraham relate, and implicitly, but no less importantly concerned with how the human speaks of the divine, it is ultimately, perhaps fundamentally, concerned with how language and meaning relate to truth in its inherent incompleteness.[3] I have attempted to show that *Fear and Trembling* does not finally answer any of these questions, at least not in any straightforward, rational, or systematic fashion. Indeed, I am suggesting that if the declaration that faith is absurd is a supreme rational gesture, then the text paradoxically and ironically invites us to see that to the extent it seeks to grasp faith on wholly rational terms, reason itself is found to be both absurd and in sin.

If the text nowhere formalizes a logic or a methodology designed to tell us precisely what the truth is and where it is to be found, it is because it frustrates any and all such efforts to do so. In other words, with an eye toward how the text functions, *reading with* the text reaches toward textual meaning without corralling the truth. My reading of *Fear and Trembling,* therefore, highlights this function, the implications of which have everything to do with the hubris of metaphysical philosophy, which, in its misplaced desire to reveal the truth, as it is in itself, oversteps and therefore transgresses the finite boundaries that necessarily limit its reach.

∿

We recall from chapters 1 and 2 that my fundamental concern was to question conventional and contraventional assumptions about *what* the text of *Fear and Trembling* communicates, *how* it communicates, and *why* it communicates in the manner it does, not to mention on *what/whose* authority. In so doing, I argued that *reading with* the text creates a space that allows it to be read differently, thus enabling it to speak differently, that is, in ways that exceed modern, orthodox readings, as well as late modern, unorthodox renderings. While chapter 1 focused its critical attention on Evans's understanding of the relationship between authorship and authority, how it connects with his reading of the pseudonym, and what the hermeneutical implication are, chapter 2 paid close attention to Derrida's treatment of the pseudonym and ultimately how it impacts his reading of the text.

After a close consideration of the relationship between authorship and authority, and its significance for a fair reading of Kierkegaard's texts, in

---

3. While the text of *Fear and Trembling* indicates that truth is never in question, what *is* at issue is the question of mediation or access to the truth. But of course this destabilizes the very notion of truth and our ability to speak of it, at least as something objective, and thus, explainable or otherwise containable through strictly rational means.

chapter 1 I showed that Evans's interpretation pivots on the division of his writings along the lines of authorship. We noted that because such a distinction employs the proper name of Kierkegaard as the veritable bottom line in all matters hermeneutical, it therefore functions as a universal principle of authority that in effect pre-exists the articulation of that principle (to borrow Hale's phrasing). In this way, the name "Kierkegaard" becomes, more or less, a master signifier that papers over the complexities of the pseudonymous texts in general, and the singularity of the pseudonyms in particular. To the extent that such a move draws its strength from the binary logic of metaphysics, I concluded that it narrows the hermeneutical scope of the text rather than opens it. Thus, when we connect Evans' philosophical assumptions to his hermeneutic methodology we better understand *how* Kierkegaard's proper name functions this way, and *why,* as such, it must *necessarily* precede the finite, particular texts that announce it.[4] In the end, my concern is that Evans gives too much credence to metaphysics and the so-called objective, foundational truth that it promises to deliver. To the extent that this focus, which entails a quest for unwavering, metaphysical veracity, eclipses the deeply critical dimensions of the text, I argue that it ironically exposes Evans's reading to the stylus tip of its critique.

In chapter 2 I focused on Jacques Derrida's reading of *Fear and Trembling* in *The Gift of Death.* There I argued that while his approach achieves a kind of openness that eludes Evans, Derrida's own reading, for all its deconstructive virtue, unduly narrows the text for surprisingly similar reasons. I demonstrated that this narrowing is due largely to his treatment of the pseudonym which, at its most basic level, follows in the footsteps of orthodox readings. The very fact that Derrida fails to make a clear, careful, and consistent distinction between the pseudonymous author and the proper name of Kierkegaard, carries with it at least two hermeneutically problematic implications: first, it serves to confuse the relationship between authorship and authority in a way that invariably reduces the pseudonymous voice to Kierkegaard's own; and second, it keeps Derrida from recognizing the significance of the faith inspired, "proto-deconstructive" function of the text.

Having shown that both Evans and Derrida assume that the world of Johannes de Silentio is, for all intents and purposes, Kierkegaard's world, in chapters 3 and 4 I questioned that assumption more thoroughly and suggested that *reading with Fear and Trembling* opens the text in a unique

---

4. For Evans, in the same way that divine commands must ontologically precede human moral obligations (otherwise there is no absolute moral ground) the name "Kierkegaard" must precede the texts that articulate it. This can only mean that the proper name functions as a universal principle of authority by which proper interpretation is secured (otherwise there is no absolute hermeneutical ground). See *E.KEL,* chapter 1.

way, thus allowing it to speak differently. In order to demonstrate this, I emphasized the importance of taking de Silentio strictly at his word as the author of the text which entails bracketing Kierkegaard from the authorial equation. In this way, it leaves the reader to wrestle with the text's tears, cross-currents and ambiguities *without* recourse to the proper name as an organizing, universal principle of authority. This shift in authorial focus then allows the textual differences to stand in their difference thus creating a space where questions can emerge. With an eye toward how the text functions, *reading with* the text reaches toward what the text means without corralling the truth, in other words, without reducing the latter to the former.

With these things in mind, I argued that *Fear and Trembling* is, from the outset, structured dualistically even as the author attempts to resist such structuration and the metaphysical pretensions inherent in it. As such, I made the claim that the text is complicit with metaphysics exemplified in the author's remedy for the ostensible chasm that exists between reason and faith, namely the "teleological suspension of the ethical." Overall, my focus in chapters 3 and 4 was on the first two thirds of *Fear and Trembling* itself, and began with a general summary of each section (up to and including Problema II) meant to highlight the tears, cross-currents and ambiguities at work in the text. Through this lens, the very fact that the text assumes an absolute distinction between the human (reason) and the divine (faith) gives us reason to pause and consider the assumptions involved as we witness de Silentio attempt first to "lyrically" understand Abraham's actions, and then to "dialectically" "perceive the prodigious paradox of faith" that transforms murder into a holy, sacrificial act (*FT*, 53, 30).

After chapter 3, and before chapter 4, we find an "interlude" or "pause" that stands between the "lyrical" and the "dialectical" structure of *Fear and Trembling* where the author begins preparing the ground for the explicitly philosophical section to come. "Dialectical lyricist" that he is here, de Silentio has a few things to say even as he continues wrestling with Abraham's actions in a way that tries to make "poetical philosophical" sense of the paradox of faith. My primary objective, however, was to show that de Silentio's lyrical dialectical creation of such figures as the "Knight of Faith" and the "Knight of Infinite Resignation," connected as they are with later notions such as "Absolute Duty to God" and the "teleological suspension of the ethical," are in fact "complicit" with the dualistic logic of metaphysics that he ironically attempts to overcome in order to make room for faith and thereby save Abraham from the judgment of ethics.

In the final chapter (5) my concern was to draw out the fact that *Fear and Trembling* takes an important, critical turn in the last third of the text— Problema III. If the focus in Problema I and II is on ethics (reason) and its relation to faith, in Problema III the author shifts that focus to esthetics and allows it to guide his inquiry as it leads inexorably to the religious. His ostensible purpose "is to have esthetic hiddenness and the paradox [of religious hiddenness] appear in their absolute dissimilarity" (*FT,* 85). But even as de Silentio's negatively conceived, comparative analysis works, on the one hand, to reinforce the stark categories of the text, on the other hand, his exploration of silence builds as a critique of that starkness as he moves from playful silence to the insidiousness of deceitful silence, and then finally to the danger inherent in demonic silence. After tracing the contours of silence, my primary task was to look closely at the anatomy of demonic concealment in the context of the story of Agnes and the merman, with a view toward showing not only how it functions against the backdrop of *Fear and Trembling,* but what the hermeneutical implications are.

Thus, embedded in the thicket of Problema III, I argue that a strong, critical current is at work, specifically in the story of Agnes and merman. With its focus on the phenomenological structure and function of sin, the story itself gives us reason to pause and reflect. When considered against the larger framework of *Fear and Trembling* my reading suggests that de Silentio's masterstroke ("the teleological suspension of the ethical") is in fact a transgressive gesture. In keeping with the split structure and conflicted sensibility of the text, I emphasized that the overall textual dynamic implicitly undermines its central argument. In other words, on the one (complicit) hand, the presenting, dualistic logic of *Fear and Trembling* assumes that reason and faith inhabit two absolutely separate economies, which means that the former is rational and the latter is irrational (or "absurd"). On the other (critical) hand, because faith, so understood, is construed and therefore judged solely on reason's own strictly rational terms, reason itself can be seen as absurd by virtue of its belief in and reach for totality—a gesture that de Silentio calls demonic concealment. To be sure, in the context of *Fear and Trembling,* the dictates of reason force faith inward (toward silence) making it necessary to suspend the very choices that are constitutive to being human. In this way, by default, the text argues that true faith is far from absurd (irrational) but in fact constitutes a foundational mode of being human. Ironically, the implicit argument here is that unquestioned faith in reason is absurd. In fact, the text suggests that unquestioned faith in reason is not only absurd, it is detrimental, even dangerous to the individual's well being.

In the end, I summarize "The Return to Abraham" and the "Epilogue," and then connect them to the overall significance of *Fear and Trembling.*

EVANS, DERRIDA, AND KIERKEGAARD

By way of summary and conclusion, it is important to reiterate not only the significant differences between my understanding of Evans's and Derrida's reading of *Fear and Trembling*, but the significance of those differences as they relate to my rendering.

As I understand Evans's reading, a central, motivating part of his interpretive strategy involves saving "Kierkegaard" from himself, which is to say, from the sharpness of the metaphysical divide that exists between faith and reason.[5] But the very fact that to interpret Kierkegaard rightly is to employ the proper name as a baseline interpretive principle, at the very least, confines Evans to a predetermined space and thereby narrows his hermeneutical field of vision.

On my reading, this interpretive posture effectively reduces the pseudonymous voice to Kierkegaard's which in turn treats the views and perspectives of the author's as if they were Kierkegaard's own. As we have seen, this pervasive, "common sense" approach, however, forces Kierkegaard to sign his own name to a text that he did not author. But it is precisely this treatment of the text, and the assumptions undergirding it, that compels Evans to rescue "Kierkegaard" from a methodological strategy that smacks *too* much of metaphysics and the sharpness of its absolute distinctions. The very fact that Evans traffics in similar distinctions, however, implicates him in de Silentio's own complicity with metaphysics and thereby hamstrings his ability to see the more critical, deeply religious dimensions of the text. But if my argument holds, and if we assume instead that de Silentio is *not* Kierkegaard and therefore *not* the author of *Fear and Trembling*, then there is no need to save Kierkegaard from his metaphysical machinations. This then frees the reader to allow the text's differences to stand in their difference, enabling us to glimpse the more radical dimensions of the text. Rather than *what* the text means based on the truth of "Kierkegaard's" intentions as a guiding interpretive principle, this hermeneutical refocus redirects our attention to *how* the text functions and *why* without abandoning textual meaning.

If Evans's orthodox rendering of *Fear and Trembling* prevents him from seeing the more critical dimensions of the text, to the extent that Derrida's own reading follows a similar trajectory, he too is prevented from

---

5. That Evans finds it necessary, therefore, to round out the sharp edges of that divide so that faith more easily fits the glove of reason indicates that he fundamentally, though not without qualification, agrees with "Kierkegaard's" project and his strategy for redressing the divide between faith and reason. Ironically enough, Evans' concern to save "Kierkegaard" is quite like de Silentio's attempt to save Abraham.

appreciating its full critical import. Nevertheless, in a manner similar to the effect that Kierkegaard's texts themselves achieve, the fact that Derrida's deconstructive approach reaches for a way of writing that addresses the linguistic space between "Yes" and "No," puts him closer to what is at issue in *Fear and Trembling*.[6] But if Derrida proposes a more strictly philosophical, humanistic way of *"thinking"* that addresses that difference, de Silentio draws on the religious and divine otherness as the source of love, connection, and redemption that calls the self by love, to (the responsibility of) love, for love.

In his exploration of what ails us in *The Gift of Death,* while Derrida readily discusses Jan Patočka's notion of the demonic, it is not insignificant that he philosophically sidesteps the notion of sin that de Silentio links directly to it. Instead, Derrida comes in through the side door of philosophy with a focus on human finitude, proposing, as we have seen, his unique deconstructive remedy. But while de Silentio's approach to the demonic in Problema III is itself deeply philosophical, he extends and radicalizes the idea in the direction of the religious and thereby highlights the connected notion of sin, intrinsic to which is the "self"/"Other" paradox. Briefly rehearsing the similarities between Derrida's and de Silentio's accounts of and approaches to the demonic will allow us to see not only their overlapping sensibilities, but their significant differences, as well. In the end these differences are meant to highlight what I contend is the uniqueness of *Fear and Trembling* and Kierkegaard's unique contribution to late twentieth and early twenty-first century thought, the inherent religiousness of which has not been fully appreciated.

In the opening pages of *The Gift of Death,* Derrida likens Levinas to Patočka who "warns against an experience of the sacred as an enthusiasm or fervor for fusion . . . as a form of demonic rapture that has as its effect, and often as its first intention, the removal of responsibility, the loss of the sense or consciousness of responsibility" (*GD,* 3). A few pages later he says that to speak of authentic religion is to say that it "comes into being the moment that the experience of responsibility extracts itself from that form of secrecy called demonic mystery" (ibid., 5). Then, in linking the demonic to primal desire, Derrida says that "the concept of the *daimon* crosses the boundaries separating the human from the animal and the divine . . ." (ibid.). Interestingly, and ultimately pertinent to our comparative analysis, he goes on to

---

6. Although it lies well beyond the scope of this dissertation my strong sense is that Derrida saw in Kierkegaard's approach to writing and authorship much more than he ever admitted. I would go so far as to suggest that his reading of *Fear and Trembling*, in fact, distracts us from just how much Derrida's own strategy is indebted to Kierkegaard.

discuss the "genesis of responsibility" as the emergence of the self and its relation to the "*gift of death*" (ibid.).[7]

What I want to briefly focus on here as it connects with de Silentio's commentary on Agnes and the Merman, is Derrida's definition or distillation of the "demonic" as that which, rooted in human desire, transgresses the boundary that separates the human from the divine. On my reading, Derrida is talking about a deeply religious gesture that claims *direct* access to, in this case, "the mystery of the sacred" (ibid., 3). In other words, the issue here, for Derrida, involves a boundary breach where concrete religion, for example, claims that, via the secret (revealed), it is privy to the mystery of the sacred, to secret divine knowledge, or to the will of God. What is interesting is that in de Silentio's account of Agnes and the merman, one finds strikingly similar language in the service of similar themes and issues, but with a very different trajectory. With that in mind we will rehearse and reconsider that difference more closely by highlighting the critical contours of that story from the latter half of the last chapter (5).

In his discussion of Agnes and the merman we remember that de Silentio summarizes the original version of the legend by telling of a merman, a seducer by nature, "who rises up from his hidden chasm and in wild lust seizes and breaks the innocent flower standing on the seashore . . ." (*FT*, 94). In de Silentio's retelling, the merman, who in the original account could only seduce and destroy, is endowed with human consciousness. Thus, when confronted with the purity of Agnes' love, the merman is faced with a choice to either *conceal* his guilt at having planned to seduce her, or *reveal* his intention and confess his sin. It is precisely at this tension filled juncture, says de Silentio, where sin insinuates itself and asserts its possibility. According to Johannes, the tension between the merman's desire to conceal or reveal his guilt stems from being awakened *by* the pure love of Agnes *to* the redemption that it promises—not to mention the freedom that it entails. But at the same time it exposes his former, sinful desires. If the merman gives in to the temptation to turn his back on love (NO ["not to be"]), thus concealing himself in inward turmoil generated by guilt and shame; if he listens to the whispering of fear that tells him such suffering is not only punishment well deserved, but indeed salvific in the long run, then the slide

---

7. On my reading, Derrida's "genesis of responsibility" is for Johannes Climacus, the moment of possibility where eternity meets temporality in the form of the "god man." See *Philosophical Fragments*, 23ff. If, for Derrida, "the experience of responsibility extracts itself from" the grip of "demonic mystery," which happens, voilà, which is also to say in a vacuum of absence or neutrality, for de Silentio, that possibility or "genesis" is birthed in love, by love, and for love. See *GD*, 5, and *FT*, Problema III, 94–99.

into sin begins.[8] If the merman repents and turns away from the darkness of concealment toward the light of love (YES ["to be"]), if he lets go of his fear and gives in to the love of Agnes, then he is saved.[9]

But when faced with the perceived greater threat of exposure, shame, and rejection in the face of love's penetrating and revealing light, the temptation is to protect oneself through silence and concealment. And this is precisely what leads one to self-deceptively attach oneself to a promise that one's finite resources can never deliver. In de Silentio's retelling of the merman legend, sin is a willful refusal of love, entailing as it does a self-enclosed embrace of self-ness, on the altar of which the other is sacrificed. Whereas sin deals in fear and is rooted in a self-absorbed relationship with oneself, love gives itself and is rooted in responsibility to the Other. Awakened and brought to life by the redeeming power and promise of love (the "genesis of responsibility" [*GD*, 5]), the emergent, divided self is tempted by fear to turn its back on love, and instead turn toward self-enclosed resources which entail its own promise of salvation. In succumbing to this temptation, the self crosses the boundary between self and other in a bid to mediate the distance. According to the text, to the extent one believes that mediation is thusly achieved, this constitutes sin or demonic concealment.[10]

On my reading, the critique of speculative philosophy in *Fear and Trembling*, as it comes to the fore in Problema III, stands or falls on the notion of sin, not to mention the connected issue of salvation from sin. Indeed, I contend that with its emphasis on the phenomenological structure, psychological deceptiveness, and the theological significance of sin, the story of Agnes and the merman is a pivotal part of a textual strategy that demonstrates the necessity, indeed, "actuality of a non-philosophical site from which philosophy can be criticized."[11] Such a strategy, therefore, is able to destabilize reason at its core and call it to account. If my argument holds that, via the "teleological suspension of the ethical," de Silentio is

8. See *Philosophical Fragments* where Climacus talks about the "procreative love" of "God"/"Teacher"/Savior" that "gives birth to the learner, or, as we have called him, one born again, meaning the transition from 'not to be' to 'to be'" (30).

9. Ibid. In this way, the merman is not saved by self or by ethics, but by the gift of love. Although Agnes is a figure of ethical salvation, she also points to the purity of love that highlights the inadequacy of ethics as means of redemption.

10. But if, for Derrida, encountering the otherness of the other is the condition of possibility for the "genesis of responsibility," one wonders how the subject rises to that responsibility encumbered as it is by sin and the self deception that it entails. On my reading, whereas Derrida's encounter with the other simply provides the condition of responsibility, de Silentio's account of the Merman's awakening to love, provides both its condition and its possibility through love's redeeming power.

11. See Weston, *Kierkegaard and Modern Continental Philosophy*, 9.

complicit with reason, then to the extent that he believes his negative strategy successfully suspends ethics and therefore mediates the space between faith and reason, the author is guilty of transgressing the boundaries between self and Other.

Conflicted, torn asunder, and complicit with metaphysics though he surely is, the author of *Fear and Trembling* recognizes, ironically enough, that our best attempts to "know" the truth and ultimately "do" the truth fall short of the ethical mark in the face of human finitude, brokenness and sin. If it is important, á la Derrida, to face up to our finitude and stare unflinchingly into the abyss of unknowing and death, for de Silentio, this is only the first step toward addressing the significance, the centrality, and inescapability of sin. And according to the text, sin is the fly in the ointment of existence that highlights our deepest needs that cannot be addressed with right philosophical thinking or right ethical action. In fact, the belief in our ability to pull ourselves up by the philosophical bootstraps, mediate the difference between the human and divine, and thereby save ourselves, is precisely what the text calls sin. In the end, such a posture of self-sufficiency only serves to conceal our need and our utter inability to ever bridge that difference. According to de Silentio, then, if we are finite, we are also broken and therefore cut off from ourselves and the other, the remedy for which is the redeeming power of love and our willingness to say, in *fear and trembling*, YES to the Other.

If, as the text of *Fear and Trembling* suggests, that the quest for truth is inextricably linked with the yearn for love and connection, then Kierkegaard might say, with Augustine, that since we were first loved, we trust and believe in order to understand, which is not far from saying that truth lies in the heart of love. If this means that we can never arrive at the truth in all of its fully revealed glory, it can and does show itself as it passes by us, glinting as it does on the frayed edges of existence.[12]

---

12. If God is truth in the fullest sense, the image found in Exodus 33:21–23 is not only beautiful but instructive: "Then the Lord said [to Moses], 'Behold, there is a place by Me, and you shall stand *there* on the rock; and it will come about, while My glory is passing by, that I will put you in the cleft of the rock and cover you with My hand until I have passed by. Then I will take My hand away and you shall see My back, but My face shall not be seen'" (*New American Standard Bible*).

Bibliography

Adorno, Theodor W. *Kierkegaard: Construction of the Aesthetic.* Translated and Edited by R. Hullot-Kentor. Minneapolis: University of Minnesota Press, 1989.

Agacinski, Sylviane. *Aparté: Conceptions and Death in Kierkegaard.* Translated by K. Newmark. Tallahassee: Florida State University Press, 1988.

Anselm, Saint. *Proslogium: Discourse on the Existence of God.* Translated by Sydney Norton Deane. 1903. Reprint, Eugene, OR: Wipf & Stock, 2003.

Augustine, Saint. *The City of God.* Translated by M. Dods. New York: Modern Library, 1950.

————. *Confessions.* Translated by H. Chadwick. Oxford: Oxford University Press, 1991.

Backhouse, Stephen. *Kierkegaard: A Single Life.* Grand Rapids: Zondervan, 2016.

————. *Kierkegaard's Critique of Christian Nationalism.* Oxford: Oxford University Press, 2011.

Bernstein, Richard. *Beyond Objectivism and Relativism.* Philadelphia: University of Pennsylvania Press, 1983.

Bowie, Andrew. *Aesthetics and Subjectivity from Kant to Nietzsche.* Manchester: Manchester University Press, 1990.

Caputo, John D. "Gadamer's Closet Essentialism: A Derridean Critique." In *Dialogue and Deconstruction: The Gadamer-Derrida Encounter*, edited and translated by D. P. Michelfelder and R. E. Palmer, 258–64. SUNY Series in Contemporary Continental Philosophy. Albany: SUNY Press, 1989.

————. *How to Read Kierkegaard.* New York: Norton, 2007.

————. "Introduction: Who Comes after the God of Metaphysics?" In *The Religious*, edited by J. D. Caputo, 1–19. Malden, MA: Blackwell, 2002.

————. *The Prayers and Tears of Jacques Derrida: Religion without Religion.* Indiana Series in the Philosophy of Religion. Bloomington: Indiana University Press, 1997.

————. *Radical Hermeneutics: Repetition, Deconstruction, and the Hermeneutic Project.* Studies in Phenomenology and Existential Philosophy. Bloomington: Indiana University Press, 1987.

————, ed. *The Religious.* Blackwell Readings in Continental Philosophy. Malden, MA: Blackwell, 2002.

————. Review of *After God.* By Mark C. Taylor. *Journal of the American Academy of Religion* 77 (2009) 162–65.

————. Review of *Religion: Cultural Memory in the Present.* Edited by J. Derrida and G. Vattimo. In *Journal of the American Academy of Religion* 68 (2000) 171–74.

Carlisle, Clare. *Kierkegaard's* Fear and Trembling: *A Reader's Guide.* Continuum Reader's Guides. London: Continuum, 2010.

Chestov, Leon. *Kierkegaard et la Philosophie Existentielle: Vox Clamantis in Deserto.* Paris: Vrin, 1972.

Come, Arnold B. *Kierkegaard as Theologian: Recovering Myself.* Montreal: McGill-Queens University Press. 1997.

Connell, George. *To Be One Thing: Personal Unity in Kierkegaard's Thought.* Macon, GA: Mercer University Press. 1985.

Conway, Daniel, ed. *Kierkegaard's* Fear and Trembling: *A Critical Guide.* Cambridge: Cambridge University Press, 2015.

Critchley, Simon, and William R. Schroeder, eds. *A Companion to Continental Philosophy.* Companions to Philosophy 12. Malden, MA: Blackwell, 1998.

Crouter, Richard. "Kierkegaard's not So Hidden Debt to Schleiermacher." *Journal for the History of Modern Theology* 1 (1994) 205–25.

Cudney, Shane R. "'Religion without Religion': Caputo, Violence and Particularity." In *Religion with/out Religion: The Prayers and Tears of John D. Caputo,* edited by J. H. Olthuis, 34–49. New York: Routledge, 2002.

D'Agnostini, Franca. "From a Continental Point of View: The Role of Logic in the Analytic-Continental Divide." *International Journal of Philosophical Studies* 9 (2001) 349–67.

Dallmayr, Fred R. "Hermeneutics and Deconstruction: Gadamer and Derrida in Dialogue." In *Dialogue and Deconstruction: The Gadamer–Derrida Encounter,* edited and translated by D. P. Michelfelder and R. E. Palmer, 75–92. SUNY Series in Continental Philosophy. Albany: SUNY Press, 1989.

de Lacoste, Guillermine. "A Feminist Interpretation of the Leaps in Kierkegaard's *Fear and Trembling.*" *Philosophy Today* 46 (2002) 3–15.

Derrida, Jacques. *Donner la Mort.* In *L'éthique du don, Jacques Derrida et la pensée du don.* Edited by Jean-Michel Rabaté et Michael Wetzel. Paris: Métailié-Transition, 1992.

——. "Faith and Knowledge: The Two Sources of 'Religion' at the Limits of Reason Alone." In *Religion,* edited by J. Derrida and G. Vattimo, 1–78. Stanford: Stanford University Press, 1996.

——. "Foi et Savoir: Les deux sources de la 'religion' aux limites de la simple raison." In *La Religion,* edited by J. Derrida and G. Vatttimo, 9–86. Paris: Seuil, 1996.

——. *The Gift of Death.* Translated by D. Wills. Chicago: University of Chicago Press, 1995.

——. *The Gift of Death.* 2nd ed. and *Literature in Secret.* Translated by D. Wills. Chicago: University of Chicago Press, 1995/2008.

——. *Of Grammatology.* Translated by G. C. Spivak. Baltimore: Johns Hopkins University Press, 1976.

——. *Positions.* Translated by A. Bass. Chicago: University of Chicago Press, 1981.

——. "Structure, Sign and Play in the Discourse of the Human Sciences." In *Writing and Difference,* Translated by A. Bass. Chicago: University of Chicago Press, 1978.

——. "Three Questions to Hans-Georg Gadamer." In *Dialogue and Deconstruction: The Gadamer-Derrida Encounter,* edited and translated by D. P. Michelfelder and R. E. Palmer, 52–54. SUNY Series in Contemporary Continental Philosophy. Albany: State University of New York Press, 1989.

————. *The Truth in Painting.* Translated by G. Bennington and I. McLeod. Chicago: University of Chicago Press, 1987.

Derrida, Jacques, and Maurizio Ferraris. *A Taste for the Secret.* Edited and Translated by G. Donis and D. Webb. Cambridge: Polity, 2001.

Descartes, René. *Meditations on First Philosophy.* Translated by D. A. Cress. Indianapolis: Hackett, 1993.

Donne, John. *Devotions upon Emergent Occasions.* CreateSpace Independent Publishing Platform, 2013.

Dooley, Mark. *The Politics of Exodus: Søren Kierkegaard's Ethics of Responsibility.* Perspectives in Continental Philosophy 20. New York: Fordham University Press, 2001.

Dunning, Stephen N. *Kierkegaard's Dialectic of Inwardness: A Structural Analysis of the Theory of Stages.* Princeton: Princeton University Press, 1985.

Edgar, Matthew. "Deer Park or the Monastery?: Kierkegaard and Hegel on Unhappy Consciousness, Renunciation, and Worldliness." *Philosophy Today* 46 (2002) 284–99.

Evans, C. Stephen. *Kierkegaard's Ethic of Love: Divine Commands and Moral Obligations.* Oxford: Oxford University Press, 2004.

Fenves, Peter D. *"Chatter": Language and History in Kierkegaard.* Meridian. Stanford: Stanford University Press, 1994.

Ferreira, Jamie M. "Faith and the Kierkegaardian Leap." In *The Cambridge Companion to Kierkegaard,* edited by A. Hannay and G. Marino, 207–34. Cambridge Companions to Philosophy. New York: Cambridge University Press, 1998.

Gadamer, Hans-Georg. "Text and Interpretation." In *Dialogue and Deconstruction: The Gadamer-Derrida Encounter,* edited and translated by D. P. Michelfelder and R. E. Palmer, 21–51. SUNY Series in Continental Philosophy. Albany: State University of New York Press, 1989.

————. *Truth and Method.* 2nd rev. ed. Translated by J. Weinsheimer and D. Marshall. New York: Continuum, 1989.

Gergen, Kenneth J. *The Saturated Self: Dilemmas of Identity in Contemporary Life.* New York: Basic Books, 1991.

Gill, Jerry. "Faith Is as Faith Does." In *Kierkegaard's* Fear and Trembling: *Critical Appraisals,* edited by R. L. Perkins, 204–17. 1981. Reprint, Kierkegaard Classsic Studies Series. Eugene, OR: Wipf & Stock, 2009.

Green, Ronald M. *Kierkegaard and Kant: The Hidden Debt.* SUNY Series in Philosophy. Albany: SUNY Press, 1992.

Hale, Geoffrey A. *Kierkegaard and the Ends of Language.* Minneapolis: University of Minnesota Press, 2002.

Hannay, Alastair. *Kierkegaard: A Biography.* Cambridge: Cambridge University Press, 2001.

————. *Kierkegaard.* The Arguments of the Philosophers. London: Routledge & Kegan Paul, 1982.

Hare, John E. *The Moral Gap: Kantian Ethics, Human Limits, and God's Assistance.* New York: Oxford University Press. 1996.

Hart, Kevin. *The Trespass of the Sign: Deconstruction, Theology and Philosophy.* Cambridge: Cambridge University Press, 1989.

Hawthorne, Gerald. *Philippians.* Word Biblical Commentary 43. Waco, TX: Word Books, 1983.

Hegel, G. W. F. *Logic.* Translated by W. Wallace. Oxford: Clarendon, 1975.

———. *Phenomenology of Spirit.* Translated by A. V. Miller with J. N. Findlay. Oxford: Oxford University Press, 1977.

———. *Philosophy of Right.* Translated by T. M. Knox. New York: Oxford University Press, 1967.

———. *Reason in History.* Translated by R. S. Hartman. New York: Bobbs-Merrill, 1953.

———. *Science of Logic.* Translated by A. V. Miller. New York: Humanities Press, 1969.

Heidegger, Martin. *The Question Concerning Technology.* Translated by W. Lovill. New York: Harper & Row, 1977.

Hirsch, E. D. *The Aims of Interpretation.* Chicago: University of Chicago Press, 1978.

———. *Validity in Interpretation.* Rev. ed. New Haven: Yale University Press, 1973.

Holy Bible. King James Version. New York: Nelson, 1972.

Husserl, Edmund. *Cartesian Meditations: An Introduction to Phenomenology.* Translated by D. Cairns. The Hague: Nijhoff, 1960.

Jegstrup, Elsebet. "Kierkegaard and Deconstruction: Is Kierkegaard *Inter Alia* Anywhere in Derrida's *The Gift of Death?*" *Søren Kierkegaard Newsletter* 41 (2001) 19–23.

———. "Text and the Performative Act: Kierkegaard's (Im/possible) Direct Communications." *Philosophy Today* 45 (2001) 121–32.

Jegstrup, Elsebet, ed. *The New Kierkegaard.* Studies in Continental Thought. Bloomington: Indiana University Press, 2004.

Kant, Immanuel. *Foundations of the Metaphysics of Morals and What Is Enlightenment?* Translated by L. W. Beck. New York: Macmillan, 1985.

———. *Religion within the Limits of Reason Alone.* Translated by T. M. Greens and H. H. Hudson. New York: Harper & Row, 1960.

Kearney, Richard. "Kierkegaard's Concept of God-Man." *Kierkegaardiana* 13 (1984) 105–21.

Kierkegaard, Søren. *The Concept of Anxiety.* Edited and Translated by R. Thomte with A. B. Anderson. Princeton: Princeton University Press, 1980.

———. *The Concept of Dread.* Translated by W. Lowrie. Princeton: Princeton University Press, 1944.

———. *Concluding Unscientific Postscript to "Philosophical Fragments."* 2 vols. Edited and Translated by H. V. Hong and E. H. Hong. Kierkegaard's Writings 12. Princeton: Princeton University Press, 1992.

———. *Concluding Unscientific Postscript.* Translated by D. F. Swenson and W. Lowrie. Princeton: Princeton University Press, 1941.

———. *Either/Or.* 2 vols. Vol. 1 translated by D. F. and L. M. Swenson. Vol. 2 translated by W. Lowrie. Princeton: Princeton University Press, 1944.

———. *Fear and Trembling and The Sickness unto Death.* Translated by W. Lowrie. Princeton: Princeton University Press, 1941.

———. *Fear and Trembling.* Edited by C. S. Evans and S. Walsh. Translated by S. Walsh. Cambridge: Cambridge University Press, 2006.

———. *Fear and Trembling / Repetition.* Edited and Translated by H. V. Hong and E. H. Hong. Kierkegaard's Writings 6. Princeton: Princeton University Press, 1983.

———. *Fear and Trembling / The Book on Adler.* Translated by W. Lowrie. New York: Everyman's Library/Alfred A. Knopf, Inc., 1941/1994.

———. *Fear and Trembling.* Translated by A. Hannay. London: Penguin, 1985.

———. *Johannes Climacus*. Translated by T. H. Croxhall. Revised and edited by J. Chamberlain. London: Serpents Tail, 2001.

———. *Papers and Journals: A Selection*. Translated by A. Hannay. London: Penguin, 1996.

———. *Philosophical Fragments/Johannes Climacus*. Edited and Translated by H. V. Hong and E. H. Hong. Kierkegaard's Writings 7. Princeton: Princeton University Press, 1985.

———. *The Point of View for My Work as an Author / On My Work as an Author*. Translated by W. Lowrie. London: Oxford University Press, 1939.

———. *Practice in Christianity*. Edited and Translated by H. V. Hong and E. H. Hong. Kierkegaard's Writings 20. Princeton: Princeton University Press, 1991.

———. *Practice in Christianity*. Translated by W. Lowrie. New York: Random House, 2004.

———. *The Present Age* and *of the Difference between a Genius and an Apostle*. Translated by Alexander Dru. New York: Harper Torchbooks, 1962.

———. *Purity of Heart Is to Will One Thing*. Translated by D. V. Steere. New York: Harper Torchbooks, 1938.

———. *Repetition* and *Philosophical Crumbs*. Translated by M. G. Piety. Oxford: Oxford University Press, 2009.

———. *The Sickness unto Death: A Christian Psychological Exposition for Upbuilding and Awakening*. Edited and Translated by H. V. Hong and E. H. Hong. Kierkegaard's Writings 19. Princeton: Princeton University Press, 1980.

———. *The Sickness unto Death*. Translated by A. Hannay. London: Penguin, 1989.

———. *Søren Kierkegaard's Journals and Papers*. Edited and translated by H. V. Hong and E. H. Hong. 7 vols. Bloomington: Indiana University Press, 1967–78.

———. *Søren Kierkegaards Papirer* [The Papers of Søren Kierkegaard]. Edited by P. A. Heiberg, V. Kuhr, and E. Torsting, 2nd aug. ed. by N. Thulstrup. Index by N. J. Cappelørn. 22 vols. Copenhagen: Gyldendal, 1968–78.

———. *Søren Kierkegaards Skrifter*. Edited by N. J. Cappelørn, J. Garff, J. Kondrup, A. McKinnon and F. H. Mortensen. 4 vols. Copenhagen: Gads, 1997.

———. *Training in Christianity*. Translated by W. Lowrie. New York: Randon House, 2004.

———. *Works of Love*. Translated by D. F. and L. M. Swenson. Princeton: Princeton University Press, 1946.

———. *Works of Love*. Translated by H. V. Hong and H. E. Hong. Kierkegaard's Writings 16. Princeton: Princeton University Press, 1995.

Kirmmse, Bruce H., Ed. *Encounters with Kierkegaard: A Life as Seen by His Contemporaries*. Translated by B. H. Kirmmse and V. R. Laursen. Princeton: Princeton University Press, 1996.

Krentz, Arthur. "Kierkegaard's Dialectical Image of Human Existence in *The Concluding Unscientific Postscript to the Philosophical Fragments*." *Philosophy Today* 41 (1997) 277–87.

Latour, Bruno. *We Have Never Been Modern*. Translated by C. Porter. Cambridge: Harvard University Press, 1993.

Levinas, Emmanuel. "Existence and Ethics." In *Kierkegaard: A Critical Reader*, edited by J. Rée and J. Chamberlain, 26–38. Blackwell Critical Readers. Oxford: Blackwell, 1998.

Lippitt, John J., and George G. Pattison. Eds. *The Oxford Handbook of Kierkegaard.* Oxford Handbooks. Oxford: Oxford University Press, 2013.

Lippitt, John J. *Routledge Philosophy Guidebook to Kierkegaard and* Fear and Trembling. London: Routledge, 2003.

———. "What neither Abraham nor de Silentio Could Say." *Aristotelian Society Supplementary Volume* 82/1.1 (2008) 79–99.

Mackey, Louis. "The Loss of the World in Kierkegaard's Ethics." In *Kierkegaard: A Collection of Critical Essays,* edited by J. Thompson, 266–88. Garden City, NY: Anchor, 1972.

———. *Points of View: Readings of Kierkegaard.* Tallahassee: Florida State University Press, 1986.

———. "The View from Pisgah: A Reading of *Fear and Trembling,*" In *Kierkegaard: A Collection of Critical Essays,* edited by J. Thompson, 394–428. Garden City, NY: Anchor, 1972.

Madison, Gary B. "Beyond Seriousness and Frivolity: A Gadamerian Response to Deconstruction." In *Gadamer and Hermeneutics,* edited by H. J. Silverman, 119–35. New York: Routledge, 1991.

———. *The Hermeneutics of Postmodernity: Figures and Themes.* Studies in Phenomenology and Existential Philosophy. Bloomington: Indiana University Press, 1988.

Mahn, Jason A. *Fortunate Fallibility: Kierkegaard and the Power of Sin.* New York: Oxford University Press, 2011.

Malabou, Catherine. *The Future of Hegel: Plasticity, Temporality and Dialectic.* Translated by Lisabeth During. New York: Routledge, 2005.

Matustik, Martin J. *Postnational Identity: Critical Theory and Existential Philosophy in Habermas, Kierkegaard, and Havel.* Critical Perspectives. New York: Guilford, 1993.

Matustik, Martin J., and Merold Westphal, eds. *Kierkegaard in Post/Modernity.* Studies in Continental Thought. Bloomington: Indiana University Press, 1995.

Meillassoux, Quentin. *After Finitude: An Essay on the Necessity of Contingency.* Translated by R. Brassier. London: Continuum.

Milbank, John. *Theology and Social Theory: Beyond Secular Reason.* Signposts in Theology. Oxford: Blackwell, 1990.

Mooney, Edward F. *Knights of Faith and Resignation: Reading Kierkegaard's* Fear and Trembling. SUNY Series in Philosophy. Albany: SUNY Press, 1991.

Nancy, Jean-Luc. *Who Comes after the Subject?* Edited by E. Cadava and P. Connor. New York: Routledge, 1991.

New American Standard Bible. New York: Nelson, 1977.

Newmark, Kevin. "Secret Agents: After Kierkegaard's Subject." *MLN* 112 (1997) 719–52.

Norris, Christopher. "Fictions of Authority: Narrative and Viewpoint in Kierkegaard's Writings." *Criticism* 25 (1983) 87–107.

Olthuis, James H. *The Beautiful Risk: A New Psychology of Loving and Being Loved.* 2001. Reprint, Eugene, OR: Wipf & Stock, 2006.

———, ed. *Knowing Other-Wise: Philosophy at the Threshold of Spirituality.* Perspectives in Continental Philosophy 4. New York: Fordham University Press, 1997.

———. "Otherwise than Violence: Toward a Hermeneutic of Connection." In *Dancing in the Wild Spaces of Love.* Forthcoming.

————, ed. *Religion with/out Religion: The Prayers and Tears of John D. Caputo.* New York: Routledge, 2002.

Pattison, George G. *Kierkegaard, Religion and the Nineteenth-Century Crisis of Culture.* Cambridge: Cambridge University Press, 2002.

————. *The Philosophy of Kierkegaard.* Continental European Philosophy. Montreal: McGill-Queens University Press, 2005.

Poole, Roger. *Kierkegaard: The Indirect Communication.* Charlottesville: University Press of Virginia, 1993.

————. "The Unknown Kierkegaard: Twentieth-Century Receptions." In *The Cambridge Companion to Kierkegaard,* edited by A. Hannay and G. Marino, 48–75. Cambridge Companions to Philosophy. New York: Cambridge University Press, 1998.

Rée, Jonathan and Jane Chamberlain, eds. *Kierkegaard: A Critical Reader.* Blackwell Critical Readers. Oxford: Blackwell, 1998.

Rumble, Vanessa. "Eternity Lies Beneath: Autonomy and Finitude in Kierkegaard's Early Writings." *Journal of the History of Philosophy* 35 (1997) 83–103.

————. "Love and Difference: The Christian Ideal in Kierkegaard's *Works of Love.*" In *The New Kierkegaard,* edited by E. Jegstrup, 161–78. Bloomington: Indiana University Press, 2004.

————. "The Oracles's Ambiguity: Freedom and Original Sin in Kierkegaard's *The Concept of Anxiety.*" *Soundings* 75 (1992) 605–25.

————. "Sacrifice and Domination: Kantian and Kierkegaardian Paradigms of Self-Overcoming." *Philosophy and Social Criticism* 20 (1994) 19–35.

————. "To Be as No-One: Kierkegaard and Climacus on the Art of Indirect Communication." *International Journal of Philosophical Studies* 3 (1995) 307–21.

Simmons, J. Aaron. "What about Isaac?: Rereading *Fear and Trembling* and Rethinking Kierkegaardian Ethics." *Journal of Religious Ethics* 35 (2007) 319–45.

Smith, James K. A. *Speech and Theology: Language and the Logic of Incarnation.* Radical Orthodoxy Series. New York: Routledge, 2002.

Solomon, Robert C. *Continental Philosophy since 1750: The Rise and Fall of the Self.* New York: Oxford University Press, 1988.

Stern, Karl. *The Flight from Woman.* New York: Farrar, Straus & Giroux, 1965.

Sweetman, Robert. "Getting in Line: Justin Martyr, Saint Augustine, and the Project of Integral Christian Scholarship." *Pro Rege* 33 (2005) 26–36.

Taylor, Mark C. *After God.* Religion and Postmodernism. Chicago: University of Chicago Press, 2007.

————. *Erring: A Postmodern A/Theology.* Chicago: University of Chicago Press, 1984.

————. *Journeys to Selfhood: Hegel and Kierkegaard.* Berkeley: University of California Press, 1980.

————. *Nots.* Religion and Postmodernism. Chicago: University of Chicago Press, 1993.

————. "Sounds of Silence." In *Kierkegaard's* Fear and Trembling: *Critical Appraisals,* edited by R. L. Perkins, 165–88. University: University of Alabama Press, 1981.

Thompson Chain-Reference Bible. New International Version. Indianapolis: B. B. Kirkbride Bible Co.; and Grand Rapids: Zondervan, 1983.

Walsh, Sylvia. *Living Poetically: Kierkegaard's Existential Aesthetics.* University Park: Pennsylvania State University Press, 1994.

Westfall, Joseph. "Saving Abraham: Johannes de Silentio and the Demonic Paradox." *Philosophy Today* 48 (2004) 276–87.

Westphal, Merold. *Becoming a Self: A Reading of Kierkegaard's* Concluding Unscientific Postscript. West Lafayette, IN: Purdue University Press, 1996.

———. "Kierkegaard and Hegel." In *The Cambridge Companion to Kierkegaard*, edited by Alastair Hannay and Gordon D. Marino, 101–24. Cambridge Companions to Philosophy. New York: Cambridge University Press, 1998.

———. "Kierkegaard's Climacus—a Kind of Postmodernist." In *Concluding Unscientific Postscript to "Philosophical Fragments,"* edited by Robert L. Perkins, 53–71. International Kierkegaard Commentary 12. Macon, GA: Mercer University Press, 1997.

———. *Kierkegaard's Critique of Reason and Society*. University Park: Pennsylvania State University Press, 1991.

———. "The Transparent Shadow: Kierkegaard and Levinas in Dialogue." In *Kierkegaard in Post/Modernity*, edited by Martin J. Matustik and Merold Westphal, 265–81. Studies in Continental Thought. Bloomington: Indiana University Press, 1995.

Weston, Michael. *Kierkegaard and Modern Continental Philosophy: An Introduction*. New York: Routledge, 1994.

Wood, David. "Much Obliged." *Philosophy Today* 41 (1997) 135–40.

Žižek, Slavoj. *The Parallax View*. Short Curcuits. Cambridge: MIT Press, 2006.

Index

Haecker, Theodor, 9
Hale, Geoffrey, 5–6, 26, 40n28
Hawthorne, Gerald, 70
Hegel, G.W.F., 28, 43, 76n25, 85n40,
    103–4, 107, 110, 127, 139, 149
Heiberg, Peter, 7
hermeneutics, 29, 31, 84, 162n62
hiddenness, 13, 16, 125n6, 127,
    137n21, 148, 151, 152n 49, 156,
    169
    See also demonic

immediacy, 76, 124n 4, 128n9
    second or later, 124n4, 150
incarnation, 46n1
individual, the single, 103–4, 107–8,
    111, 113, 115, 117–19, 123,
    127, 137n21, 139, 141, 147–49,
    152–54, 157, 159n57, 161
interpretation, 4n7, 6n13, 7n14, 8,
    10n16, 14, 17, 23, 25, 31–32,
    34–36, 44, 46, 70, 73, 85n42,
    105n4, 167
Iphigenia, 130, 159
irony, 2, 7, 11–12, 34n21, 76, 119, 139,
    155–56, 160
irrational, 16, 35, 41n21, 155, 169
irrationalism, 35, 39–40, 105, 153
irrationalist, 12, 36n24, 109n9,
    116n12, 165
Isaac, 10–11, 39, 51, 55–56, 58, 71,
    76–77, 82, 84, 90–92, 94–95,
    97n11, 101, 104–5, 108n8,
    112–14, 125, 158, 159n 58, 160,
    164

Jaspers, Karl, 9
Jepthah, 105–6

Kierkegaard, 1–10, 12, 14–15,
    21–30, 32–35, 37, 41, 43n31,
    45–49, 51–54, 56–61, 65–66n1,
    67–69, 72n18, 94, 103n2, 109n9,
    113n10, 116, 119n18, 141n27,
    146–47n37, 153, 155, 159n58,
    162n62, 164–65, 167–68,
    170–71n6, 174

Knight, of infinite resignation, 16, 38,
    66, 82, 95–96, 98, 106, 114, 168

Levinas, Emmanuel, 49, 58–59, 171
Lippitt, John, 129, 147
Lukács, Georg, 8
lyrical, 11, 15, 55, 65–86, 89–90, 100,
    161, 168

Mackey, Louis, 5n11, 9, 106
meaning, 3–6, 10, 15, 22n1, 23n3,
    25–30, 32, 34–35, 40n28, 61,
    66–67, 71, 100, 103n2, 109, 112,
    118–19, 142n29, 147n37, 160,
    164, 166, 170, 173n8
mediation, 10–12, 25n10, 28, 31, 41,
    43n31, 46n1, 61, 66n1, 72–73,
    76, 104, 113, 118
merman, *See* Agnes
meta-ethical, 14, 22, 41–42
metaphysics, 11–13, 22n1, 23–25, 31,
    33n19, 36n24, 47, 49, 53–54,
    56, 59, 66–68, 74n21, 76n25,
    77n28–29, 84–85n43, 95n9,
    98n12, 116n13, 118, 125, 165,
    167–68, 170, 174
    critique of, 84
    Greco-Cartesian, 141
    Hegelian, 23n3
    Platonic, 42–43, 76n24
modern, 1–2, 12–13, 21, 48, 53,
    73–74, 127–28, 166
    late, 5, 13, 21, 166
modernity, 3n4, 74

negative, 24n7, 34–35, 99, 109, 116n
    13, 118, 125, 129, 132, 135,
    138–39, 141–42, 149–50, 154,
    156–57, 159n57, 174
logic, 13n17, 37, 77n29, 79–81,
    83–85n43, 102, 116, 119, 124,
    126, 132, 137n21, 142, 150, 152,
    154
Nietzsche, Frederick, 8n15

objective, 2
    truth, 14, 35, 167
    logic, 23

Made in the USA
Monee, IL
14 April 2022

94762901R00118